# Bureaucracy, policy, and the public

# Bureaucracy, policy, and the public

**STEVEN THOMAS SEITZ**

Department of Political Science
University of Illinois at Urbana-Champaign
Urbana, Illinois

*with* 129 *illustrations*

**THE C. V. MOSBY COMPANY**

Saint Louis    1978

Cover photograph from *American Education* magazine,
courtesy Institute for Political and Legal Education.

The C. V. Mosby Company
11830 Westline Industrial Drive, St. Louis, Missouri 63141

**Library of Congress Cataloging in Publication Data**

Seitz, Steven Thomas, 1947-
    Bureaucracy, policy, and the public.

    Bibliography:  p.
    Includes index.
    1.  Bureaucracy.  2.  Policy sciences.
I.  Title.
JF1501.S44        350′.001        77-26656
ISBN  0-8016-4482-8


GW/M/M   9  8  7  6  5  4  3  2  1

FOR

**J. David Greenstone,**
**Benjamin Evans Lippincott,**
**and**
**W. Phillips Shively,**
*who know the excitement of doing social science.*

# Preface

Because the bureaucracy and public administration literature is vast and ever-growing, a justification for the present contribution is in order. *Bureaucracy, Policy, and the Public* is unusual in several respects. First, the book draws heavily from political science, sociology, anthropology, business administration, criminal justice, economics, psychology, and history. More important, it attempts to synthesize materials from these disciplines, which makes the book interdisciplinary rather than multidisciplinary. Second, bureaucracy is approached as a process. Too often, research on bureaucracies focuses on the static structural dimension of bureaucracy to the exclusion of regard for its macro- or micro-dynamic functions. Allowing a contrast between the static and dynamic, the process perspective provides new insights and a more comprehensive analysis of bureaucratic organizations than might be possible if bureaucracy were considered merely an abstract idea or "thing." Third, the book is both theoretical and empirical. Its theory provides a structural-functional framework that integrates middle-range theory, previous research, and new data analyses into a comprehensive overview of bureaucracy, policy, and the public. Equally important, the theory has practical relevance to professional administrators because it provides key insights to the bureaucratic experience. Empirically, the book relies heavily on both qualitative and quantitative data, most of which are either historical or comparative. Some of the quantitative data derive from secondary analyses and some derive from original data collection. In addition, the book presents several illustrative examples and contains an overview of important cases in United States administrative law.

The book is divided into three parts. In Part one the macrodynamics of bureaucracy are examined. Chapter 1 is a historical review of bureaucracy in both ancient and modern societies. Chapter 2 presents a general theoretical statement about the function of bureaucratic organization and why it tends to appear with increasing social complexity. Chapters 3, 4, and 5 apply this theoretical statement to the problems of economic production, social control, and international relations. Part two shifts attention to the microdynamics of bureaucracy. In Chapter 6 I examine the proliferation of bureaucracies in industrial society, why this occurs, and the dynamics of interagency coordination. In Chapter 7 I try to show how different systems of recruitment and personnel policies might enhance bureaucratic power. In Chapter 8 a detailed analysis of communication as a means for shaping and sharing power, both within a bureaucracy and between a bureaucracy and its environment, is presented. Chapter 9 presents a process perspective on management, concentrating on those devices that allow a bureaucracy to stabilize its environment and operations, yet allow it to make radical adjustments when conditions require. Chapter 10 synthesizes the chapters in Part two through an analysis of bureaucratic decision making. In Part three (Chapter 11) the role of bureaucracy in the American democracy is discussed.

Some comment concerning the style and format of the book is necessary. Whenever possible, jargon has been avoided. Those technical terms that are indispensable have been included in a glossary. The longer sections of the book are followed by encapsulated summaries, as are the chapters themselves. Further, the reader can easily outline each chapter by following the headings and subheadings provided in the text. The footnotes draw on the vast body of literature relevant to various portions of the argument. The statistical materials have been simplified so that those with only modest background can readily read the graphs and tables. Although the book does assume the reader has some social science background, it should be understood easily by college students.

As with many projects of this scope, the demands on time and resources have been enormous. The University of Illinois Research Board provided computer time, allowing me to prepare, process, and analyze the 15 or so data banks used here. During the past 2 years, Marion Carter of the Social Science Quantitative Laboratory has built a fine data archive, which made access to relevant data much easier. The outstanding library at the University of Illinois also proved to be a critical resource.

Several graduate students have been enormously helpful throughout the final stages of this project. James Beachell, Bette Hughes, Gary Kebbel, and John Robertson read several chapters and provided critical comments helpful in elaborating and elucidating portions of the argument. As a professional copy editor, Gary Kebbel was extremely helpful in putting the manuscript in more presentable form. John Robertson did the pantograph work found throughout the book. Jim Beachell and Bette Hughes also assisted in proofreading and collating the final draft. With her incredible energy, Bette Hughes helped at every stage of preparation of the final manuscript. Marla Liberman and Mary Weisenberg typed the final manuscript. Maria made some critical editing revisions that have improved the final version.

Finally, I must offer very special gratitude to Gerald M. Pops, West Virginia University, and Rod O. Julander, Weber State College, reviewers of the manuscript, and to my colleague Lester Seligman at the University of Illinois. The reviewers raised some important issues that, once resolved, refined the argument and improved its quality. Professor Seligman took time to review several chapters. He cautioned against my tendency to use metaphor and simile, and to the extent that these have been removed from the final draft, the book is less mystical and more concrete. Those who know Easton or Parsons will recognize the value of that suggestion.

Several years ago I heard Truman Capote comment that he never finishes a book; someone simply takes it away. I now know what he meant. I must assume responsibility for the errors that remain.

**Steven Thomas Seitz**

# Contents

# PART ONE

# Macrodynamics of bureaucracy

# CHAPTER 1

# Birth of bureaucracy

A cross-cultural and historical survey of bureaucracies reveals several characteristics that distinguish the form of bureaucratic organization and its primary social function. As societies become more complex, major social problems demand solutions that favor bureaucratic organization over more traditional forms of social organization. Several of these major social problems help explain the development of bureaucracy in the United States.

## A NOTE ON METHOD

The rudiments of bureaucratic organizations have existed in all but the most simple human societies. Long before Europeans invaded the African continent in the nineteenth century, for example, several Bantu tribes had established bureaucracies (Fallers, 1965). Before Columbus discovered America, the Cheyenne Indians had a prototype of modern bureaucratic organization (Hoebel, 1968:127-168). Of course, the Bantu, Cheyenne, and other early bureaucracies cannot match the more developed bureaucracies of ancient Egypt, Greece, Rome, and China. Nor can the bureaucracies of these ancient civilizations excel those that arose with the modern nation-state in the sixteenth century. Still, as the Bantu and Cheyenne examples illustrate, bureaucratic organizations are not unique to the Greco-Roman tradition in the Western World, and these organizations predate the bureaucracies of the nation-state.

### Postponing definitions

Of the many ways we might survey the birth of bureaucracies, two are fairly common. First, we could define bureaucracy and then set out to find organizations that conform to our definition. This approach is somewhat risky. There are almost as many definitions of bureaucracy as there are scholars of bureaucracy. If we choose one of these definitions, we might restrict our survey in ways that we would later regret. Even worse, we might never see aspects of bureaucratic organization that are essential for understanding the role of bureaucracy in modern society.

How can we survey bureaucracy without first defining it? Most of us already have some ideas about bureaucracy; otherwise, the term would not make sense in common language. Even if we postpone a rigorous definition, we still have some general ideas to guide our search for bureaucracies. For comparison, consider the color "red." We have a pretty good idea of what red is. On the color spectrum, it represents a range of light rays with specific lengths. As we move toward the boundaries of what we perceive as red on the color spectrum, we become less sure whether the color is actually red! For a concept such as bureaucracy, imagine how difficult it is to establish the definitional boundaries for what is and what is not a bureaucracy! Lest we exclude something near the borderline that we later wish to include under the concept of bureaucracy, we will postpone a formal definition until our survey is complete.

### Natural history

Natural history is the second way to survey bureaucracies. Because we already have some ideas about bureaucracy, we will look at a variety of social organizations in both a comparative and a historical perspective. This is the methodology of natural history. The method helps us identify cross-cultural characteristics of bureaucracy. Using this approach, we broaden our vision of bureaucracy while avoiding the premature closure that a formal definition might impose. Rather than defining a bureaucracy and then looking for it, we will first look at the boundaries of bureaucracy, guided by our existing ideas, so we can better define bureaucracy. (This approach is often termed a posteriori investigation. For a classic illustration, see Dewey, 1946.)

## SOCIAL PROBLEMS

Bureaucracies have appeared in many societies throughout recorded history. Although some writers might explain the appearance and reappearance of bureaucracy as a random social accident or part of some divine plan, we shall consider bureaucracy as a social device used when certain problems require solutions that other social devices cannot effectively provide. In this book, we will not concern ourselves with the alternate explanations, which would take us beyond the normal range of social science explanation.

Three questions are directly relevant to our explanation of bureaucratic development. What social problems require bureaucratic organization? Why does bureaucracy provide solutions that other social devices cannot provide? What type of social device is bureaucracy? We will find a number of answers to these questions throughout this chapter and the remaining chapters in Part I of this book.

All societies must resolve certain basic social problems. Three of these are particularly important. First, people must coordinate their behavior to secure survival against the forces of nature. The material world provides people with food and shelter. Unlike paradise, nature does not give people these items. In fact, the history of human technology illustrates continued efforts to expand the boundaries of human existence against a nature that is uncooperative and sometimes hostile. From the Stone Age through the Iron Age to the modern electronic age, people have struggled against the forces of nature in battles for food, shelter, and the pleasantries of life. The history of human technology also is the story of human cooperation. When left alone, without the help of relatives, neighbors, and friends, people are far more vulnerable to the forces of nature. Together, people complement their strengths and weaknesses; provide for one another during youth, sickness, injury, and old age; and bring to bear on social problems more strength and cunning than one person could produce alone. We will further examine this problem in Chapter 3.

Second, people must regulate social conflict. Some writers, particularly the anarchists, do not believe that conflict is an inevitable result of society. However, anthropologists have found no society where all people freely respect the rights and privileges of others. Nor have anthropologists found any society where people are such slaves of habit and tradition that conflict disappears. Even in the most simple societies, the personal interests of some might conflict with the interests of others, especially when people seek scarce resources and power. To regulate social conflict, all societies have rules of behavior, whether formal or informal. And all societies have some mechanism for enforcing these rules. From the gossip of a small community to the police of our modern cities, people rely on several means to maintain order and regulate conflict. We will further examine this problem in Chapter 4.

Third, societies must govern their relations with other societies. Except for a few simple societies, most societies periodically encounter conflicts with other societies. These conflicts can be very severe, including the threat of invasion and conquest. In addition, most societies rely on some form of trade to secure desired goods from other societies and to find a market for their own goods. We will further examine this problem in Chapter 5.

### Bureaucratic coordination

All societies face basic social problems, but the scope, intensity, and frequency of these problems vary considerably from one society to another. One reason for these differences is the relative complexity of a society. Imagine a continuum from very simple to very complex societies. At one end, the simple societies have very small populations, where one person knows almost all the other people in that society and what they do. Here there is little division of labor, the economy is near subsistence level, and there is very little social diversity. At the other end, the complex societies have relatively large populations, where the vast majority of people do not know one another or what most other people are doing. Here there is an extensive division of labor, the economy is relatively sophisticated, and there is a fair degree of social diversity.

Social complexity implies that the relations between people and nature and the relations among persons have become increasingly complicated. Complex societies have complex technologies: increasingly sophisticated means through which people battle nature. Also, complex societies imply complex social relations: intricate patterns of rights, privileges, and obligations. At some point the relations between people and nature and the relations among people become so complex that the simpler mechanisms of society no longer are adequate to secure human coordination. The following discussion illustrates that this complexity is itself a source of new problems for social coordination. As the problem of human coordination increases in scope and intensity, bureaucracies help fill the void left by primary, but less adequate, social arrangements. What are these primary social arrangements? How do bureaucracies help fill the void created by social complexity?

### LEVELS OF BUREAUCRATIC DEVELOPMENT

All societies might be located on a continuum, ranging from the most simple societies to the modern complex nation-states of the twentieth century. For convenience, however, we will examine three major sections of this continuum: simple societies, rudimentary states, and bureaucratic states. Among the bureaucratic states, we will further distinguish beginning bureaucratic states, intermediate bureaucratic states, and advanced bureaucratic states. As we move across these levels of bureaucratic development, we will see the primary social arrangements that help secure human coordination, and we will see how bureaucratic organizations augment and then replace primary social arrangements.

### Simple societies

Bureaucracies are not found in the simplest societies. Two such societies are the Siriono Indians of Bolivia and the Comanche Indians of the early United States. Although both the Siriono and Comanche recognize leaders, these leaders excel in the skills required of everyone else (see Hoebel, 1968; Holmberg, 1969). Outstanding hunters, for example, are likely candidates for leadership. These leaders exercise subtle influence over their bands, but they have little formal authority. Sanctions exercised by leaders and tribe members alike normally are limited to the withdrawal of reciprocity. That is, leaders and tribe members enforce certain behaviors by failing to fulfill their usual obligations toward the erring individual. Apart from the minimal influence of leaders, coordination in these societies rests on self-help tempered by the economic duties and conflict negotiations imposed by kinship. Here the primary social arrangement to secure coordination is the kinship institution.

### Rudimentary states

Somewhere between the simplest societies and those with recognizable bureaucracies are societies with minimal governments. Drawing from Africa before its colonization, the Ashanti of West Africa and the Gusii of East Africa provide examples of this stage of social organization (see Hoebel, 1968:211-254; Mair, 1962:109-112). Both of these societies have a form of institutionalized authority: procedures for vesting authority in certain people. In both cases, the emergent political structure rests on kinship lineages. Ashanti and Gusii leaders can delegate authority. Where authority is not institutionalized, this is impossible. In addition to the withdrawal of reciprocity, Ashanti and Gusii leaders can back the exercise of authority with material and coercive sanctions. Coordination in these societies rests on the authority exercised by established political leaders, tempered and augmented by immediate kinship duties and ancestral obligations. Here the primary social arrangements to secure human coordination are political authorities and the kinship institution. Political authority is linked to the kinship institution through ancestral worship. The legitimacy of political authority derives from the leader's kinship link with sacred ancestors. Like their counterparts in simple societies, individuals owe economic duties to their kin.

### Bureaucratic states

The range of states with some form of bureaucratic organization is quite wide. Some, such as the beginning bureaucratic states, differ only slightly from the rudimentary states, such as the Ashanti and Gusii. Others, such as those with which we are most familiar, are drastically different from rudimentary states. Still, some common themes tie bureaucratic states together and make them distinct from the rudimentary states. Let us search for these common themes.

*Beginning.* The political authority in beginning bureaucratic states still rests on a network of kinship obligations. Unlike political authority in rudimentary states, however, the network of kinship obligations is augmented by a patronage system that creates its own client-patron obligations. The Soga of Eastern Africa illustrate the early bureaucratic states. The early Busoga state is organized around patrilineal kinship, ascribed rank, a patron-client system, and an ancestral cult (Fallers, 1965:126, 134). Busoga rulers govern through an administrative staff, often composed of commoners of unusual ability, to whom are delegated certain subdivisions of the state (Fallers, 1965:127). Compared with rudimentary states, The Busoga increasingly delegate authority. Among the Busoga it is not unusual to find the patron-client relation secured through marriage, or affinal kinship (Fallers, 1965:135). Hence the commoners to whom authority is delegated might become part of the ruler's family through marriage. In descending order, the political hierarchy in the Busoga includes the ruler, princes, chiefs, headmen, and advisors. These authorities form a military, judicial, and tribute-gathering organization (Fallers, 1965:137). From headmen to princes, each is expected to make tribute payments and to provide military aid to their superiors in the political hierarchy. And each is expected to recognize the judicial decisions of superiors. Failure to do so invites sanction and reprisal (Fallers, 1965:137). Although authority is legitimized in part through ancestral lineage, Busoga political authority transcends both the ancestral cult and the kinship institutions on which it rests. Failure to pay tribute or to recognize judicial decisions is deliberate secession. And the possibility of secession illustrates a loose bond between political authority and the primary social arrangements in rudimentary states.

*Intermediate.* In the intermediate bureaucratic states, the political system becomes increasingly divorced from kinship duties, although an ancestral cult often plays a limited role in the political myths of the state. Not only is authority increasingly delegated in these states, but the delegation generally follows identifiable lines of specialization. Further, the material and coercive sanctions backing the exercise of authority become increasingly extensive and effective and less restrained by ancestral cults and other religious beliefs. To examine these themes, we will discuss five intermediate bureaucratic states: the ancient Egyptian Kingdom, the Athenian Empire, the Roman Empire, the Sung dynasty in China, and Medieval Christendom. These examples highlight several ways that bureaucracies help people solve social problems. Later in the chapter, we will see how similar social problems contributed to the growth of American bureaucracy between 1870 and 1950.

*Egypt.* The Nile Valley of Egypt was one of the earliest centers of human civilization. Its geographic conditions are among the most favorable to human society: the land is rich, and the weather is very predictable. Under these conditions, the population density rapidly increased, requiring Egyptian officials to adopt land- and water-use programs. These programs helped increase productivity in the fertile valley, thereby providing more food for the growing population. About 300 BC, a powerful bureaucratic state emerged. The bureaucracy essentially controlled land, water, and food in the valley. So extensive were these resource programs that Egyptians developed an early writing system and a civil service of scribes (Omer-Cooper et al., 1968: 5-9). The top political figure was the pharaoh. In theory, the pharaoh owned all the land. Together with his ancestors, he was thought responsible for land fertility. Together with his civil servants and priests, he exercised immense power over the Egyptian commoner. With slave labor and exacting tribute from commoners, political

authorities in Egypt created some of the most impressive monuments known, not the least of which are the pyramids, tombs for the pharaohs.

*Greece.* Like Egypt, the geographic conditions around Athens favored uniting a large territory under one political center (Rostovtzeff, 1963:82). By 450 BC, Athens had consolidated a political empire over her onetime confederates. Across the empire, Athens imposed obligatory coinage, weights, and measures, all supported by a growing administrative staff (Rostovtzeff, 1963:151). During that time, Greek science rapidly improved agricultural production and manufacturing. Although her science and philosophy are hallmarks of Western civilization, the city-state remained integrally bound with religious practices and customs (Robinson, 1948: 191-192). Athens' greatest scholar, Socrates, was sentenced to death for supposed heresies against the ancestors and existing customs. And although the city gave birth to one of the earliest plebiscitarian democracies known, its imperialist policies toward other city-states required a huge administrative apparatus and considerable delegation of authority to maintain law and order, to exact tribute, and to secure the economic dominance of Athens.

*Rome.* The Roman Empire was the largest political system to emerge before the rise of the nation-states in the sixteenth and seventeenth centuries. And it supported one of the largest, most extensive bureaucracies outside modern times. As the empire expanded, religion became increasingly separated from state actions, although the emperor did claim divine sanction. Administratively, the Roman government had several departments, constituted on functional and geographic grounds (Rostovtzeff, 1960:226). These departments reported to the emperor and his central office. The emperor maintained an organized police force in Rome, and military police protected communication routes throughout Italy and the provinces.

Given the size of Rome, about 1 million inhabitants, the emperors also implemented planned urban growth and urban renewal, sanitation and water systems, garbage collection, and drainage systems. Programs were implemented to secure a plentiful food supply for the city, and early measures were developed to distribute food to the poor. In addition, places of amusement, such as public baths, were built to absorb leisure time (Rostovtzeff, 1960:232). To no small extent, the life of ancient Rome rested on its public bureaucracy.

*China.* Confucian China developed many of the personnel policies common to public bureaucracies in the modern state (Kracke, 1953:1). These policies include recruitment, promotion, and control of patronage. The Chinese state governed an empire roughly comparable in size to the Roman Empire. Although its programs were less extensive than those in Rome, its art of public administration was unexcelled until modern times. Apparently, the impetus toward civil service derives from Confucian doctrine. With its philosophic egalitarianism, Confucian thought emphasized the conditional nature of imperial authority (Kracke, 1953:20-21). Granted by heaven, the imperial throne could be withdrawn from an unworthy occupant, with the common people making the ultimate judgment (Kracke, 1953:21). In addition, Confucian doctrine held that government office should go to people of proved merit and ability (Kracke, 1953:4). Qualified people in turn had a duty to accept office (Kracke, 1953:22). Facing military pressures, economic problems, and a growing population, The Sung bureaucracy proved remarkably resilient.

*Medieval Christendom.* The public bureaucracy of the Middle Ages was a regression from the level achieved under the Roman Empire of the first and second centuries. Absent the strong Roman military, political power rapidly decentralized, reflecting the terrain of Europe. Environ-

mental features, such as marsh, mountain, and forest, placed natural limits on the scope of governmental power (Southern, 1953). By the thirteenth century, many political functions had become ecclesiastical functions as well. For example, the military system of knighthood particularly fell under church control (Southern, 1953: 112). In fact, the church hierarchy became the single thread holding together the increasingly fragmented societies of the Middle Ages. The Pope maintained some semblance of ecclesiastical stability through roving ambassadors and civil service administrators who fulfilled specialized activities within the papal household (Southern, 1953:145). Through this apparatus the Pope expanded his authority, holding councils throughout Europe, hearing and settling disputes, and administering the justice that secular rulers found increasingly difficult to deliver in the established secular courts (Southern, 1953:146-150). In addition to the central administration in Rome, the monasteries of the church played a key role in administering religion, peace, and strict laws to the countryside of Europe in the absence of effective political authority (Southern, 1953:151-155).

***Advanced.*** The advanced bureaucratic states generally are characterized by the total secularization of politics: the transference from ecclesiatical to civil authority (see Smith, 1970).* This level illustrates the full meaning of Max Weber's "rationalization of authority" (see Weber, 1964). The father of modern bureaucratic theory, Max Weber (1964:328) argued that advanced administrative organizations exercised authority because those affected accept the normative rules as legal and accept the commands of those in authority as an exercise of a legally derived right.

---

*Countries like Franco's Spain would likely fall on the border between intermediate bureaucratic states and advanced bureaucratic states, given state policy under Franco and the alliance with the Catholic Church.

Obvious examples of advanced bureaucracies include the secular constitutional governments of the United States, Britain, France, Germany, and the Soviet Union. The basic characteristics of these states are well known: (1) they have the power to enforce commands with coercive sanctions; (2) they govern through massive delegations of specialized authority; (3) they sever the link between kinship and politics; and (4) they exercise secular, not ecclesiastical, political authority.

## Overview

Review some changes that occur as we move from simple to complex societies. Simple societies lack formal authority apart from very personalized leadership. Rudimentary states have made the transition to institutionalized authority, although, like simple societies, the political structure is intricately bound with kinship relations. And institutionalized authority allows its delegation. In rudimentary states, sanctions extend well beyond the withdrawal of reciprocity to include the positive use of material and coercive sanction. With bureaucratic states, we find further institutionalization of authority, allowing both delegation and considerable specialization of authority. The bureaucratic state also makes extensive use of positive sanctions. Among bureaucratic states, we ses a rapid decay of the fusion between kinship structures and the political structure. Table 1-1 summarizes these points of comparison.

Simple societies rely heavily on self-help and kinship as a means through which individuals resolve social differences and exploit their natural environment. Rudimentary states superimpose institutionalized authority and positive sanctions on both kinship and self-help. Bureaucratic states mark a rapid deterioration of the link between politics and kinship, while further institutionalizing authority through massive specialization as well as delegation.

We have also noted a process of differentiation within bureaucratic states. In earlier bureaucratic states, the linkage between politics and kinship is strained by a client-patron relation, but the link is not completely broken. In addition, these states tend to fuse religion and politics. Intermediate bureaucracies finally sever the link between kinship and politics, and the religious system becomes a countervailing power for political institutions. With ad-

**Table 1-1.** Birth of bureaucracy

|  | SIMPLE SOCIETIES | RUDIMENTARY STATES | BUREAUCRATIC STATES |
|---|---|---|---|
| Disintegration of link between kinship and politics | No | No | Yes |
| Specialization of authority | No | No | Yes |
| Delegation of authority | No | Yes | Yes |
| Use of positive sanctions | No | Yes | Yes |

**Table 1-2.** Differentiation of bureaucratic states

|  | BEGINNING BUREAUCRACY | INTERMEDIATE BUREAUCRACY | ADVANCED BUREAUCRACY |
|---|---|---|---|
| Separation of religion and politics | No | No | Yes |
| Separation of kinship and politics | No | Yes | Yes |

vanced bureaucratic states, politics is largely secularized and rationalized. Table 1-2 summarizes these comparisons.

## DEFINITION OF BUREAUCRACY

The natural history of bureaucracy suggests that bureaucracy is far more than a complex social organization pursuing its goals. To be sure, bureaucracy is a special form of social organization, but to concentrate on the *form* of organization might lead us to overlook its social *functions*. Hence, our definition of bureaucracy should include its characteristic form and function. In the preceding pages we have seen that bureaucracy is a procedural device for delegating specialized authority and that it helps structure political action by elaborating and administering substantive guidelines set by policy makers. Consistent with these points, we shall define bureaucracy as a special form of social organization that provides procedures to elaborate and administer substantive guidelines for structuring political action through the delegation and specialization of authority. In Part I of this book, we shall concentrate on the social function of bureaucracy; in Part II we shall discuss its form and relate that form to its functions.

We can use our definition of bureaucracy to summarize the preceding discussion. First, in simple societies and rudimentary states, religion and kinship determine the substantive guidelines for political action and provide mechanisms for enforcing these guidelines, such as ecclesiastical authority and kinship obligations. Second, in bureaucratic states, politics is increasingly divorced from religion and kinship and hence more autonomous. By implication, substantive guidelines that once were fixed by kinship and religion are now determined by an autonomous political process. In turn, bureaucracy provides a procedural device for enforcing these guidelines through a secular (or, in Weber's terms, rational) delegation of specialized author-

ity. Third, within bureaucratic states there is a continuum of political autonomy. In beginning bureaucratic states the political process still is encumbered by ecclesiastical authority and kinship obligation, even though there are visible trends toward more secular authority. In intermediate bureaucratic states the political process is encumbered by ecclesiastical authority, but the trend toward secular authority is stronger than that found in beginning bureaucratic states. In advanced bureaucratic states the political process is relatively autonomous and secular authority is the primary mechanism for enforcing substantive guidelines.

## CAUSES OF CHANGE IN SOCIAL ORGANIZATION

Our account of bureaucracy thus far has been static, for we have only compared different levels of development. Before discussing the theory of bureaucratic development (see Chapter 2), we must examine the dynamics of bureaucratic change. For example, what are the social problems whose solutions favor bureaucracy over kinship and religion? How are religion and kinship inadequate, and how is bureaucracy more adequate? How do transitions occur from one level of development to another?

### Need to delegate authority

Authority in simple societies derives largely from traits of the individual rather than from official positions or offices. The Comanche braves, for example, see their leaders excel at the tasks they also are obliged to do. In this case, the chiefs are better hunters, better warriors. Clearly, authority that derives from prestige such as this cannot readily be delegated to another. And there is little need to do so, because most members of the community have regular personal contacts with one another. But as societies expand and occupy larger and larger geographic areas, this personal contact becomes less likely. As societies become very large or geographically dispersed, the subtle influence of personal authority begins to wane. Alternately, authority becomes increasingly fragmented across the society. For a common political bond to continue, authority must be attached to offices, not to individuals. Here the positions of authority take on a meaning that transcends a particular individual.

Increased social complexity does more than tax simple authority systems. It also exacerbates basic social problems, particularly the need for material resources, the level of social conflict, and the relations among societies. As a society becomes larger or covers a greater geographic area, its coordination problems—the balance of private and public ends—increase accordingly. With more people there are more chances for quarrel and more people to pursue private interests over common interests. As population increases, there are greater demands against nature for food, clothing, and shelter, and consequently greater demands for coordination. The volume, intensity, and quality of these problems makes it increasingly difficult for public opinion or a single authority figure to exercise control. When authority is institutionalized—attached to offices, not to individuals—officials can delegate authority to representatives, often kinsmen, who exercise influence, judgment, and sanctions on behalf of the leader and his or her council.

### Inadequacy of kinship

In simple societies, kinship relations, particularly the system of economic duties and privileges supported by feelings of belonging and responsibility for one's own kind, provide a natural setting from which leaders emerge. Outstanding leaders exceed the requirements expected of them by providing for kinsmen in ways that merit the acclaim of others. But kinship also provides a blueprint for political action in primitive societies. Kinship might determine where one lives, whom one marries, and to whom primary and secondary obligations are due. These two functions are united as authority is institutionalized. With the emergence of the rudimentary state, institutionalized authority continues to reflect the kinship foundations within which it arose. Kinship sets bounds around the exercise of power, links the ruler to subjects through lineage and ancestral ties, provides a means for replacing leaders and recruiting representatives of the central leadership, and helps secure loyalty between the leader and his or her designated representatives. But in many instances kinship is inadequate when authority is institutionalized; it is particularly ineffective in recruiting talented officials for administrative offices, especially when these offices are highly specialized. Among the beginning bureaucratic states, the patron-client system provides an alternative for recruiting talented officials. Still, client loyalty to a patron is not always assured, and patrons often cement this bond through marriage.

Even after kinship is separated from the political structure, as in the intermediate bureaucratic states, the residual effects of this early bond continue. In several states, seventeenth century France among them, the functional administrative and judicial offices are separated from the lineage of the king, only to become the hereditary property of the few families occupying these offices (Strauss, 1961:180). In France, these officials assumed power and authority independent of the king. When they failed to execute his commands, Louis XIV found it necessary to circumvent and supplant these established offices (Strauss, 1961:181). Similar events occurred in Prussia and Russia.

All told, the kinship institution provides ineffective solutions to the severe problems of complex societies, leading to failures in human coordination and further fragmentation of political power. Although kinship helps maintain loyalty between leader and representative, the kinship institution provides a poor method for recruiting specialized talent. And although kinship provides a means for replacing old leaders, it sets a precedent that encourages administrative officials to make their offices hereditary as well. When this happens, as it did in seventeenth century France, Prussia, and Russia, authority is fragmented and the bureaucracy becomes a power countervailing that of the royal family.

## ADVENT OF BUREAUCRACIES

The inadequacies of kinship do not explain the advent of bureaucratic states. When do bureaucracies emerge? The real impetus toward bureaucratic development appears to be conditions of social crisis or rapid social change. For convenience, we will divide these conditions into two categories: those intrinsic to the society and those largely extrinsic to it.

### Intrinsic conditions

Five intrinsic conditions appear particularly relevant to the advent of bureaucratic development: economic disaster, economic boom, domestic violence, religious conversion, and democratization.

First, economic disaster might foster bureaucratic development. We have already seen that human society requires considerable coordination to secure people's efforts against nature. In societies with less developed economies, the occurrence of natural disasters such as droughts and floods, crop diseases, and even unusual seasonal variations can threaten the source of vital foodstuffs needed to sustain an existing population. To protect against these problems, people turned early to bureaucratic planning and administration. As economies become more differentiated and specialized, the need for administrative planning becomes even more acute. In the present American economy, for example, a shortage of natural gas at one plant can

stop production at 25 plants located across the United States, put thousands of workers off the job, result in millions of dollars in lost productivity each day, and require considerable start-up costs to get the complex systems running smoothly again. Imagine what happens when an energy shortage hits several states simultaneously!

The second intrinsic condition is economic boom. Several problems accompany unexpected economic prosperity. These include rapid population growth, either by natural expansion or through immigration; more available material resources than can be absorbed readily through existing economic institutions, as happened in the boom towns of the Old American West; and a desire to maintain the new levels of prosperity, coupled with continued efforts to stimulate economic growth. In all these cases, bureaucratic administration, particularly through the specialization of authority it allows, helps people gain control over a situation that might otherwise court disaster. Both more developed economies and less-developed economies have vested interests in controlling these sharp peaks and potential troughs in the economy. Even under the laissez-faire system in early America, the government never fully abandoned regulation of the economic order.

The third condition advancing bureaucratic development focuses on the increasing complexity of relations among people. All societies have some degree of internal conflict. As societies become increasingly large and sophisticated in property rights, civil regulations, and criminal law, the demands on political institutions for regulating conflict geometrically increase. In more than a few societies, the development of these political institutions lags behind the demands they face. On occasion these discrepancies erupt into protests and collective violence. When internal conflict erupts into tribal or class warfare, bureaucratic development advances very rapidly.

The fourth intrinsic factor is religious conversion. Although many religions do not have a well-developed component of public law, others do, including Moslem, Hindu, and Christian religions. As these religions took hold in their respective areas of the world, there emerged strong ecclesiastical pressures to guide behavior in accordance with religious precepts. Depending on religion and locality, religious conversions might provide an important impetus to the development of bureaucratic apparatuses that serve to connect peoples of similar faith and increase ecclesiastical control over the conduct of people.

The final intrinsic factor is democratization. As the enfranchisement in modern democratic states expands to include larger and larger portions of the citizenry, the quality of demands on political institutions and the expectations of these institutions rapidly change. Enfranchisement of the lower classes, as happened in early Rome, leads to state policies for distributing food and shelter to the poor. In more advanced economies, such as those of Great Britain and the United States, the extensive enfranchisements create pressures for measures that partially redistribute wealth from the richer to poorer sectors of society. These measures, plus the demands for equal protection under the law, enhance the growth and importance of bureaucracies.

### Extrinsic conditions

Three extrinsic conditions advancing bureaucratic development are particularly important: (1) conquest or threat of invasion, (2) imperialism, and (3) trade.

We will consider conquest an extrinsic factor because it represents an exchange between one society and a second external to its territorial borders and existing political structure. Under threat of conquest or invasion, a state rapidly must muster its resources, protect its foodstuffs, and place unusual demands on its citizenry, at least for the duration of threat. The planning and regulation so required often enhance the institutionalization of authority, its del-

egation, and its specialization. Failure to do so, particularly if the invading force is well prapared, well equipped, and well organized, will likely mean defeat. Under such conditions of threat or seizure, bureaucratic military arrangements allow the unusually high levels of coordination required for protection.

The second extrinsic condition is the mirror image of the first: imperialism. For whatever reasons, including internal problems with which they cannot cope, many states turn to conquer their neighbors. But to do so, the imperialist state must secure the necessary weaponry, food, transport facilities, and manpower. To do this on a grand scale, to undertake battles that might involve thousands of persons and consume several years, requires an apparatus for continued coordination of the war effort at home to provide needed resources for those on the battlefield. Like the response to conquest or invasion, imperialism requires extraordinary coordination among people and intensive exploitation of nature. These requirements exceed the fixed blueprint of kinship and some religions and the vagueness of other religious doctrines. Bureaucracies, on the other hand. allow the authority structure to centralize power and alter substantive guidelines while increasing effectiveness and efficiency through the delegation and specialization of authority.

The final extrinsic factor is trade. Among the early bureaucratic states in Africa, for example, trade was an important impetus to bureaucratic development and bureaucratic regulation. By the seventeenth century, the city-states in the Niger Delta Area of West Africa had developed complex forms of trade supplemented by what appears to be an early civil service system (Davidson, 1966:224-229). Trading companies, only partly based on kinship, emerged in these city-states, providing economic regulation throughout the delta area. Eventually, the early trade in gold, ivory, cotton, animal hides, and kola nuts were overshadowed by the trade in slaves. But the bureaucratic arrangements of this house trade system made it easy for the indigenous peoples to maintain control over trading routes, limiting European access to the coastal areas.

## RISE OF ADVANCED BUREAUCRATIC STATES

Advanced bureaucratic states are a product of relatively recent history. We tend to identify them with the modern nation-state and an industrial economy. Scholars since Karl Marx have worried about the transition from intermediate to advanced bureaucratic states and in particular the political transition from feudalism to modernity. Although several theories have been proposed to explain the transition from intermediate to advanced bureaucratic states, two catch our attention. These are the "big-push theory" and the "countervailing-power theory."

### Big-push theory

The big-push theory suggests that political officials in underdeveloped countries decide to industrialize their countries. To do so, these officials consolidate political authority or renovate the remnants of colonial administrations. Using bureaucratic administration, these officials consolidate resources and control over the citizenry to revolutionize the existing economic system. Through bureaucratic agencies, these officials delegate and specialize authority for controlling the production, distribution, and consumption of resources vital to industrialization. To varying degrees, this theory helps explain the political activities in many countries of the Third World today.

### Countervailing-power theory

The countervailing-power theory argues that economic development more easily occurs if the economic sector is largely insulated from the actions of the political sector. Here economic authorities are free to pursue their activities because state regulation is held to a minimum. Through multiple centers of power, the central state authority is fragmented, with various political authorities checking the actions of others. One such example is a state administration independent of the royal family. Countervailing-power theorists claim that technological innovations and the diffusion of these innovations will occur faster and more extensively if government regulation is held to a minimum. In short, they believe that economic competition fosters industrialization better and faster than the guiding hand of the state (see Holt and Turner, 1965). Eventually, bureaucratic administrations expand to help regulate the industrial economy, but the origin and development of the industrial economy is best left free of these administrative regulations. It is generally thought that this theory helps explain the early emergence of the industrial economy in Great Britain and Japan (Holt and Turner, 1965:292-335).

### Development in the United States

Neither the big-push nor the countervailing-power theory adequately explains the observed patterns of bureaucratic development in the United States. As a measure of bureaucratic development, we will use the number of federal bureaucratic employees per 100,000 population in the United States. And as a measure of industrialization, we will use the per capita gross national product (GNP), expressed in constant dollars. If the big-push theory is adequate, we should find the GNP measure lagging behind changes in the ratio of federal bureaucratic employees per 100,000 population. If the countervailing-power theory is adequate, we should find the ratio of federal bureaucratic employees lagging behind per capita GNP. As Fig. 1-1 illustrates, neither is true.

In the United States, the growth of per capita GNP parallels very closely the

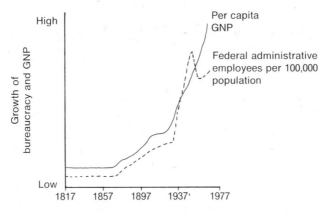

**Fig. 1-1.** Bureaucratic development in United States, 1821 to 1971. Data from U.S. Bureau of the Census. Per capita GNP is calculated in constant 1929 dollars. Federal administrative employees exclude military personnel. Data are reported in 10-year intervals from 1821 to 1971.

growth of federal administrative employees per 100,000 population. This pattern implies a synchronous development of economy and federal public administration. Since 1821 there have been at least two points where the rate of growth of per capita GNP and public administration changed sharply. The first followed the depression of the 1870s and the second followed the Great Depression of the 1930s.

The evidence from the United States suggests an organic model of economic development in advanced bureaucratic states and the expansion of the public bureaucracies. Although data are severely limited from other countries, semblances of the U.S. pattern also may be seen in some of the continental European countries, particularly Germany. From this data it appears that neither polity nor economy develop too far without pulling the other along. Just as we found an organic fusion of economy, kinship, and personalized leadership in simple societies, so also we have some evidence of an organic fusion between economy and institutionalized authority in advanced bureaucratic states. The economic depressions of the 1870s and 1930s might represent crisis points in this organic fusion, followed by sharp ad-

justments in both the economic sphere and public administration at the federal level.

The history of bureaucracy in the United States closely conforms to our description of the dynamics of bureaucratic development. The United States at the beginning of the eighteenth century might be classified as an intermediate bureaucratic state. Recall that intermediate bureaucratic states separate kinship and politics but tend to fuse religion and politics. When Americans fled the clerical oppressions of the Old World, they sought freedom to practice their own religions, but they did not seek freedom from religious influence. These diverse religious groups had extraordinarily rigid canons of orthodoxy, they imposed religious authoritarianism at the local level, and they were grossly intolerant of nonconformity. Among these groups were the Puritans and later the Mormons, Amish, Mennonites, and Brethren (see Roche, 1956:13).

The religious grasp on political power in the United States did not decline until the latter part of the nineteenth century. In part, this decline followed the Civil War, during which the federal government drastically increased its direct contact with individual citizens. The shift of power to the federal government that occurred during the 1860s subsequently was maintained through the growing federal bureaucracy administering Reconstruction in the South and attempting to address the economic panic of 1873. Once power began shifting from the state governments to the federal government, the religious domination at the local level slowly was replaced by increased national regulation of community life. This shift in power allowed the federal government to set standards that might apply to all communities, regardless of religious persuasion, and permitted the federal government to directly protect individuals from the intolerance of local communities. As Weber has argued, this form of "rational" social action is the domain of bureaucracies.

From our list of intrinsic and extrinsic conditions, five factors are particularly important in describing the growth of bureaucracy in the United States from 1870 to 1950: economic disaster, economic boom, protest and collective violence, war, and trade. During this 80-year period, these factors continued shifting power to the federal government and continued expanding the federal bureaucracy. Fig. 1-2 presents clear evidence of the transition from an intermediate to advanced bureaucracy in America.

The graph in Fig. 1-2 identifies several points directly relevant to bureaucratic development in the United States:

1. Bureaucratic expansion followed the Civil War.
2. The sharp upturn in collective violence and the imbalance of U.S. trade during Reconstruction and following the panic of 1873 directly correspond to the first important change in size of the federal bureaucracy.
3. This expansion continued, closely following the pattern of trade balances and collective violence, until 1929. During this period, in 1887 the Congress passed the Act to Regulate

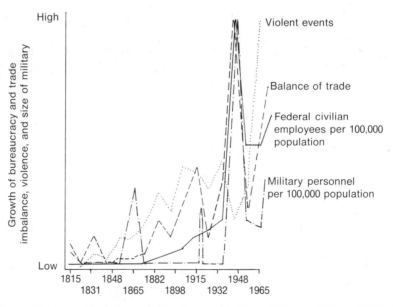

**Fig. 1-2.** Impetus toward bureaucratic development in United States, 1821 to 1971. Collective violence represents number of events per decade. Trade imbalance is absolute values of exports divided by imports. Military, bureaucratic employee, and trade data from U.S. Bureau of the Census. Violence data from Levy (1969:84-100).

Commerce, creating the Interstate Commerce Commission (see Sharfman, 1931).* This act marked the beginning of massive federal regulative activities. Earlier, in 1883, the Congress adopted a civil service system for federal civilian employees.

4. The second major turning point in the growth of the federal bureaucracy occurred during the Roosevelt Administration. This renewed growth corresponds to the economic depression of the 1930s, the level of social unrest, and the unfavorable trade imbalance.

5. The Second World War exaggerated the trend of bureaucratic growth. During that period the trade situation dramatically improved, the proportionate size of the army drastically increased, but the incidence of social unrest declined.

6. After the Second World War, the growth of the federal bureaucracy reversed until the 1960s.

7. During the 1960s, renewed growth in federal civilian employment paralleled the escalation of collective violence, the growing trade imbalance,

_____
*The major court case establishing governmental authority in regulation was *Munn* v. *Illinois* (1876).

and the increase in military personnel as the Vietnam War began.

**CONCLUSION**

Using a natural history approach to the study of bureaucracies, we have examined the types of social conditions and political organizations from which bureaucratic organizations appear to emerge. Central to each stage of development is the need to coordinate people's behavior in their struggles against nature, the need to coordinate behavior for controlling social conflict, and the need to govern the relations among societies. Among bureaucratic states, we have found a secondary pattern of development leading from beginning bureaucratic states to advanced bureaucracies. A series of intrinsic and extrinsic factors helps account for these observed changes. Finally we have seen that, even within advanced bureaucracies such as the United States, there might be a pattern of development that drastically increases the size and scope of administrative regulation. Fig. 1-3 illustrates a composite of the stages of development from simple societies through advanced bureaucracies.

The wavy line in Fig. 1-3 represents a series of S curves linked one to another. The plateau of delegation and specialization at one stage of development becomes

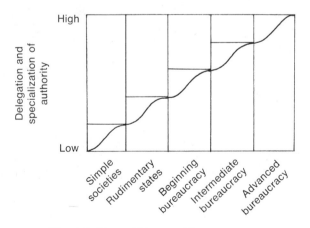

**Fig. 1-3.** Natural history of bureaucracy.

the starting point for the next stage. The **S** curve in Fig. 1-1 can be superimposed on the final **S** curve in Fig. 1-3, representing the course of administrative development within advanced bureaucracies. The curve for the United States suggests that the U.S. is approaching the upper plateau of administrative development. If so, coming generations might see levels of administrative organizations emerge that are greater than those we know today.

## REFERENCES

Davidson, B. *A history of West Africa.* New York: Doubleday & Co., Inc., Anchor Books, 1966.

Dewey, J. *The public and its problems.* Chicago: Henry Regnery Co., Gateway Editions, 1946.

Fallers, L. *Bantu bureaucracy.* Chicago: University of Chicago Press, 1965.

Hoebel, E. A. *The law of primitive man.* New York: Atheneum Publishers, 1968.

Holmberg, A. *Nomads of the long bow.* Garden City, N.Y. American Museum Science Books, 1969.

Holt, R., and Turner, J. *The political basis of economic development.* New York: D. Van Nostrand Co., 1965.

Kracke, E. A., Jr. *Civil service in early Sung China —960-1067.* Cambridge, Mass.: Harvard University Press, 1953.

Levy, S. G. A 150-year study of political violence in the United States. In H. D. Graham and T. R. Gurr (Eds.), *The history of violence in America: a report to the National Commission on the causes and prevention of violence.* New York: Bantam Books, Inc., 1969.

Mair, L. *Primitive government.* Baltimore: Penguin Books, Inc., 1962.

Omer-Cooper, J. D., Ayandele, E. A., Afigbo, A. E., and Gavin, R. J. *The making of modern Africa* (Vol. 1). Atlantic Highlands, N.J.: Humanities Press, Inc., 1968.

Robinson, C. E. *Hellas.* Boston: Beacon Press, 1948.

Roche, J. P. We've never had more freedom. *New Republic,* 1956, *134,* 13.

Rostovtzeff, M. *Rome.* New York: Oxford University Press, Inc., Galaxy Books, 1960.

Rostovtzeff, M. *Greece.* New York: Oxford University Press, Inc., Galaxy Books, 1963.

Sharfman, I. A. *The Interstate Commerce Commission.* New York: Commonwealth Fund, 1931.

Smith, D. *Religion and political development.* Boston: Little, Brown and Co., 1970.

Southern, R. W. *The making of the Middle Ages.* New Haven, Conn.: Yale University Press, 1953.

Strauss, E. *The ruling servants: bureaucracy in Russia, France—and Great Britain?* New York: Praeger Publishers, Inc., 1961.

Weber, M. *The theory of social and economic organization* (T. Parsons, ed. and trans.). New York: Free Press, 1964.

# CHAPTER 2

# Foundations of bureaucracy

People structure political action to solve social problems. Although there are many devices for structuring political action, some are more flexible and might help a society make adjustments to radical social change. Social crises and radical change impel increased social complexity, bureaucratic development, innovations that might generate more social crises, and the growth of science and the secularization of authority.

## BUREAUCRATIC DEVELOPMENT

Bureaucracy is a special form of social organization that provides procedures to elaborate and administer substantive guidelines for structuring political action through the delegation and specialization of authority. Of course, bureaucracy is not the only means of structuring political action. In simple societies, for example, the web of kinship is the primary means of structuring political action. And in more complex societies ecclesiastical authority and rudimentary bureaucratic organization are the primary means of structuring political action. However, only in the more advanced bureaucratic states does bureaucratic organization assume a central role in structuring political action. But even in these advanced states, as we shall see more clearly in Part III of this book, bureaucratic organization is tempered by a variety of other means to structure political action. Democracy and totalitarianism are two of the more important complements of bureaucratic organization.

### Natural history

The natural history of bureaucracy reveals an important fact: bureaucracies do not appear suddenly; rather, bureaucratic organization emerges and develops quite slowly. Rudiments of bureaucracy appear when individual authority is transformed into institutionalized authority. Slowly, authority is delegated to specialized agents. Even more slowly, delegated and specialized authority becomes divorced from the web of kinship obligations and ecclesiastical authority. In the social history of a culture, these changes generally are cumulative. As illustrated by Fig. 1-3, a clear pattern of increasing delegation, specialization, and secularization of authority underlies the natural history of bureaucracy. But why is this pattern so consistent in social history?

### Toward a macro theory of bureaucracy

The natural history of bureaucracy illustrates several consistent themes underlying bureaucratic development:

1. In simple societies, kinship supplies a blueprint for political action through its system of duties and privileges.
2. As authority becomes institutionalized (i.e., attached to positions, not individuals), kinship patterns become the natural setting from which officials emerge, and kinship continues to guide political action.
3. As societies become more complex, kinship fails to recruit needed talent, its system of duties and privileges lim-

**19**

its the range of permissible action, and the bond between kinship and institutionalized authority disintegrates.

4. Simultaneously, social crises and rapid social change impel bureaucratic development.
5. As bureaucratic organization becomes increasingly autonomous, it becomes increasingly secular. In this chapter we will put these themes together.

## STRUCTURING POLITICAL ACTION

From our definition, bureaucracy is a special form of social organization to structure political action. Like bureaucracy, the web of kinship is another form of social organization that structures political action. But what is "social organization"? Social organization implies that social life occurs within a framework of common goals, rules, and a status system (see Silverman, 1971:8). Hence social organization means a systematic coordination of human activities, often replete with defined duties, privileges, rights, and common goals. A status system suggests that these duties, privileges, and rights are not equally distributed among all members of society. We know of no society where all individuals equally enjoy duties, privileges, and rights. Even in primitive societies we find status systems that distinguish natural leaders from ordinary persons, children from adults, the aged and weak from the strong and healthy, and males from females. Together with common rules and goals, the status system makes *social* life possible.

What, then, is "political action"? Clearly, political action is a special form of human action. It alludes to people's deliberate efforts to attend to the arrangements of society (see Oakeshott, 1962). Hence, political action enables people consciously to maintain or change social arrangements. These arrangements include the distribution of duties, privileges, and rights. Now here is a curious twist! How can social organization structure political action when the target of political action is this framework of common goals, rules, and a status system? Actually, the dilemma has two dimensions. First, both Freud (1961) and Malinowski (1964), among others, have pointed out that no group of people, whether savage or civil, submits slavishly and spontaneously to the social constraints needed to secure human coordination. In short, there always are some discrepancies among observed behaviors and the expected behaviors derived from common goals, rules, and a status system. Political actions are conscious attempts to bring observed behaviors closer to expected behaviors. Second, in a few extraordinary circumstances, political action might help change expected behaviors (see Seitz, 1978). To do so, the social organization guiding political action must be independent of existing duties, privileges, and rights. By implication, these social organizations differ from traditional organizations that incorporate existing arrangements when guiding political action. We will examine this distinction in the following discussion.

### Why structure political action?

People structure political action for several reasons, but three of them are particularly relevant. First, structured political action helps people coordinate their efforts to gain food, shelter, and energy from nature. Second, structured political action helps people coordinate their relations with each other, particularly in controlling conflict. Third, structured political action helps people govern their relations with other societies. As we saw in Chapter 1, these are three of the basic social problems facing most societies. Every society has at least two dynamic processes continually at work: the interactions of people with nature and the interactions among people. Most have a third process: the interactions among societies. Because these processes continually fluctuate, the problem of human coordination demands continual political action. As old problems recur and as new problems arise, people face the question, What are we to do? When social organization structures political action, it provides either a procedure for answering this question or substantive guidelines for answering the question, or both.

In simple societies, the privileges and obligations fixed by the kinship web become substantive guidelines for solving social problems. In such simple societies, however, there are no autonomous procedures for handling social problems, save through the leadership of unusual people, because authority is not institutionalized. But in rudimentary states, regular procedures for handling social problems accompany institutionalized authority. Here both the procedures and the substantive guidelines for handling social problems largely derive from the kinship web and from ecclesiastical doctrines. With bureaucratic states, procedural devices increasingly become autonomous of specific distributions of duties, rights, and privileges. In fact, we can distinguish between procedural devices that make or abolish substantive guidelines, such as democracy and totalitarianism, and procedural devices that elaborate and administer these legal norms and rules, such as bureaucracy.

### Procedure and substance

The distinction between procedures to structure political action and substantive guidelines to structure political action is really quite important. In less complex societies, social organizations, such as kinship and ecclesiastical authority, fix substantive guidelines and supply procedures for enforcement. But in advanced bureaucratic states, other social organizations permit regular change of substantive guidelines and furnish procedures to enforce these changing guidelines. In fact, the distinction parallels a common division in modern societies between policy making and policy administration. Policy making

refers to the procedural devices through which people decide what should be done about a particular social problem. Policy administration refers to the elaboration and application of substantive guidelines, usually in the form of legal norms and rules, which emerge from the policy-making process.

***Kinship.*** The kinship web fixes duties and privileges among people. These duties and privileges become guides for political action, but they cannot consciously be changed without disrupting the moral sentiments that make kinship an effective form of social organization. This point is crucial if we want to understand the basic differences between kinship duties and privileges and legal norms and rules. The kinship web slowly evolves over time and is not the deliberate product of policy makers. Similarly, the moral sentiments underlying kinship allow limited variation in elaborating or applying these duties and privileges to particular cases. These sentiments establish "right ways" for enforcing duties and obligations.

In simple societies, where kinship is the primary guide for political action, there is little provision for policy making and only limited discretion in policy administration. In rudimentary states, however, we do find devices for making policy. However, the kinship web sets bounds around the exercise of power; links rulers to subjects through lineage and ancestral ties; governs the means for recruiting officials and their representatives; secure loyalty between ruler and representative; and continues to influence where one lives, whom one marries, and to whom primary and secondary social obligations are due.

Now it should be clear why the kinship web becomes less effective as societies become more complex and the quality, frequency, and intensity of social problems change. First, kinship is a poor device for recruiting talented officials. Second, the moral sentiments that support it grow weak with increased population size and increased geographic distance among relatives. As the psychological bond of kinship disintegrates, the attendant economic privileges and obligations become less compelling. Third, kinship provides no procedural device for making policy. And fourth, kinship allows very little discretion in policy administration. In addition, this administration is the function of most members of the society, and the authority to administer substantive guidelines is seldom delegated or specialized.

**Ecclesiastical authority.** Most major religions have developed doctrines of public law and a social organization for promulgating and enforcing ecclesiastical law. In Christianity, for example, the Ten Commandments function as public law, the church promulgates its law to nonbelievers and enforces its law among believers (see Troeltsch, 1960). Like kinship duties and obligations, the core of ecclesiastical law cannot be changed at will, lest the claims for supernatural origin and sanctity fall under popular suspicion. Ecclesiastical authority rests on beliefs that the gods make law, authorities are representatives of supernatural powers, and failure to observe these laws invites both human and divine sanction.

The prototype of ecclesiastical authority lies in the ancestral cults reinforcing the kinship web in simple societies and rudimentary states. Ecclesiastical authority becomes a primary factor directing political action in beginning bureaucratic states. Here special agents symbolize ecclesiastical authority and apply ecclesiastical law to particular cases. Such agents might include witch doctors, medicine chiefs, and priests. These agents and doctrines they espouse force political officials to limit the range of alternative actions. In addition, these ecclesiastical authorities might threaten divine sanction if policy makers exceed the boundaries of legitimate action.

In intermediate bureaucratic states, the church might claim ecclesiastical authority to elaborate and administer ecclesiastical law. Here the church often performs both an administrative and a quasi-legislative function. In addition, the church severely limits the secular power of officials. In the Middle Ages, for example, political leaders held positions of authority approved by the church and sanctioned under ecclesiastical authority. In early seventeenth century England, when the balance of power began shifting from the church to the royal family, the king still found it necessary to claim divine right through the Fourth Commandment. As father of his country, the king claimed the same honor and respect due one's natural parents. Although this seems farfetched today, the doctrine of divine right actually was taught as part of the church's catechism.

**Bureaucracy.** The transition to advanced bureaucratic states requires two critical changes in the processes structuring political action. First, policy makers deliberately might change the laws and rules guiding substantive action. For example, policy makers can make, amend, or abolish laws. Similarly, these policy makers can amend a written constitution. Second, policy administration functionally becomes separated from policy making. The first change means that ultimate authority is vested in procedures for making laws rather than in the laws themselves. In advanced states, bureaucracy is the procedural device for policy administration, while democracy or totalitarianism are procedural devices for policy making. Of course, bureaucracies do have a quasi-legislative function. However, this function is usually secondary and is limited by explicit or implicit legislative intent.

**Democracy and totalitarianism.** In advanced bureaucratic states, democracy and totalitarianism complement bureaucracy. For our purposes, we will define totalitarianism as a special form of social organization that provides procedures for policy making through an authority system where *officials* recruit other officials and determine the general course of public policy. Democracy is a special form of social organization that provides procedures for policy making through an authority system where *the citizenry* recruits officials and determines the general course of public policy (see Dahl and Lindblom, 1953).

*Summary.* Fig. 2-1 illustrates the distinctions made in the preceding discussion. As guides to political action, the kinship web and ecclesiastical authority fuse procedure with substance and focus attention on the elaboration and administration of existing substantive guidelines. During the transition to more complex political devices, procedure and substance still are fused, but these transitional vehicles help people establish new substantive guidelines for political action. In complex societies, procedural devices, such as democracy and totalitarianism, are independent of specific laws and rules for guiding political action, and these devices can make, amend, or abolish specific laws and rules. Similarly, bureaucracy is a procedural device in complex societies that is autonomous of specific laws and rules and hence elaborates and administers substantive guidelines as they are made or amended by policy makers.

## FLEXIBILITY

Increased social complexity causes (1) a shift in the locus of authority, from specific obligations and doctrines to procedures for making laws and rules, and (2) a separation of policy-making from policy-administering functions. Why do these trends occur? Clearly, there must be something about democracy, totalitarianism, and bureaucracy as procedural devices for structuring political action that makes them more effective than kinship or ecclesiastical authority. What is this "something"?

The key to our puzzle is flexibility. As a structuring principle for political action, kinship and ecclesiastical doctrine are relatively inflexible; bureaucracies, democracy, and totalitarianism are more flexible. Why is this so? Why does the need for flexibility diminish the importance of kinship and ecclesiastical authority and increase the secularization of bureaucracy?

### Need for flexibility

All societies require some system of coordination. But this system of coordination is not a mere mechanical device, like pistons in the cylinders of an engine. Rather, it is dynamic, permitting a variety of adjustments to disturbances of coordination. In some respects, the system of coordination in society parallels that in human organic

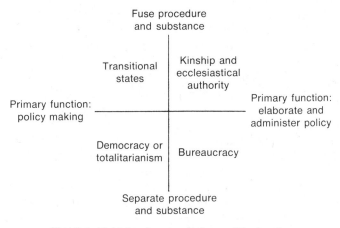

**Fig. 2-1.** Vehicles for structuring political action.

systems. The human body, for example, maintains a relative constant temperature and water distribution, despite great fluctuations in the external environment. The dynamic system of coordination in society establishes such an equilibrium; that is, the society has adequate adjustive mechanisms to absorb the usual disturbances from within and without (see Gluckman, 1968:316). Typical disturbances include the usual conflicts among people (internal) and temporary changes in the availability of food, water, shelter, and energy from nature (external) (Gluckman, 1968:316).

Unfortunately, some disturbances overtax and exceed the capabilities of these adjustive mechanisms. Like the dinosaur, whose environment changed more rapidly than its genetic adaptation, some societies might be threatened with extinction if internal and external disturbances become too great. Other societies, perhaps slightly more fortunate, might survive only through radical transformations of existing social arrangements. In short, these extraordinary disturbances exceed the existing capacities of a social equilibrium. Earlier, we divided these unusual disturbances into two categories: intrinsic and extrinsic. Intrinsic conditions include economic disaster, economic boom, collective violence, religious transformation, and democratization. Examples of extrinsic conditions are conquest or invasion, imperialism, and trade. These conditions require forms of social organization capable of great flexibility in structuring political action. Apparently, kinship and ecclesiastical authority are less flexible than secular bureaucracies when radical change becomes necessary.

Why is secular bureaucracy capable of wider ranges of adjustment than either kinship or ecclesiastical authority? Certainly, under more normal circumstances, kinship, ecclesiastical authority, and bureaucracy all provide some adjustive mechanisms to maintain a dynamic equilibrium. But why does radical change render ineffective the adjustive processes of kinship and ecclesiastical doctrine? Why are individual leadership and institutionalized authority, limited and guided by the web of kinship and ecclesiastical doctrine, often inadequate under conditions of social crisis and rapid social change?

## Tradition

The web of kinship privileges and obligations rests on tradition. When behavior violates expectations, social devices, such as rumor, gossip, ostracism, blood feuds, withdrawal of reciprocity, and simple negotiations, help maintain a dynamic equilibrium by bringing disruptive behaviors closer to expected behaviors. For the most part, these are procedural mechanisms for resolving conflict or deciding what to do about a social problem. These procedural mechanisms are intricately bound with substantive guidelines for political action. Quite often, the legitimacy of these procedural mechanisms derives from their congruency with the substantive guidelines of tradition. But tradition, especially the web of kinship, changes very slowly, often requiring several generations for modest change.

Tradition defines the expected arrangements of society. When radical change occurs, however, it often alters existing distributions of duties, privileges, and status. The growing disparity among the emerging arrangements of society and those expected on traditional grounds eventually undermines the legitimacy of tradition. Because tradition is an end in itself for the members of less complex societies, it does not provide procedures for its own change. Hence, tradition falls victim to change beyond its limited flexibility (see Beattie, 1964:246-247). Although speaking of the late Middle Ages in Europe, Lindsay (1962: 69) observes that social changes made the slow development of custom inadequate for the changing needs of the time. Tradition became ineffective against the new social conditions. Administrative activities and governing power were exalted above the law. Only unfettered law-making and law-administering bodies could do what was required when social change quickened its pace. When disturbances to a society's co-ordination become excessive, tradition becomes a very ineffective guide to political action. Fig. 2-2 illustrates this relation.

Tradition places strict boundaries around the exercise of political power. Acts that exceed these boundaries no longer may claim the legitimacy of tradition. Under conditions of crisis, therefore, there are pressures toward political actions that may, if taken, trigger a crisis of legitimacy as well. Sometimes, extraordinarily popular leaders might generate their own source of legitimacy, perhaps sufficient to carry a society through periods of crisis. Such leaders have what Weber (1964:324-392) calls "charismatic authority." However, because such leadership is highly individualized, and hence its legitimacy rests more on personality than on office, it cannot permanently replace tradition as a guide to political action. Lacking a succession of charismatic leaders, the basis of legitimacy in a society undergoing rapid change eventually must shift to a form of legitimacy divorced from both tradition and charisma. Otherwise, the crisis of legitimacy eventually would immobilize most political action.

### Ecclesiastical guidance

Ecclesiastical authority suffers many of the shortcomings found with kinship. Ec-clesiastical authority is tied to substantive religious doctrines, and given the supernatural sanction on which it rests, those ecclesiastical laws change only modestly over long periods. Unlike kinship, however, ecclesiastical authority is more appropriate to large societies and societies covering large geographic areas, because ecclesiastical doctrine shifts the psychological bond from one among people to one between people and their gods. And because ecclesiastical authority can bind people through civil and criminal codes that are more extensive than the privileges and obligations of kinship, they have a definite advantage over kinship as societies become more complex.

Of course, neither kinship nor ecclesiastical authority disappears with a bang. Rather, they continue to structure political action long after their primary utility is exhausted in complex societies. Unlike kinship, ecclesiastical authority often responds to increasing demands by becoming more general and more spiritual and hence less particular and worldly in its social teachings (see Troeltsch, 1960).

Neither particular nor general ecclesiastical doctrines are very effective in guiding political action through excessive disturbances in human coordination, because one is too inflexible and the other loses contact with concrete social problems. Like kinship, ecclesiastical authority does not have mechanisms for drastically changing ecclesiastical doctrines, although many churches do have procedures for slowly modifying their social teachings. Very general doctrines provide little direct, substantive guidance for political action. As Fig. 2-3 illustrates, universalistic, or general, ecclesiastical doctrines provide only minimal substantive guidelines, while particularistic doctrines provide maximal substantive guidelines.

Eventually, ecclesiastical authority as a guide to political action suffered the same fate that befell kinship. Consider, for example, the altered role of religion in Ameri-

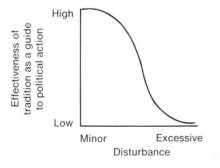

**Fig. 2-2.** Social disturbances and effectiveness of tradition.

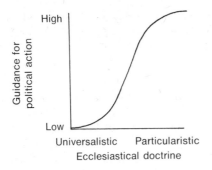

**Fig. 2-3.** Ecclesiastical doctrines and guidance for political action.

can politics. Before the Civil War, American Christians had accepted ecclesiastical law as the given nature of community life (Hadden, 1969:4). Contemporary Christians, however, witness a number of competing explanations of humanity and society. More important, they see policy makers respond to crucial events with increasingly pragmatic decisions divorced from explicit ecclesiastical justifications.

### Rational-legal authority

In complex societies, bureaucratic organization becomes increasingly secular; that is, bureaucracy becomes increasingly divorced from ecclesiastical authority. In advanced societies, few people glorify the substantive guidelines of bureaucracies as ends in themselves. Rather, people generally transfer faith and legitimacy from these substantive guidelines to the procedural mechanisms for making these substantive guidelines. Hence, rational authority has two important dimensions: (1) bureaucratic guidelines for administering political action are authoritative because they derive from duly established legal norms and rules; and (2) these legal norms and rules derive in turn from a procedural device, such as democracy, to which a good portion of the citizenry grants legitimacy. Whether it be a totalitarian party or a constitutional democracy, legitimacy in advanced bureaucratic states focuses more on the procedural function and less on the

substantive guidelines for structuring political action.

Here is the key to the flexibility of bureaucratic organization. Faith in procedures, rather than guidelines, allows faster change and greater flexibility than faith in substantive guidelines alone. Because the content of laws and rules is separate from the procedures for making them, and because faith inheres more in the latter than the former, advanced bureaucratic states find it much easier to radically change substantive guidelines. The same does not hold for those states bound by kinship or ecclesiastical doctrine. Equally important, changes in substantive guidelines in advanced bureaucracies are less likely to trigger crises of legitimacy. Again, the same does not hold for less complex societies.

Bureaucracies become increasingly secular to cope with social crises and rapid social change. Bureaucratic organization is more flexible than either kinship or ecclesiastical doctrine because it rests on legal norms and rules that the citizenry does not consider to be ends in themselves. This does not mean that individual bureaucratic agencies are flexible. As we will see in Part II, individual bureaucracies are not very flexible at all. It does mean that bureaucratic organization, when compared with either tradition or religion, is more flexible as a guide to political action.

### CRISIS, COMPLEXITY, AND INNOVATION

Social crises impel the development of bureaucratic organizations. At the same time, social crises and rapid social change usually impel greater social complexity. By their very nature, social crises and rapid social change suggest that existing social devices might not be sufficient to maintain social equilibrium. Here we can draw an interesting analogy between radical change in social arrangements and genetic mutation. When behavior is tied closely to its genetic base, unusual pressures from a changing environment favor selective adaptations of the gene codes, facilitating some mutations over those presently governing behaviors. In human societies, social organizations assume the adaptive functions of such genetic drift. Rather than await gene mutation and selection, people have the capability of improvising new social organizations needed in the struggle to coordinate human behavior (see Geertz, 1965:93-118). Without these improvisations, people may expect continued setbacks by social crises and rapid social change. As Durkheim (1964) noted long ago, these improvisations tend more toward complex organizations, particularly through the division and specialization of labor and the increasing reliance on regulation and restitution over simple repression.

Social crises might produce radical social change. But seldom does this social change completely restructure the social arrangements of a society. Rather, some arrangements are maintained, while others are sacrificed for new, better, or more efficient adjustive mechanisms. Normally these new adjustive mechanisms are more complex than their predecessors, requiring more intricate coordination and more delegation and specialization of authority. In sum, this is why social crisis impels both bureaucratic development and increased social complexity.

### Crisis and innovation

Conditions of social crisis might mean that existing ways of coordinating human behavior are inadequate to the tasks facing a society. When people improvise different organizations, they hope to reestablish a new level of social equilibrium. It is hoped the improvisations are sufficient to address or resolve the social crisis before them. But there is another side to this coin. Improvisations and innovations can foster new social crises.

**Innovations.** Innovations involve mechanical, applied, and social inventions that affect the arrangements of a society and its subsequent history (see Ogburn, 1964:62-77). Mechanical inventions such as the plow, applied sciences such as radio, television, and electricity, and social inventions such as new religious forms or new systems of property rights all have a dramatic impact on existing arrangements of a society. Not surprising, such inventions often lie at the root of theories on social change. Without question, the most famous theory of social change is that of Karl Marx. In *The German Ideology,* Marx argued that changing tools and means of economic production create tensions in the relations among people using these tools. The means of production and relations of production constitute, for Marx, the economic structure of society. As change occurs in this economic structure, it forces changes in laws, political institutions, morality, and ideology. The legal and political institutions of a society, together with its morality and ideology, constitute the superstructure of society.

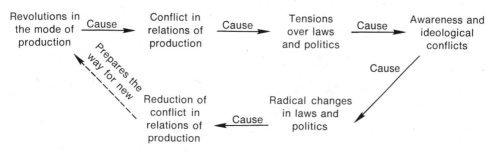

**Fig. 2-4.** Marx's theory of social change.

Fig. 2-4 illustrates Marx's model of social change. Because tools and the means of economic production are the means through which people exploit the environment, there are continued efforts to revolutionize both tools and production to expand society's control over nature. But the use of tools and means of production requires certain social organizations. As the tools and means of production change, these social arrangements also must change. As the tension in the economic structure between the means of production and the relations of production becomes more intense, it causes new pressures on laws and the political system that attempts to enforce these laws. Finally, people become aware of these tensions and pressures. Moral and ideological battles erupt within a society until the laws and political institutions are adjusted to reflect the emerging changes in the economic structure.

*Another model of social change.* The natural history of bureaucracy suggests some modifications of Marx's model. This model emphasizes the importance of unusual conditions, both intrinsic and extrinsic, that exceed the ability of existing adjustive mechanisms to maintain social equilibrium. Here there are two mainsprings for radical social change: (1) in the relations among people and nature, innovations in tools and means of production create social ferment that disrupts existing patterns of human coordination, and (2) in the relations among people and among societies, normal conflicts begin to escalate, eventually disrupting existing patterns of human coordination. This escalation creates social ferment, which in turn increases the likelihood of new innovations. Why would normal conflicts escalate? Although there are a large number of reasons, three are particularly important. First, as societies become more complex, competition among people and among societies for privileges, resources, power, and status increases. Greed and the availability of resources feed on one another (see McKenzie, 1968). Second, as societies become more complex, the sheer volume of ideas that emerge increases both the range and diversity of human conflict (see Hegel, 1967). Third, as societies become more complex, the intensity and variety of human interactions increase the possible points of friction among people and among societies (see Wolff, 1950; Geiger, 1969; Mead, 1964).

Fig. 2-5 illustrates this model of social change. Innovations in the tools and means through which people exploit nature might escalate social conflict or introduce into society disruptions that undermine existing patterns of human coordination. Social

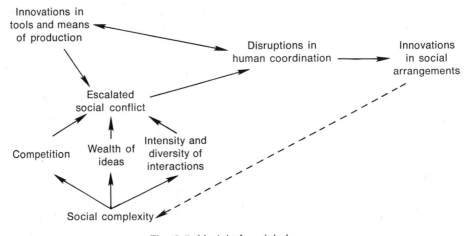

**Fig. 2-5.** Model of social change.

complexity might increase competition, the wealth of ideas, or the intensity and diversity of human interactions, thereby escalating social conflict. Escalated social conflict disrupts existing patterns of human coordination. Disrupted patterns of human coordination might encourage new revolution in the tools and means of production. Disrupted patterns of human coordination might encourage more innovations in social arrangements.

*Innovations in social arrangements.* Of course, there are a large number of innovations in social arrangements that could follow from radical social changes. We have been interested primarily in those innovations impelling bureaucratic development. And in Fig. 2-5 we now have a schematic idea of how social problems such as the relations among people and society and the relations of people to nature might impel bureaucratic development. The pattern underlying the natural history of bureaucracy has its roots in the dynamics of radical social change. Among kinship, ecclesiastical authority, and bureaucratic organization, only bureaucratic organization is capable of shifting its substantive guidelines for political action as the demands of radical social change require. Weber recognized the inherent flexibility of bureaucratic organization. The once existing apparatus, he points out, has an objective indispensability, easily made to work for anybody who gains control over it (Gerth and Mills, 1958: 229).

### Science

Our account of bureaucratic development thus far has ignored the role of science. What is its role in bureaucratic development? How does the development of science relate to radical social change?

*Science and theology.* Is science a body of knowledge uniquely different from theology? If not, how is science distinguished from theology? In many respects, science and theology are similar. Both science and theology reflect social experiences as they are conditioned by habitat and technology. And both science and theology provide guidelines for interpreting and using social experience (White, 1949:3; 1959:359).

But science differs from theology in some critical respects. Although science reflects social experience, it is less bound by time and space than theology. Developed theologies are more fixed, more clearly reflecting their origins in a particular point in time. Careful reading of the symbolism in the Bible, for example, reveals how closely Christianity is tied with an agrarian economy. In Greece, where modern science first emerged, the topological, geographical, ecological, and social and cultural factors favored a freedom of mind unusual in ancient times. This freedom of mind is essential to the development of science (White, 1959:366). With this freedom of mind, science begins to surpass theology when it can provide people with a greater knowledge of the real world than that provided by theological doctrine (see Mazur, 1968:196).

But freedom of mind is not, in itself, sufficient to distinguish science from theology. As it develops, science comes to rely increasingly on the empirical methods of validation. And scientists supposedly subject their "truths" to continued investigation and reexamination. Here science differs most markedly from theology, for theology fuses procedure and substantive beliefs. Established truths are not subject to further question except in extraordinary instances. Not coincidently, the same distinction emerges between bureaucratic organization and tradition or ecclesiastical doctrines. Tradition and ecclesiastical doctrines fuse procedure with substantive guidelines, and these guidelines for political action become ends in themselves. Hence there is a strong congruence between science as a source of knowledge and bureaucracy as a form of social organization to structure political action.

Given its emphasis on procedure, scientific knowledge changes more rapidly than does religious doctrine (see Whitehead, 1948:163; Gerth and Mills, 1958:129-156). Although both science and theology provide guidelines for interpreting and using social experience, science is better able to cope with radical change (Whitehead, 1948:163, 171). Like the guidelines of bureaucratic organization, the guidelines of science are not immutable. Like bureaucratic organization, science has become more and more important in Western civilization. In fact, the growth of science and the decline of ecclesiastical authority in structuring political action parallel the development of bureaucratic organization.

*Science and secularization.* Science and secularization go hand in hand. Because of its emphasis on scientific procedure, science cannot accept social experience as a self-contained truth. Nor can it accept the sacredness and inviolability that theology or tradition impose on human experience. Relying on procedure over substance, science can strive to strip the metaphysical aura from human events and social experiences. Events and practices no longer are thought to be necessarily beyond the control of persons. But this is precisely what the process of secularization implies. Secular guidelines for political action are not self-justifying. And in consequence, they might be seen as human contrivances subject to human change. The spirit of secularization follows in the shadow of science.

*Science, innovation, and complexity.* As science develops, its knowledge becomes increasingly specialized. Even apparently simple phenomena are seen in more complex ways. But we already have seen that bureaucratic organization becomes increasingly specialized as society becomes more complex. Again, science goes hand in hand with bureaucratic development. Bureaucratic organization involves both the delegation and specialization of authority. As authority becomes specialized, its

needs for information specialize accordingly. While ecclesiastical doctrines cannot specialize sufficiently to provide the knowledge required by bureaucracies, science can. In fact, specialized authority requires this specialized knowledge. Hence it should not be terribly surprising that the natural history of science bears a strong resemblance to the natural history of bureaucratic organization.

With its freedom of mind and healthy agnosticism, science can challenge the boundaries of social experience and even develop beyond those boundaries. By so doing, it allows people greater latitude for innovation. The Keynesian revolution of the twentieth century is just one example. As we move from simple societies to advanced bureaucratic states, pure and applied science increasingly become the handmaiden of people in their efforts to expand the boundaries of human society against the forces of nature and in their efforts to effect new forms of cooperation and control over conflict. The relation between science and politics is a matter of historical record. Not only did the ancient Greeks give birth to science, they also produced the first scientific study of politics.

## CONCLUSION

Why is bureaucracy more effective than kinship and ecclesiastical doctrine as a structuring principle of political action? Why does bureaucratic organization become increasingly secular?

Bureaucracy is more effective than kinship and ecclesiastical doctrines because it is a more flexible form of social organization for structuring political action. And bureaucracies become increasingly secular because scientific knowledge is more subject to change and revision through conscious procedures than is theology. All societies have mechanisms for maintaining social equilibrium as normal disturbances disrupt the social process. But not all societies have adjustive mechanisms capable of handling radical social change. Societies require a great deal of flexibility to handle radical change, the types of disturbances that tradition and ecclesiastical authority cannot absorb while maintaining social equilibrium. Divorcing procedure and substance, bureaucratic organization is better able to handle these disturbances, certainly more so than kinship or ecclesiastical authority. In short, secular bureaucratic organization, coupled with other procedural devices for making laws, provides a set of mechanisms for reestablishing a social equilibrium or for establishing a new social equilibrium when the old one is undermined by changes both internal and external to society.

## REFERENCES

Beattie, J. *Other cultures*. New York: Free Press, 1964.

Dahl, R., and Lindblom, C. *Politics, economics and welfare*. New York: Harper & Row, Publishers, Torchbooks, 1953.

Durkheim, E. *The division of labor in society*. New York: Free Press, 1964.

Freud, S. *Civilization and its discontents*. New York: W. W. Norton & Co., Inc., 1961.

Geertz, C. The impact of the concept of culture on the concept of man. In J. Platt (Ed.), *New views of the nature of man*. Chicago: University of Chicago Press, 1965.

Geiger, T. *On social order and mass society* (R. Mayntz, ed.). Chicago: University of Chicago Press, 1969.

Gerth, H. H., and Mills, C. W. (Eds.). *From Max Weber*. New York: Oxford University Press, Inc., Galaxy Books, 1958.

Gluckman, M. *Politics, law and ritual in tribal society*. New York: New American Library, Inc., Mentor Books, 1968.

Hadden, J. *The gathering storm in the churches*. New York: Doubleday & Co., Inc., Anchor Books, 1969.

Hegel, G. W. F. *The phenomenology of mind*. New York: Harper & Row, Publishers, Torchbooks, 1967.

Lindsay, A. D. *The modern democratic state*. New York: Oxford University Press, Inc., Galaxy Books, 1962.

Malinowski, B. *Crime and custom in savage society*. Totowa, N.J.: Littlefield, Adams & Co., 1964.

Mazur, A. The littlest science. *American Sociologist*, 1968, *3*, 196.

McKenzie, R. *On human ecology* (A. Hawley, ed.). Chicago: University of Chicago Press, 1968.

Mead, G. H. *On social psychology* (A. Strauss, ed.). Chicago: University of Chicago Press, 1964.

Oakeshott, M. *Rationalism in politics*. New York: Basic Books, Inc., Publishers, 1962.

Ogburn, W. F. *On culture and social change* (O. D. Duncan, ed.). Chicago: University of Chicago Press, 1964.

Seitz, S. T. The political structure of criminal justice. In B. Wright II and V. Fox (Eds.), *Criminal justice and the social sciences*. Philadelphia: W. B. Saunders Co., 1978.

Silverman, D. *The theory of organizations*. New York: Basic Books, Inc., Publishers, 1971.

Troeltsch, E. *The social teachings of the Christian churches* (Vols. 1 and 2). New York: Harper & Row, Publishers, Torchbooks, 1960.

Weber, M. *The theory of social and economic organization* (T. Parsons, ed. and trans.). New York: Free Press, 1964.

White, L. *The science of culture*. New York: Farrar, Strauss & Giroux, Inc., 1949.

White, L. *The evolution of culture*. New York: McGraw-Hill Book Co., 1959.

Whitehead, A. N. *Science and the modern world*. New York: New American Library, Inc., Mentor Books, 1948.

Wolff, K. H. (Ed.). *The sociology of Georg Simmel*. New York: Free Press, 1950.

# CHAPTER 3

# Bureaucracy and production

Technology and bureaucracy have elevated people from captives to captors of the ecological process. Industrialism has had a devastating impact on the ecological web and has brought about major changes in society. Coupled with policy decisions to minimize costs rather than the side effects of production, modern production organizations have created new social problems, including a potentially lethal ecocrisis.

## FUNCTIONS

Bureaucracies help people solve basic problems of social coordination. Three are of particular interest. First, bureaucracies help coordinate human behavior to secure survival against the forces of nature. That problem is examined in this chapter. Second, bureaucracies help coordinate the relations among people within a society (see Chapter 4). Third, and a composite of the first and second functions, bureaucracies help one society coordinate, control, or exploit its relations with other societies (see Chapter 5). Fig. 3-1 summarizes these simultaneous processes.

## BACKGROUND

Although people are part of a vast ecosystem, their role in that ecosystem has changed since humans first appeared. Two related factors help explain this change from total dependence on the forces of nature to skilled exploitation of natural forces. First, technical processes permit people to perform simultaneous and successive physical activities on raw materials to produce a given commodity (see Udy, 1959:

582). These processes have created demands for and have given people greater access to natural resources. Second, bureaucratic organization provides the coordination necessary for synthesizing these technical tasks into a coherent production process, because its characteristic delegation and specialization of authority allows the division of tasks among several people and the synthesis of task-products resulting from the division of labor. In turn, innovations in technique and social organization have created new social problems. The changing role of people in the global ecosystem is examined on the following pages.

### Two life processes

The global ecosystem is a web of physical, chemical, and biological processes that sustain life and create the foundations of evolutionary development (see Commoner, 1970:3-4). The earliest life process to appear converted inorganic elements from the planet's surface to organic matter. Plants, for example, convert certain minerals, carbon dioxide, and sunlight to organic compounds. Unlike the inorganic matter from which they arose, these life forms were self-sustaining and self-renewing. That is, life forms have some means, however primitive, of adjusting to environmental changes and some means of reproduction. From the second law of thermodynamics we know that matter tends toward maximum entropy, toward its least ordered state; it tends to disintegrate over time. The life process reverses the second law, if only for a time and under relatively

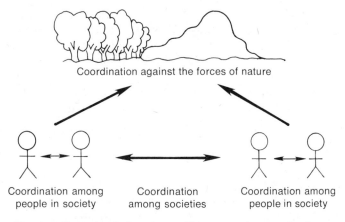

**Fig. 3-1.** Some basic functions of bureaucratic organizations.

**Fig. 3-2.** Early stages of our ecosystem.

restricted circumstances. Life brings matter into more ordered states.

Still, life as we know it today could not exist if the life process relied solely on inorganic matter as the source of life-sustaining nutrients. During any life process, forms of inorganic matter are converted chemically into new compounds, and quite often these new compounds cannot be used again by similar life forms. Because the earth has a finite amount of inorganic matter, this chemical conversion of needed raw materials into unusable forms could have become the ecosystem's fatal flaw.

Happily, a second life process emerged in the course of evolutionary history, checking this potentially fatal flaw. This life process converts one form of organic matter to another. With the second life process, new life forms can make use of the chemical compounds produced by the first life forms. Most animal life, for example, relies on or-

ganic matter for survival. From this point forward, life processes sustained each other. Slowly, the ecosystem became a complex causal nexus, with one form of life converting or reconverting the raw materials necessary to the existence of other life forms. The interrelationship is completed by the second law of thermodynamics: organic material dies and decomposes to inorganic materials. This allows the ecosystem to perpetuate itself. Fig. 3-2 illustrates this critical change in our ecosystem. The first diagram in the figure depicts the simple causal chain when life first emerged on our planet. The second diagram depicts the complex causal nexus when both life processes began supporting one another.

When nature dominates people, human behavior becomes part of the complex ecological web. However, when people dominate nature, their behavior might disrupt the ecological web. Do technical processes and their attendant bureaucracies have this impact?

### Prehistoric human life

People appeared late in our ecosystem's evolution. Fossil evidence of protohuman forms dates from about 250,000 years, but the present form of Homo sapiens dates from about 40,000 years (see Poirier, 1977: 272). Unlike other animals, people are poorly adapted physically for survival. We are not strong, swift, or well protected, and we lack natural tools such as claws or sharp teeth (see Childe, 1951:26-27). For example, people can run only about 25% faster than a charging elephant. Lacking genetically endowed protections, people substituted tools, techniques, and social organization—products of their brains, not their physiques. During their first 25,000 years, people primarily were nomadic hunters, gatherers, and scavengers. Human population remained sparse because the ecosystem in typical human habitats only could support about ten people per square mile, based on simple hunting and scavenging (Mumford, 1961:10).

*Permanent settlements.* During their first 25,000 years, people were part of a dominant ecosystem. Then about 15,000 years ago, people's place in the ecosystem began to change. Slowly, we began to dominate other life forms. The first important change occurred when people began to live in permanent settlements. To do so, people required a rudimentary agricultural technology, some domesticated animals, better fishing technology, and higher levels of social organization than family and kinship (Mumford, 1961:10). Then about 10,000 to 12,000 years ago, a second agricultural revolution began. Now people could gather and plant seeds for grasses and vegetables. No longer did they rely primarily on roots dug from the ground. Further, people increasingly relied on larger herds of domesticated animals (Mumford, 1961:11). All

this required, in turn, more advanced forms of social organization to coordinate economic efforts and to govern the relations among people. Here some of the rudiments of bureaucratic organization were born. About 10,000 years ago, people began to master the art of controlling the ecosystem in the pursuit of food and shelter.

*The city.* About 4,500 years ago, the first city appeared among the Sumerians of Mesopotamia (Mumford, 1961:79-80). The city was able to survive only because of its elaborate forms of social organization. The Sumerians had to turn vast tracts of swampland into fertile farmland, controlled by a vast system of drainage canals and dykes. This massive public works project required the coordination of thousands of people during lengthy periods. The resulting abundance of food made city life possible. But there were other requirements. Near their farms the Sumerians had little available stone for tools and little available lumber (Childe, 1951:114-115). These materials had to be imported. Here we find the roots of a complex economy. Regular trade, systems for transportation, public works for drainage and irrigation, and sustained agricultural production for home use and for trading commodities required a centralized economic system, made possible by early forms of bureaucratic organization (Childe, 1951:115). But it was in Egypt, not Mesopotamia, where this centralized economy and substantial social coordination first precipitated an intermediate bureaucratic state (Childe, 1951:126).

### Modern people

The history of present-day human society begins about 250 years ago. Before 1750, people relied largely on human, animal, and hydraulic power as the basic sources of energy to sustain human civilization. But shortly after 1750, coal rapidly replaced these sources of energy as the "prime mover" of human civilization. With coal came the Industrial Revolution. Its impact on the ecosystem, human population, and social organization has been immense.

**Impact on the ecosystem.** The use of coal, and later petroleum, has left an indelible scar on the earth's ecosystem. First, the growing industrial machine consumes organic matter at a rate thousands of times faster than that built up by the ecosystem over millions of years. Coal and petroleum are the long-term deposits of a thriving ecosystem at work for millions of years. People consume these supplies at a frightening rate, so that today we speak of available coal and petroleum reserves in terms of decades. Second, people's use of these reserves has not easily fed back into the ecosystem like the use of reserves by other life forms. Third, in gaining access to these reserves, people destroyed or permanently altered large segments of the ecosystem, particularly through careless mining and careless manufacturing. Fourth, the very use of these supplies altered the balance of organic and inorganic matter, particularly the levels of carbon dioxide, phosphates, and even ozone. Pollution has become the ecological by-product of technological progress. On the land surrounding our great industrial centers, for example, agricultural production begins to decline because the pollutants from the industrial machine have altered the ecosystem. Rivers, lakes, and perhaps the ocean become less able to support fish and other game.

**Impact on human population.** The industrial revolution did more than directly alter the global ecosystem. In country after country, industrialization has meant rapid population growth and expansion. In England, where the industrial revolution was born, the population growth curve took a rapid shift upward after 1750. From 1500 to 1750, the population growth had been rather nominal (Childe, 1951:18). Fig. 3-3 illustrates a similar growth pattern in the United States after the industrial revolution began here in the middle part of the

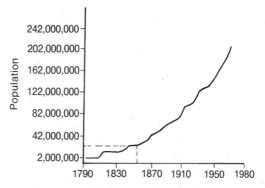

**Fig. 3-3.** Population growth in United States. Data from U.S. Bureau of the Census.

nineteenth century. Clearly, such dramatic shifts in human population size place new demands on the ecosystem for food, shelter, and raw materials for production. In turn, the by-products of this growing population permanently alter that ecosystem. People need more land, more water, more raw materials, and more energy. These come largely at the cost of an ecosystem that people had begun to master only 10,000 years earlier.

**Impact on social organization.** The ascent of people over nature occurred through five major changes in human social organization:

1. About 15,000 years ago, people established permanent settlements.
2. About 10,000 to 12,000 years ago, people began to create an ecosystem through agricultural planting and domesticated herds.
3. About 4,500 years ago, the city emerged, replete with complex economic institutions, major public works, trade relations, and abundant agricultural goods. The beginnings of bureaucratic organizations emerged to accommodate the growing industry.
4. About 3,000 years ago, the proto-types of modern science and modern bureaucratic organization were established.

5. About 250 years ago, the Industrial Revolution began, demanding escalated use of bureaucratic organization (see Ellul, 1964:43).

Fig. 3-4 illustrates these changes in people's relations to the ecosystem.

Of all these S curves in the social history of humankind, the last one is the steepest, involving the fastest and most extensive changes known to our civilization. Platt (1973:2) points out that, within the last century, communication speeds have increased by a factor of $10^7$, travel by a factor of $10^2$, data processing by a factor of $10^6$, energy resources by $10^3$, weapon power by $10^6$, and ability to control diseases by a factor of approximately $10^2$.

## PRODUCTION AND ECOLOGICAL PROCESS

As elements within the ecological web change, there emerge new pressures of competition, adjustment, and coordination among existing life forms. Before the ascent of humans, the ecological process changed slowly, often taking millennia for noticeable changes to appear. But people have denied the ecological process its most fundamental component: time. People are noticing the changes they have brought to the ecosystem. With the rapid change induced by the industrial machine during the past 250 years, people have become concerned with the "idea of progress." But human progress, if it means control over the ecosystem, is not a simple blessing. In gaining ascendency over nature, people

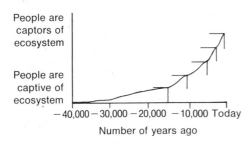

**Fig. 3-4.** People and the ecosystem.

have exploited it brutally. Even more disturbing, people have created an artificial ecosystem that is more threatening to their existence than the nature they conquered. Pollution, overpopulation, and nuclear war are imminent threats to future life. What has been done to the ecosystem?

### Ecological process

Under the old ecosystem, before the brutal victory of humans, how did competition, adjustment, and coordination lead to increasingly interdependent life processes and life forms? How has industrial victory affected this ecological process?

The mainspring of the old ecological process was competition: the battle among competing life forms for organic and inorganic matter and their subsequent adjustments to one another. From competition among life forms, Darwin derived his famous thesis on natural selection and survival of the fittest: that the struggle for survival gives selective advantage to organisms that vary in ways profitable to propagation and life (Darwin, 1966:5). Still, natural selection and survival of the fittest are only broad contours of the ecological process. More specific components include concentration, dispersion, specialization, centralization, segregation, invasion, and succession (McKenzie, 1968:23-24). To appreciate what humans have done to the ecological process, let us examine these specific components carefully.

*Concentration.* For farmers, droughts and floods are potentially disastrous, particularly if people are dependent on nature for food or for fodder for their animals (Childe, 1951:105). To get stable supplies of food and water, early people tended toward physical environments where these goods were abundant or where some control over flood and drought could be exercised (Childe, 1951:67). The ancient Sumerians and Egyptians concentrated in areas where there was abundant water and food and where they could exercise flood control and irrigation. Only as the changing climate shifted rain from North Africa and Arabia did Europe become a favored spot for large concentrations of people. To gain access to and use of these favored locations, people faced serious struggles with their natural predators. Being weak and physically ill-protected, they required tools and a social organization beyond the simple family to compete effectively.

Historically, the largest form of human concentration is the city. And as we already have seen, with the city came early forms of bureaucratic organization. But it was industrialization that made the city the dominant form of human population concentration. Indeed, it was industrialization that made bureaucratic organization dominant among other forms of social organization (see Toffler, 1973:317; Weber, 1964). Fig. 3-5 shows the stunning population concentrations following the industrial revolution in the United States. Apart from the Great Depression, when productive capacity was underutilized, note the strong parallel between urbanization and heavy industry, particularly steel and cement production.

Looking back at Fig. 1-1, we can easily see that bureaucratic development in the United States closely follows urbanization. As Mumford (1961:536) observes, monopolistic organizations, particularly banking and manufactures, gravitate to the metropolis.

*Dispersion.* As life forms concentrate more and more in one region, the normal reproductive processes produce more of the life form than can be sustained by the ecological niche. (An ecological niche is a portion of the ecological web where one life form can live and reproduce relatively free from competition of other life forms in the area. In many cases, these ecological niches are symbiotic: the life forms in one niche supply materials needed for life forms in another.) Under the old ecosystem before the industrial revolution, plants and animals—even people—dispersed from the centers of concentration. Of course, the population density would decrease with distance from the more preferred ecological niches.

Before the industrial revolution, the dispersion of human population from centers

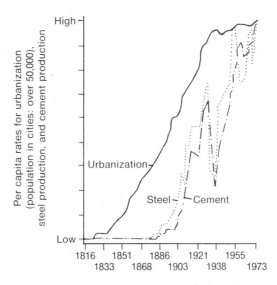

**Fig. 3-5.** Urbanization and industrialization in United States. Data from Inter-University Consortium for Political and Social Research, originally collected by Arthur Banks for *Cross-National Time-Series Archive*.

of population closely followed this pattern. The needs for greater food supplies and building materials in the cities continually forced people to improve agricultural production, regulate agricultural production and the import of needed raw materials, and expand the amount of land used for agricultural production and the acquisition of raw materials. But the limits of communication and transportation made it increasingly difficult for people to claim new lands for these purposes. Hence human population density decreased as people moved farther from the centers of population concentration.

But the industrial revolution upset the pattern of dispersion in the old ecosystem. New techniques for agricultural production and better means of transportation, particularly the steamboat and the railroad, allowed people to venture farther and farther from the major concentrations of population. Still there were some limits on the population dispersion, at least until the advent of electricity.

The use of coal as a source of energy helped spark the industrial revolution. But coal is heavy and cumbersome, requiring considerable concentrations of machinery and furnaces to make its use profitable. Although the railroad and the steamboat allowed some population dispersion along the main traffic arteries into the hinterlands of America, coal usually bound the energy explosion to the major population centers. But electricity removed this limitation. Electricity allowed people to produce energy in one area and to transmit it over vast distances. In areas outside major population concentrations, electricity allowed the intermittent use of power without huge capital investments in machinery and furnaces. Hence electricity made secondary centers of human concentration possible and permanently altered the old ecosystem's relation between the concentration of human population and dispersion.

Even with the rapid territorial expansion of the United States during the nineteenth century, electricity left its mark on the distribution of human population. The electrical revolution began here around 1880. From that time forward, the population density in the United States rose very sharply. Fig. 3-6 illustrates the impact of electricity on the U.S. population density. Note the sharp difference in the density curve, when compared with the population growth curve in Fig. 3-3. Also note the parallel between population density in Fig. 3-6 and bureaucratic development in Fig. 1-1.

Electricity allowed secondary urban centers to proliferate and grow, thereby helping to increase the population concentra-

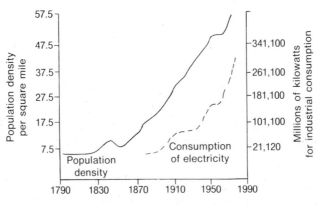

**Fig. 3-6.** Population density in United States. Data from U.S. Bureau of the Census.

tion and dispersion between the East and West Coasts. Consider the city of Chicago and the state of Illinois. Chicago was incorporated in 1837 with a population of 4,137. In 1850, the city had a population of close to 30,000. But from 1850 to 1900, the city grew to nearly 1,700,000 people. The population of the central city peaked in 1950 at 3,620,962. Two factors help explain the rapid growth of Chicago: Southern Illinois coal and the railroads. However, there is a different picture for the state as a whole. While the city had reached half its present size by the turn of the century, the state population continued to increase dramatically, spurred by the ability to transfer energy through electricity. Fig. 3-7 illustrates the growth of Illinois and Chicago. By 1900 the two growth curves begin to separate rapidly, with the state growth far exceeding that of its major city.

The advent of electricity did more than undermine the ecosystem's relation between human population concentrations and their dispersions. It became the vehicle for transporting bureaucratic organization from the city to the countryside as well as further expanding the control of bureaucratic organization over work in the city. The production, distribution, and consumption of electricity requires both regularity and planning to ensure efficiency.

These requirements escalated the extension of bureaucratic organization into more segments of American life. With electricity, the countryside moved into the rational, planned era ushered in by the industrial revolution. Rosenberg (1972) points out that electricity allowed decentralization in production facilities and made possible the reorganization of work to use mass-production techniques.

***Specialization.*** Specialization closely follows population concentration. Under the preindustrial ecosystem, concentrations of populations meant potential competition among life forms for available raw materials. Selective advantage went to those life forms that could specialize their needs for raw materials. Over millions of years, life forms in areas of concentration come to occupy ecological niches—a complex stratification of life forms where competition among species is minimized by the specialization of need for raw materials, the by-products of one life form become essential ingredients of the life processes of others, and these complex interdependencies evolve from competition among life forms to symbiotic relations among many life forms.

To reiterate, life forms specialize under conditions of competition for scarce resources. For life forms low on the phylo

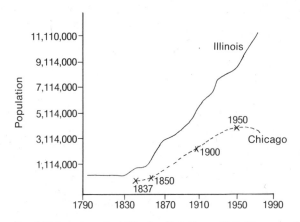

**Fig. 3-7.** Growth of Chicago and of Illinois. Data from U.S. Bureau of the Census.

genetic ladder, the specialization occurs almost entirely in relation to other life forms. As we climb the phylogenetic ladder, the specialization occurs both in relation to other life forms and in terms of social organization. Many animal species, including some fish, birds, and monkeys, develop rudimentary forms of social organization (see Hinde, 1974).

Poorly suited for physical competition, humans triumphed over nature and lower life forms by use of their growing intelligence. Finding strength in numbers, people organized and then specialized for production efficacy. In his critically important essay on the division of labor in society, Durkheim (1964:262) argues a close relation between population growth and population density and the increasing specialization of tasks among people.

*Industrialization and specialization.* Industrialization brought greater concentrations of human populations. Use of electricity increased population densities outside the major centers of population concentration. Both factors, according to Durkheim, force greater specialization of social organization. This occupational specialization did, in fact, occur. As Fig. 3-8 illustrates, the proportion of people employed in American agriculture drastically declined with the advent of industrialization in the United States. Today, over half

of those employed in the United States work in service professions. America was the first nation where less than half of the employed population was involved in the production of food, clothing, shelter, and other tangible goods (Bell, 1973:263).

*Centralization.* According to Mumford (1961:35), the existence of cities hinges on the centralization of political power. Centralized policy making requires bureaucratic organization to rationally administer, plan, and monitor the course of human events. Rudimentary forms of bureaucratic organization appear when cities appear. So do the rudiments of centralized power. More developed forms of bureaucratic organizations appear with empires and nation-states. Finally, with industrialization, bureaucracy becomes the dominant form of social organization. Bureaucratic organizations are vehicles for the exercise of centralized political power (Lindsay, 1962: 181).

Centralized power drastically increases people's control over the ecosystem. With centralized power, Mesopotamia and Egypt could claim swamplands from nature and turn them into fertile farmlands. But compare these deeds with the canals, dams, and irrigation systems of the twentieth century! Or consider the Russian collective farms, where mass-production organization first was introduced to agriculture (see

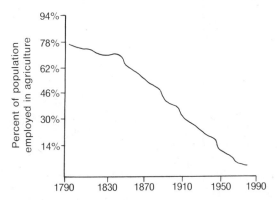

**Fig. 3-8.** Agricultural employment in United States. Data from U.S. Bureau of the Census.

Drucker, 1962:3). Other equally impressive feats include the Soviet fishing fleet, the mechanized cotton plantations in the Mississippi Delta, the vegetable cooperative in the California Central Valley, and the modern mining industry (see Drucker, 1962:3; Helin, 1967:45-70). Together with science, bureaucracy has helped people take captive the old ecosystem by combining the explosive force of technique with the coordinating power of bureaucracy (see Price, 1965:43).

*Human mistakes.* New social problems, however, have been created by these innovations. The Mesopotamians ruined their topsoil by irrigation that allowed saltwater to contaminate the soil. And closer to home, agricultural malpractices helped create the disastrous Dust Bowl of the 1930s in the United States (Rosenberg, 1972:197-198). Strip-mining has virtually destroyed the ecosystem on thousands of acres of land. Phosphate mining in Florida threatens available fresh water supplies for several central Florida communities. Water pollution has virtually killed Lake Erie and turned many streams and rivers into flowing sewage channels. And insecticides, herbicides, and other toxic substances continue to upset the ecological balance far beyond the limited purposes for which they were originally employed. Unfortunately, these are but a few of the negative consequences of human victory over the ecosystem.

Consider some of the environmental impacts of the modern steel industry in America. Open hearths emit a yellowish dust. Pickling steel operations emit acid wastes. The industry uses around 8 billion gallons of water a day, primarily for cooling. Hot water is subsequently returned to lakes and streams. Oil slicks and other contaminants, such as those dumped into the Cuyahoga River and which flow into Lake Erie, have made the Cuyahoga a fire hazard (Davenport, 1970:45). Even today, only some of these problems are being addressed

through environmental regulation. For another example, consider the impact of electric power generation. It produces 13% of our annual pollution tonnage: 50% of the sulpher dioxide, 27% of the oxides of nitrogen, and about 30% of the particulates. With increased use of soft coal to generate electricity, under the present energy crisis, these figures likely will increase (Alexander, 1970:123). In short, high technology might be lethal to human society (Editors of *Fortune*, 1970:8).

*Segregation.* People have overcome some of the old "laws" of our ecosystem, primarily through massive bureaucratization and applied science. This has wasted the ecosystem in a few generations, comparable to the impact of climate changes during several millennia. We have robbed the ecosystem of its essential ingredient for adjustment: time. So what has come of the life forms foreign to this artificial environment?

Threatened life forms are being segregated. Like the American Indian reservations, we have set aside game and forest preserves where we try to keep intact the few wilderness areas left after civilization's brutal assault on the environment. We have, in short, segregated small portions of the old ecosystem from the ecosystem created and dominated by humans. But there are ironies in this segregation. Starved for a glimpse of the old ecosystem, people crowd the nation's wilderness areas each year, leaving behind the traces of human refuse that supposedly make these areas different from the Cuyahoga River. But the difference is only in the quantity of pollutants, not the quality of a virgin ecosystem. On a miserable day the pollutants from Los Angeles may be smelled in Phoenix. The global ecosystem makes this attempted artificial segregation of life forms little more than a passing fancy.

*Invasion.* The human assault on ecology has other, even less desirable consequences. One is the continued invasion of the remaining portions of the old ecosystem, claiming more and more for human purposes and competing with whatever life forms stand in the way, whether they be buffalo or redwood trees. The westward expansion of the nineteenth century in America invaded millions of acres of virgin timberland. Moving across the continent, Americans wasted more lumber than their European counterparts had at their disposal. American milling procedures wasted large parts of lumber being cut into planks. And the abundance of lumber made it an economical substitute for coal in powering the steam engine.

**Succession.** People exaggerated the process of ecological segregation and the process of ecological invasion. Vast portions of the ecosystem that nature took millions of years to build were ravaged and destroyed in a few hundred years. By so doing, people distorted yet another ecological process: succession. In the old ecosystem, life forms competing for various ecological niches eventually replaced those life forms with less advantage in the struggle. But human victory over the ecological web replaces not one, but a host of life forms in the areas claimed for human exploitation. Together with rats and other scavengers of human civilization, people brought less diversity to the ecosystem. Superior social organization helped create in a few hundred years the ecological nightmare that nature avoided by slow ecological processes over millions of years. One thing is sure: the old ecological process cannot save us, because we have altered that process into a caricature of its former self. Advances in human social organization and knowledge, particularly bureaucracy and science, gave people the ability to conquer the old ecosystem. Ironically, these same advances are our best hope for sustained life on this planet.

**Production organizations**

Now that we have charted the impact of industrialism on the ecological web, let us more closely examine the anatomy of this industrial economy. Although more abstract, a brief discussion of the economic foundations of industrial production might provide added insight into the changing role of bureaucracy or production organizations during the last 250 years.

Production organizations are bureaucracies that administer technical processes (see Udy, 1959:583). In the preceding discussion, we have found that technical processes include factors of production, or those raw materials available for processing, and production techniques, or tools available for procuring raw materials and transforming them into given products. Combined with an administrative system to coordinate work activities, production factors and techniques define what economists call a production function: the maximum amount of output capable of being produced by each and every set of production factors (see Samuelson, 1970:516). Hence this production function reflects the limits of existing technology and administration. (The set of production factors processed by a production organization might be determined by market mechanisms or government planning boards.)

We have seen that industrialism represented a qualitative advance over earlier production functions. This advance became possible when people learned to harness energy, thereby improving access to raw materials and improving tools for transforming raw materials into given products. The bureaucratic development that accompanied these improvements might be explained in terms of the production organizations necessary to administer these new technological processes.

The production organizations that ushered in the Industrial Age illustrate a relation between work complexity and the structure of authority. In particular, mass production is a principle of work organization that minimizes the number of separate tasks each worker must perform, even though the tasks performed by the total production organization are diverse and complex. In turn, supervisors might monitor more employees, because the amount of attention required is limited by the range of activities monitored (see Blau, 1970: 210). This principle allows economies of scale, where the cost per item in production decreases in large organizations when compared with smaller organizations. Note that large production organizations integrate tasks through administration that individuals must integrate in smaller organizations. That is, of course, the consequence when specialized authority is delegated in large-scale production organizations. The growing size of production organizations and other bureaucracies introduces another social problem: motivation in work organizations. Because this topic is complex, we will discuss it further in Part II of this book.

## CONCLUSION

Bureaucracies help people coordinate human behavior to secure survival against the forces of nature. Bureaucracy and technology are successful—too successful. With their technological society, made possible through the rational structuring of social action, people conquered the ecosystem. But this victory was shortsighted. The damage to our ecosystem is a direct result of human decision making. Bureaucracies merely provide processes through which these decisions are elaborated and executed. But such decisions ignore many options, preferring to maximize production and efficiency while minimizing production costs, regardless of the external social costs accrued. Bureaucratic organization makes pollution possible, but it did not cause people to pursue this option. The fault lies with short-sighted decision making and, in many instances, the lack of more adequate knowledge of unseen consequences. Service to society, Henry Ford II observed, requires a short-run sacrifice of business profit. But we have failed to de-

vote adequate resources to seek ways for reducing side effects, and we have selected alternatives that are less costly in money outlays but more costly in their side effects (Rosenberg, 1972:200-201).

## REFERENCES

Alexander, T. Some burning questions about combustion. In Editors of *Fortune, The environment*. New York: Harper & Row, Publishers, Perennial Library, 1970.

Bell, D. Notes on the post-industrial society. In F. Tugwell (Ed.), *Search for alternatives*. Cambridge, Mass.: Winthrop Publishers, Inc., 1973.

Blau, P. M. A formal theory of differentiation in organizations. *American Sociological Review*, 1970, 35, 210.

Childe, V. G. *Man makes himself*. New York: New American Library, Inc., Mentor Books, 1951.

Commoner, B. The ecological facts of life. In R. Disch (Ed.), *The ecological conscience*. Englewood Cliffs, N.J.: Prentice-Hall, Inc., 1970.

Darwin, C. *On the origin of species*. Cambridge, Mass.: Harvard University Press, 1966.

Davenport, J. Industry starts the big cleanup. In Editors of *Fortune, The environment*. New York: Harper & Row, Publishers, Perennial Library, 1970.

Drucker, P. *The new society*. New York: Harper & Row, Publishers, Torchbooks, 1962.

Durkheim, E. *The division of labor in society*. New York: Free Press, 1964.

Editors of *Fortune*. *The environment*. New York: Harper & Row, Publishers, Perennial Library, 1970.

Ellul, J. *The technological society*. New York: Random House, Inc., Vintage Books, 1964.

Helin, R. Soviet fishing in the Barents Sea and the North Atlantic. In H. Roepke (Ed.) *Readings in economic geography*. New York: John Wiley & Sons, Inc., 1967.

Hinde, R. *The biological bases of human social behavior*. New York: McGraw-Hill Book Co., 1974.

Lindsay, A. D. *The modern democratic state*. New York: Oxford University Press, Inc., Galaxy Books, 1962.

McKenzie, R. *On human ecology* (A. Hawley, ed.). Chicago: University of Chicago Press, 1968.

Mumford, L. *The city in history*. New York: Harcourt Brace Jovanovich, Inc., Harbinger Books, 1961.

Platt, J. What must we do? In F. Tugwell (Ed.), *Search for alternatives*. Cambridge, Mass.: Winthrop Publishers, Inc., 1973.

Poirier, F. *Fossil evidence* (2nd ed.). St. Louis: The C. V. Mosby Co., 1977.

Price, D. K. *The scientific estate*. Cambridge, Mass.: Harvard University Press, 1965.

Rosenberg, N. *Technology and American economic growth*. New York: Harper & Row, Publishers, Torchbooks, 1972.

Samuelson, P. *Economics* (8th ed.). New York: McGraw-Hill Book Co., 1970.

Toffler, A. The coming ad-hocracy. In F. Tugwell (Ed.), *Search for alternatives*. Cambridge, Mass.: Winthrop Publishers, Inc., 1973.

Udy, S. H., Jr. The structure of authority in non-industrial production organizations. *American Journal of Sociology*, 1959, *64*, 582, 583.

Weber, M. The theory of social and economic organization (T. Parsons, ed.). New York: Free Press, 1964.

# CHAPTER 4

# Bureaucracy and social control

Complex societies increasingly have made use of criminal justice bureaucracies to control the breach of social rules. Key policy changes and advanced social science technology have encouraged the growth of regulatory agencies that allow governmental intervention in the economy. Complex societies increasingly have suppressed outbursts of collective violence through bureaucratic law-enforcement agencies.

Two important sources of conflict threaten coordination among the members of a society: (1) the breach of rules of good conduct, and (2) struggles over the social arrangements in society, particularly the distribution of basic needs for subsistence and the desires for rights, privileges, prestige, and power. However primitive, all societies have mechanisms to regulate both sources of social conflict.

## SOCIAL CONTROL

All societies require coordination among members, but coordination is seldom, if ever, automatic. Social conflict occurs in all societies known. Some, like the anarchist Michael Bakunin (1970), believe that people can live in spontaneous harmony with their neighbors, without conflict, if only they first are free to discover and obey the laws of nature. Still, few people are quite so optimistic as Bakunin. Of all societies known, all suffer periodic disturbances in social relations, and none has been successful in preventing social conflict.

For example, crime occurs in all societies. Breaches in rules of good conduct occur in all societies, from simple to complex (see Gluckman, 1968:xix). Similarly, all societies have a system for distributing rights, privileges, prestige, power, influence, and obligations among their members. But this system of distribution seldom is acceptable to all members. Accordingly, conflicts over the distribution of food, shelter, clothing, power, and prestige occur in both simple and complex societies (Gluckman, 1968:86).

### Breach of rules

Rules are control mechanisms for governing human behavior (see Geertz, 1965: 107). Human societies have a wide variety of such rules, including the rules of etiquette, moral prescriptions, and the important body of rules commonly known as law.

Commenting on rule-governed conduct, Richard Flathman (1972:67) suggests that rules of conduct indicate some pattern in the activities of people. Further, rules presuppose that people have a choice of whether to conform to them. And rules are standards of proper action. Finally, people must have good reasons for asserting rules and conforming to them.

But why do such rules exist? First, because human behavior is not totally determined by genes or habit, people have some capacity and opportunity for decision making and the assertion of their individual wills. Human behavior, then, theoretically might vary infinitely under similar circumstances. If an infinite variety of behaviors did occur under similar circumstances, social interaction would be extremely chaotic. Herein lies a fundamental problem of

**45**

human interaction. How can people interact with one another if the range of possible behaviors to a particular stimulus is infinite? Second, and consequent to the first reason explaining why rules exist, people cannot interact effectively if they cannot predict the behavior of others (Geiger, 1969:39; see also Mead, 1934).

Rules exist because people need to limit the number of behavioral responses to particular stimuli in order that they will behave in similar fashions that are therefore predictable. For example, I can coordinate my behavior with yours only if I have some idea of how you will react to my conduct, your reaction is consistent with my expectations, and my conduct falls within your expectations (Geiger, 1969:39). Coordination is possible when social actors fulfill the expectations of others, at least to some minimal degree.

**Interaction.** A breach of rules indicates that somebody violated the expectations of another. These rules might be explicit or implicit, the former being specified and the latter being unformulated but still part of social understanding. All societies have mechanisms for addressing a breach of rules. However, these mechanisms might vary considerably from simple to complex societies. In the simple societies public opinion, rumor, and gossip and often sufficient to correct a breach of rules. But as societies grown in complexity, early forms of a judiciary emerge to supplement the more simple mechanisms for addressing a breach of rules. Why?

First, there are relatively few rules to violate in simple societies. Second, there are basic limitations on the number of people with whom one comes into contact. Third, as population density increases, particularly in the city when compared with rural life, the interactions of people become more varied and frequent (see Simmel, 1950:409-424). In the city there are more diverse rules and more chances to violate them. Thus, three factors make it increasingly difficult for traditional mechanisms of social control to maintain social order in more complex societies: the increased frequencies of human interactions, the increased number of rules governing social relations, and the increased opportunity for violating these rules. To handle the problem, bureaucratic judiciaries and other bureaucratic organizations supplement traditional mechanisms for social control. Fig. 4-1 illustrates the relation between the complexity of social interactions (including increased frequency of interaction, the increased number of rules governing interactions, and the increased opportunities for violating rules) and the impetus toward bureaucratic control over the breach of rules.

**Simple judiciaries.** All bodies of law include a large number of rules governing several areas of human behavior. These rules are not necessarily related logically (Gluckman, 1972:17). Like the more advanced judiciaries, the simple judiciary system selects and applies the rule or rules that give justice to a case at trial. However, unlike more advanced judiciaries, judicial decisions are not made simply on the application of rules to specific, legally relevant facts. For in simple judiciary systems, deliberations might also include matters of etiquette and morality in conjunction with legal violations. Judges attempt to assess the overall reasonableness of an action, given the social position of the actor.

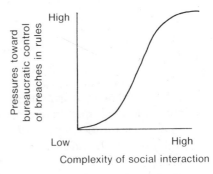

**Fig. 4-1.** Interaction and bureaucratic control.

Among the Barotse of Northern Rhodesia, for example, Gluckman (1972:17) found that the choice of rule and how it was applied was influenced by the extent to which partners fulfilled or had broken moral obligations, observed proper etiquette, and conformed to ritual prescriptions.

**Complex judiciaries.** In theory, the modern bureaucratic judiciary confines its attention to the application of stated rules to legally relevant facts. Ideally, judges should arrive at the same decision in a particular case, because they are supposed to weigh questions only of law and of legally relevant fact. In Sweden, for example, lower-court judges are penalized if superior judges overturn their decisions on a particular case. Of course, in practice, to achieve the type of consistency demanded by the strictly rational model of a complex judiciary system is difficult (Gerth and Mills, 1958: 219-220). No matter how many rules we make, there always will be situations in which the rules do not fit the offense. Then judicial discretion becomes very important. Still, the modern judiciary differs from the simple judiciary system among the Barotse.

### Social integration

Breach of rules is not the only hindrance to social coordination. Another is the ongoing struggle in every society over the arrangements of power, prestige, rights, subsistence, and obligations. The unequal distribution of rewards and obligations can be reflected in a variety of ways, including different social roles ascribed by sex, age, achievement, occupation, or race and ethnicity. Depending on their social roles, people have unequal access to subsistence, power, prestige, privilege, and rights. Similarly, obligations fall more heavily on some than on others. In some societies these inequalities are cumulative: people who have one reward have others, and people who bear one obligation bear several. In other societies, these inequalities are dispersed. Here different people enjoy different social rewards and different people bear different social obligations. Under a system of dispersed inequalities, all people get some rewards and all people bear some social obligations (see Dahl, 1961).

The distribution of social rewards and social obligations comprises the social stratification. Regardless of the distribution of these rewards and obligations, whether cumulative or dispersed, all societies have some mechanisms to maintain this stratification. But these mechanisms drastically differ from simple to complex societies. In simple societies people share common traditions, gods, and "natural" leaders. These are powerful forces supporting existing social arrangements. Under normal circumstances, these are sufficient to maintain the arrangements of a society and hence some level of social integration among its members. But complex societies increasingly turn toward bureaucratic organizations to maintain some level of social integration. Why?

**Social differentiation.** In simple societies, social differentiations are minimal. That is, there are relatively few categories that distinguish the members of society, and hence there are relatively few structural bases on which social rewards and social obligations are distributed unequally. Tribal societies recognize ascribed distinctions that derive from sex, age, strength, or ability and perhaps from differences in occupation. Slightly more complex societies add distinctions based on matters such as lineage and ethnicity. In complex societies the division of labor introduces new social distinctions, which derive from specialized work tasks. Occupational specialization makes people more functionally interdependent; that is, overall productivity requires the coordination of labor among several different categories of workers. Of course, this is what occupational specialization implies: different people perform different work functions, and these different functions must be recombined to produce a finished product. In complex societies, there are few jacks-of-all-trades.

In simple societies, mutual expectations hold society together. But in complex societies, the functional interdependency among workers becomes so important that it replaces mutual expectations as the primary bond of society (see Durkheim, 1964). That does not imply that mutual expectations are unimportant. But it does mean that doing what your neighbors, friends, and acquaintances expect of you will not inherently integrate your work functions and those of others whom you never have met. This functional interdependency among members of complex societies requires new forms of social organization unknown and unnecessary in simple societies.

*Civil law.* When rules are breached, complex societies increasingly turn toward bureaucratic judiciaries and a complex set of organizations to administer penal law. But threats to the functional interdependency in complex societies go beyond violations of expected behaviors in settings of social interaction. In fact, functional interdependence does not require those dependent on one another to interact directly. With the growth of functional interdependence has come a growth in a second body of law: civil law. In contrast to criminal law, civil law involves commercial, constitutional, procedural, and administrative rules, all aimed at maintaining some level of functional interdependency and hence social integration (Durkheim, 1964:69). Over time, the growing importance of civil law has contributed enormously to the expansion of bureaucratic control in complex societies.

One obvious example is the increased intervention of government in the economic order. Today, governments attempt to remedy deficiencies in the market economy, regulate production and distribution, sometimes regulate consumption, provide a host of social services and welfare transfers, and even promote employee develop-

ment and relocation of personnel (see Carson et al., 1973). To do so, governments require extensive civil codes and extensive bureaucracies to administer these codes.

*Social order.* Apart from criminal law, the primary target of which is the individual offender, complex societies need additional mechanisms to maintain social order and some level of social integration. Increased functional interdependencies make complex societies more vulnerable to the effects of civil disorders, such as revolts, disobedience, collective violence, and other reflections of social instability. Hence, complex societies respond to these dangers by further bureaucratizing their control over the social order. These mechanisms may include professional police, militia, and the more subtle constraints and inhibitions of welfare bureaucracies. Each of these is examined more closely in the sections that follow.

### Overview

Bureaucracies help coordinate the behavior of individuals in complex societies. Three problems of coordination are particularly relevant to bureaucratic social control. First, bureaucracies help control the breaches of rules through criminal law. Second, bureaucracies help maintain functional interdependencies through civil law. Third, bureaucratic organizations, such as the police and militia, help control unusual social disorders, such as riots and protests.

### BUREAUCRACY AND CRIMINAL LAW

Some semblance of criminal law exists in all known societies. In simple societies, these laws are not written or codified. Rather, they exist in "trouble cases," historical recollections of disputes, trouble, grievances, and what was done about them (Hoebel, 1968:12). But, regardless of form, whether codified or trouble cases, all societies have rules governing property and personal security. And all societies are concerned with protecting life and property

(Mair, 1962:36). Simple societies differ from complex societies in the diversity and content of rules governing property and personal security and in the mechanisms used to administer these rules. Even Adam Smith (1973:22-23), the father of laissez-faire economics, saw a strong need for greater administration of justice in complex societies.

## Criminal justice administration

In simple societies recurring disputes and grievances make social control a major problem (Gluckman, 1968:xviii). However, complex societies compound this problem because the diversity of social interaction increases and the amount of property increases. In turn, complex societies have more rules governing property and personal security.

**Number of rules.** In complex societies the number of rules governing personal security and property makes it increasingly difficult to rely on memory and "trouble cases." In fact, increasing social complexity and increasing amounts of property have created types of crimes relatively unknown in simple societies, such as white collar crime and organized crime. The judicial mechanisms in less complex societies are ill-equipped to administer the diverse rules protecting person and property in complex societies. In fact, complex societies increasingly use specialized bureaucracies to administer criminal law, such as juvenile courts, traffic courts, misdemeanant courts, felony courts, and federal courts. Further, we have developed an impressive array of asylums for handling those who breach rules of good conduct (see Rothman, 1971; Platt, 1969).

In American history, the growing use of penitentiaries, almshouses, insane asylums, and reformatories corresponds to a period of increasing social change in the middle of the nineteenth century (Rothman, 1971:xviii). As urbanization, and hence the amount of visible deviancy, spread in the

United States, so did the use of asylums for social control. But there was a second cause for the proliferation of asylums and the concomitant bureaucratization of these new forms of social control. In the eighteenth century, Americans believed crime and delinquency were ordained parts of the social order. But in the nineteenth century, Americans came to believe that a science of society could provide the technology for rehabilitation of individuals and the means to correct the social conditions causing crime, delinquency, insanity, and other forms of behavior that broke rules of good conduct. Here again, bureaucratization accompanied the growth of social science and technology.

**Violations of rules.** We have seen that complex societies have more rules governing personal security and property than do simple societies. In addition, complex societies also have proportionately more violations of rules. Two reasons are particularly important in explaining this increased rate of violation. First, more rules mean more chances for people to violate a rule. Virtually every American has violated one or more rules that could subject him or her to criminal sanction. Each year, between 4.5% and 5% of all Americans are arrested for criminal offenses.* Second, people interact with more people and in more diverse ways in complex societies, as compared with simple societies. Hence people have more opportunities for breaches of rules defined as criminal behavior. Of course, the problem is compounded by the enormous number of rules defining good conduct.

Consider the distinction between rural and metropolitan areas in the United States. Suppose we calculate the average rural crime rate for the 50 states, and sup-

---

*Figures based on calculations of data reported by the Federal Bureau of Investigation in *Uniform Crime Reports,* 1975. Although crime data are questionable, these estimates are likely smaller than the actual percent arrested each year.

pose we calculate the average metropolitan crime rate in all the states. A comparison of these two averages is particularly revealing. For violent crimes, the metropolitan crime rate is almost three times higher than the rural crime rate. Similarly, the property crime rate in metropolitan areas across the 50 states is almost three times higher than the property crime rate in rural areas. Table 4-1 presents these averages for 1975.

In general, metropolitan areas have more laws and statutes governing human behavior and greater diversity of social interactions, when compared with the rural areas of each state. Clearly, these figures illustrate the enormous burden placed on criminal justice agencies in the large metropolitan areas. And not surprising, these metropolitan areas normally have more bureaucratized criminal justice administrations than do rural areas in the same states. Freud (1961:92) once argued that the fateful question for the human species is whether people's cultural development could master the disturbances of communal life by the instinct of aggression and self-destruction. But the figures above shift the question somewhat. Perhaps the real question is whether bureaucratic organizations should continue to administer so many laws making citizens de facto criminals.

### Law enforcement

Bureaucracies are capable of administering a large number of rules under various circumstances. Fortunately for most of us, law enforcement is not quite so efficient. Still, the professional police force is one way modern society chooses to increase the efficiency and effectiveness of social control. In fact, there is a striking trend toward increasing police protection when crime rates increase. Fig. 4-2 illustrates this relation. The graph reports 1970 trends in 845 U.S. cities of over 25,000 persons. Increases in crime rates per 100,000 popula-

**Table 4-1.** Average crime rates for the 50 states: 1975*

| | METROPOLITAN AREAS | RURAL AREAS |
|---|---|---|
| Violent crimes per 100,000 population | 463.0 | 168.8 |
| Property crimes per 100,000 population | 5,612.8 | 1,981.8 |

*Based on calculations generated from tabulations and projections reported by the Federal Bureau of Investigation in *Uniform Crime Reports,* 1975.

tion show corresponding increases in the number of police officers per 100,000 population.

*Ecology of crime.* Unlike other life forms in the ecological process, humans did not specialize their needs for raw materials when competing with other species for survival. Rather, people increasingly specialized their relations with others. One form of this specialization is the division of labor in society (see Chapter 3). But there is a second, less obvious specialization within human society. Under conditions of competition among people, the ecological process helps determine the geographic relations among them, that is, where they live. Like the competition among life forms in the environment, the ecological processes of segregation, invasion, and succession affect the location of people and, by implication, affect the social order as well. As McKenzie (1968:19) suggests, the spatial distribution and social life of society are part of one complex.

*Cities.* Cities are the focal point of human ecological processes. Racial, religious, ethnic, occupational, and economic groups come to occupy their own neighborhoods, jealously guarding against the invasion of other races, religions, ethnic groups, or social classes. Here we see the natural process of segregation at work. But we also know that the physical structure of neighborhoods—the streets, the buildings, the schools—all deteriorate with age, and some

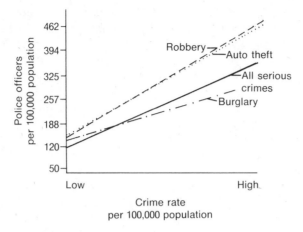

**Fig. 4-2.** Crime and police protection. Correlations here are rather strong, particularly given a data base of 845 cities. All coefficients are significant at .00001. Pearson correlations between police per 100,000 population and each crime rate are:

| | |
|---|---|
| All serious crimes/100,000 | .44 |
| Robbery/100,000 | .55 |
| Burglary/100,000 | .38 |
| Auto theft/100,000 | .48 |

Graph reflects regression lines for each plot. Data from *City and County Data Book* (1972).

urban neighborhoods grow faster than others. Taken together, these factors help explain the pressures toward invading neighborhoods by "outsiders" and their eventual conquest of an old neighborhood. Here the natural processes of invasion and succession are at work. Although urban renewal programs have attempted to alter these natural processes, they have not been very successful.

**Decay, stability, growth.** When the process of segregation balances the pressures toward invasion and succession, the social life of the city is relatively stable. Relative to population and economic activity, the city is in a state of equilibrium. But when the processes of segregation are overwhelmed by pressures toward invasion, succession rapidly follows. Here the city is in disequilibrium; its social and physical characters rapidly change. Typically, this has occurred in America's older cities. Succession usually accompanies aging physi-

cal structures, population declines, and economic deterioration. But there is a third category of cities as well. In these cities, most of them relatively new, the process of population concentration and population segregation is not yet complete. Here we find rapid population growth and rapid economic expansion. Neighborhoods still are consolidating, still evolving a character and threat of invasion and succession still is weak, primarily because the urban physical and social character has not assumed a stable identity. Poor and rich might be located in pockets scattered throughout the city and not be segregated into the ghettos that typically characterize older American cities. Fig. 4-3 illustrates these three stages of the urban ecological process.

**Crime.** Is there any relation between the urban ecological process and crime? Under stable urban systems, residents have relatively fixed access to the amenities available in the city, whether that be choice of neighborhood or economic opportunity. Under systems of decline, the old physical plant of the city offers little diversity, and economic opportunities continue to decline. But under new urban systems, the choices of neighborhood and economic opportunity generally are higher than the other two urban forms. To the extent that property crime is related to opportunity, we might expect to find crime rates distributed like those shown in Fig. 4-4. This is a reverse J curve. As achievement opportunities decline, property crime rises sharply. But as these opportunities expand, property crime decreases accordingly.

*Population change.* One measure of declining cities is negative population growth. Conversely, new cities will have rapid population growths. Does crime in these cities follow the expectations in Fig. 4-4? Fig. 4-5 illustrates the relation between population change from 1960 to 1970 and the total serious-crime rate in 845 American cities of more than 25,000 persons. Similar graphs obtain when we compare population change to rates of auto theft, rates of aggravated assault, and robbery rates. Clearly, the expectations hold remarkably well.

*Economic growth.* Another measure of declining cities is slowed economic production. Conversely, economic productivity in new cities is rapidly expanding. Fig. 4-6 shows the relation between the change in the value added through manufacturing production from 1963 to 1967 with the total serious-crime rate for the 845 American cities of more than 25,000 persons in 1970. A similar graph obtains when we compare change in value added through manufacturing production with burglary rates, auto theft rates, aggravated assault rates, and robbery rates. Again the pattern is extremely close to that proposed in Fig. 4-4.

**Social control.** But what has all this to do

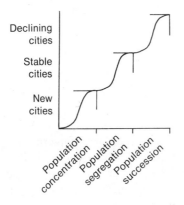

**Fig. 4-3.** Urban ecological process.

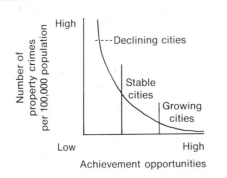

**Fig. 4-4.** Achievement opportunities and property crime.

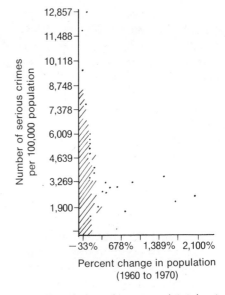

**Fig. 4-5.** Population change and total rate of serious crime. Data from *City and County Data Book* (1972).

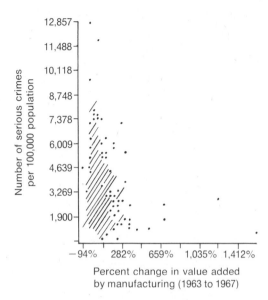

**Fig. 4-6.** Economic growth and total rate of serious crime. Data from *City and County Data Book* (1972).

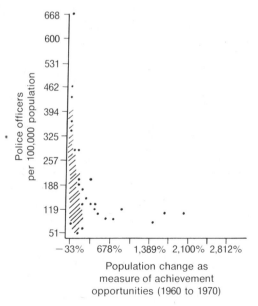

**Fig. 4-7.** Achievement opportunities and social control. Data from *City and County Data Book* (1972).

with social control? Our model of the urban ecological process describes relations among people in urban settings and the broad contours of change in these relations. Clearly, changes in the levels of social integration in the city also might affect the level of social disorder. The data in Figs. 4-5 and 4-6 suggest that social control problems are highest in declining cities and lowest in new cities. So does the urban ecological process affect the levels of bureaucratic control needed through law enforcement?

Fig. 4-7 clearly illustrates that the urban ecological process directly affects the perceived need for social order, reflected in higher per capita police protection. Comparing Fig. 4-7 with Figs. 4-5 and 4-6, we readily can see that the number of police officers per 100,000 population directly parallels these crime curves. Declining cities have more police protection, growing cities have consistently less. And the same holds when we look at economic growth. In cities where economic productivity is declining, more police protection is made available. Where economic production is expanding, lower per capita levels of police protection are made available.

## Overview

In complex societies, bureaucratic organizations serve important functions in administering the criminal law. Complex social interactions and increased affluence lead to larger numbers of rules protecting persons and property. The increased number of rules in turn requires higher levels of bureaucratic control in criminal justice, because there are more rules to violate and more opportunities to do so. One important function of criminal justice bureaucracies is law enforcement, particularly through the modern urban police system. Police protection is directly related to the level of crime in a city. And levels of police protection tend to reflect urban growth and decay.

## BUREAUCRACY AND CIVIL LAW

Civil law includes a variety of juridical rules, ranging from administrative law to specific subjects, such as labor law, commercial law, trade regulations, land use, social welfare and even procedural law (see Durkheim, 1964:69; Gellhorn and Byse, 1974:1). When social problems arise in complex societies, whether they involve commerce, land use, welfare, or other matters, modern governments use administrative agencies to address problems of growing public concern. Consider, for example, the origin of the Interstate Commerce Commission in the United States. Since 1887 the ICC has regulated railroads and other common carriers in the United States. But the commission was created in large part to redress private and public grievances against the railroads. And as a classic case of administrative control, the Interstate Commerce Commission has effects reaching far beyond the railroads, to include control over private enterprise and intrastate commerce (Sharfman, 1931:3).

### Administrative agencies

Today a vast array of administrative agencies oversees the administration of civil rules in the United States. An exhaustive list would include hundreds of agencies and commissions at each of the local, state, regional, and national levels (see Derthick, 1974). The following list shows some of the more important major agencies in the federal government and the dates they were established.*

Major federal administrative agencies and date established*

*Executive office of the President*
  The White House Office
  Council of Economic Advisors (1946)
  Central Intelligence Agency (1947)
  National Security Council (1947)
  Office of Science and Technology Policy (1962)

---

*Based on U.S. *Government Organization Manual*. Some agencies, such as the Office of Management and Budget, succeed earlier agencies.

Office of Special Representative for
  Trade Negotiations (1963)
Council on Environmental Policy (1969)
Office of Telecommunications Policy (1970)
Office of Management and Budget (1970)
Domestic Council (1970)
Council on International Economic Policy (1971)
Federal Property Council (1973)
Energy Resources Council (1974)
Office of Drug Abuse Policy (1976)

*Executive departments*
  Department of State (1789)
  Department of Treasury (1789)
  Department of Justice (1789)
  Department of the Interior (1849)
  Department of Labor (1884)
  Department of Agriculture (1889)
  Department of Commerce (1903)
  Department of Health, Education, and
    Welfare (1953)
  Department of Housing and Urban
    Development (1965)
  Department of Transportation (1966)

*Independent agencies*
  U.S. Postal Service (1789)
  Library of Congress (1800)
  U.S. Botanical Garden (1820)
  Architect of the Capitol (1851)
  Government Printing Office (1860)
  U.S. Civil Service Commission (1883)
  Interstate Commerce Commission (1887)
  Federal Reserve System (1913)
  Federal Trade Commission (1914)
  Farm Credit Administration (1921)
  U.S. International Trade Commission (1916)
  General Accounting Office (1921)
  Veterans Administration (1930)
  Federal Power Commission (1930)
  Tennessee Valley Authority (1933)
  Federal Communications Commission (1934)
  National Labor Relations Board (1935)
  Civil Aeronautics Board (1940)
  Federal Mediation and Conciliation Service (1947)
  General Services Administration (1949)
  National Science Foundation (1950)
  Small Business Administration (1953)
  U.S. Information Agency (1953)
  National Aeronautics and Space
    Administration (1958)
  Federal Maritime Commission (1961)
  National Foundation on the Arts and the
    Humanities (1965)
  Environmental Protection Agency (1970)
  Cost Accounting Standards Board (1970)
  Community Services Administration (1974)
  Energy Research and Development
    Administration (1975)

Federal Elections Commission (1975)
National Transportation Safety Board (1975)
Nuclear Regulatory Commission (1975)

As can be seen, administrative control extends into most areas of the social order. In early 1977 there were some 1,900 federal agencies and 1,175 advisory panels (as reported in the *Wall Street Journal,* April 4, 1977, p. 1). In reviewing the names and dates of establishment of the agencies listed above, two points are clear: the social impact of industrialization and urbanization made necessary the proliferation of administrative agencies, and advances in applied sciences made possible this proliferation (see Reagan, 1963). Further, note that the dates agencies were established tend to coincide with the historical periods in which social problems required the attention provided by the new agency. In some instances, particularly among economic agencies, new agencies appear because older agencies have failed to resolve social problems.

Each of these agencies has executive or legislative (or both) mandates regarding the functions they are expected to fulfill. But these agencies do not merely administer rules established by the executive branch or the legislature. More often than not, the President or Congress establishes broad guidelines for activity, and the agencies are permitted wide discretion in (1) interpreting their mandates, (2) elaborating broad guidelines through specific policy directives, and (3) accepting or rejecting jurisdiction over a variety of matters that might be brought before them. In short, these agencies do more than simply administer civil law; they also help evolve civil rules and regulations.

### Government and the economy

One important problem following the industrial revolution was the increasing severity and extensiveness of economic ebb and flow. During the first two thirds of the nineteenth century, business cycles lasted about ten years. In Great Britain, home of the industrial revolution, troughs occurred in 1825, 1839, 1847, 1857, and 1866 (Henderson, 1968:3). From 1870 onward, long periods of unemployment and poor trade replaced these short panics (Henderson, 1968:3). Major depressions occurred from 1873 to 1896 and from 1929 to 1933, and both were worldwide in scope.

***Crisis of social order.*** The sustained economic crises after 1870 brought social and political turmoil to the affected industrial nations. In the United States, radical movements among laborers and farmers multiplied in number and size. The Populist movement of the 1890s in America was only one example of the political consequences following severe economic slumps late in the nineteenth century (see Hicks, 1961). By 1936, Franklin Roosevelt found one third of the American people ill-clothed, ill-fed, and ill-housed, largely a consequence of the economic disaster of 1929. This depression encouraged proto-Fascist, Communist, and Anarchist movements and increased major civil unrest.*

The increased severity of the economic slumps no longer permitted governments the luxury of predicting "prosperity around the corner." Like the Roosevelt transformation in the United States, industrial countries across the world took various steps to control the impact of economic slump, even if they could not control the economic cycle itself. After 1936 the Keynesian revolution in economic thought gave governments the hope and technology needed to control the economic cycle itself, at least enough to soften the extreme fluctuations observed from 1870 to 1935 (Keynes, 1935). Within a few short decades, the Keynesian doctrine, or some elaboration of the Keynesian doctrine, became a key element of economic policy in industrial nations throughout the world. Even

---

*For a discussion of the situation in England before and during the Second World War, see Beveridge (1943).

Milton Friedman, a long-time advocate of limited government management in the economy, admitted that "in one sense, we all are Keynesians now" (Samuelson, 1970: 207).

*Government spending.* Regardless of label, whether Keynesian, neo-Keynesian or post-Keynesian, modern economists generally agree that government intervention in the economy has helped check the severity and extensiveness of economic cycles in the industrial world. In part the key lies in government policies to stabilize the economy by controlling total production, whether through federal spending or monetary and credit policies. These controls in turn require greater government planning and forecasting and hence more administrative agencies to monitor, manage, and administer government economic policies.

Why does government spending help insulate a society from wide economic fluctuations? Why are severe economic slumps less likely if a government controls one third of the country's gross national product? Consider a very simple macroeconomic model. Suppose total product $(P)$ is equal to the sum of consumer spending $(C)$, investment spending $(I)$, and government spending $(G)$: $P = C + I + G$. Clearly, when a government has considerable control over a nation's resources, it is possible to increase total production (at least in theory) by increasing government spending $(G)$. Hence, when consumer spending or investment spending declines, governments can partly offset their impact on total production by increasing government spending. Alternatively, governments can provide incentives toward greater consumer spending (for example, tax rebates) or certain investment credits.

In the United States, government expenditures, measured as a percentage of the total gross national product, have continued to rise since the Great Depression of the 1930s. Except for the obvious jump during World War II, the government steadily has expanded its control over total production by controlling an increasingly larger share of total spending. Fig. 4-8 illustrates the trend in the United States from 1900 to 1975. In addition, and depending on the administration in power, Americans have tried a variety of other economic policies to stimulate or dampen economic growth to avoid wide fluctuations in the economic cycle, such as those experienced from the 1870s to 1930s.

*Personnel development.* In 1962 the President's Council of Economic Advisors urged not only measures of economic stabilization, but also measures to reduce employment and underemployment by matching available workers with available jobs. Today, personnel training and development in the United States is an important area of government intervention in the social order. Even before Walter Heller and his poverty programs, the state was investing in employee training through colleges and universities. In 1900 there were only 24,000 college teachers, in 1920 only 49,000, but by 1970 the figure rose to 48,000 (Galbraith, 1974:155; see also Price, 1965).

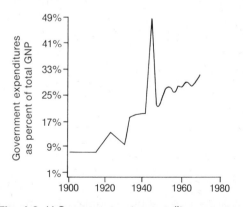

**Fig. 4-8.** U.S. government expenditures as percent of gross national product. Data from U.S. Bureau of the Census, *U.S. Census of Government* (1967), *Historical Summary of Government Finances in the United States* (1967), and *Economic Report of the President* (1971 to 1976).

## Overview

The second large category of control through bureaucratic organization is civil law and economic management. Administrative agencies in the United States have proliferated drastically during the twentieth century, reflecting (1) new and increasingly severe social problems following industrialization and urbanization, (2) the growth of technical expertise and knowledge in the applied sciences, especially economics, and (3) the need to reallocate and retrain people to match the demands of a changing social structure. In particular, government in the United States maintained considerable bureaucratic control over the social order through economic stabilization policies, research subsidies to universities and other foundations, and personnel training and development, particularly through its universities, but also through a host of service programs designed to provide the unskilled with vocational training. Ultimately, of course, these efforts reflect continued attempts to secure social order and enhance the level of social control in complex societies. More subtle than criminal law, these government efforts help secure the functional interdependencies among people in complex societies by expanding the scope of adjustment mechanisms governments have at their disposal when faced with disruptions of the social order.

## BUREAUCRACY AND SOCIAL DISORDER

All political societies involve at least three action systems to control collective violence: policy-making systems; administrative systems to apply rules, protect rights, and exact dues, and action systems of competition for power, prestige, and other social rewards (Gluckman, 1968: 196). Seldom are these three systems complementary. Bureaucracies, such as those in nineteenth century Russia and Prussia, attempt to resist changes introduced by policy makers. Even in the United States a new President finds the bureaucracy slow and resistant to new directions. Both policy-making systems and administrative systems attempt to check or regulate the competition for power, prestige, and other social rewards. If this system of competition gets out of hand, revolts against established authorities and incidents of civil disorders may ensue.

However, it would be wrong to say that policy-making systems and administrative systems establish and maintain social order, while competition for power, prestige, and other rewards is a force toward social disintegration. In fact, our market economy attempts to harness competition for the social good; similarly, democratic procedures attempt to harness the competition for power and other rewards in socially productive ways. That is, in modern democracies we wish to count heads more often than break them. According to Gluckman (1968:173), the system of competition for power and prestige may be beneficial to less complex societies as well.

## Integration

Functional interdependence in complex societies requires that the system of rules governing the relations among people helps form some level of social equilibrium. These rules and the social roles that result from them must in some respects be compatible. When they are not, social stress and strains appear. In complex societies, for example, the rules and roles comprising the complex web of occupations must be relatively complementary (see Durkheim, 1964; Parsons, 1951). But there are some respects in which social rules and social roles are not compatible. Marx spoke of social tensions between the bourgeoisie and the proletariat. Today another serious tension is that between producers and consumers (Greenstone, 1969). Producers in the modern economic system typically seek to maximize production, maximize profit, and minimize cost. But consumers seek decision rules that might conflict with those of producers, particularly regarding consumer protection and environmental management.

The simple fact is, of course, that all societies have complementary social rules and, to a lesser extent, incompatible social rules. In turn, the social equilibrium of any society rests simultaneously on organic union and conflict and coercion (see Dahrendorf, 1959:257-265). Mechanisms to maintain social equilibrium must control the conflict, lest it get out of hand and seriously disrupt the existing level of social integration.

Social integration—the degree to which social roles are held together—does not imply social harmony. Whether social roles are complementary or in conflict, bureaucratic organizations help complex societies maintain integration by controlling disturbances of the social order. Three matters are particularly important. First, because of the volume of social roles in complex societies, the chances of social conflict are higher. Second, extensive social conflict among groups and classes in complex societies disrupts functional interdependencies and hence undermines social integration. Third, pressures toward disruption and disintegration increases the demand for bureaucratic control over these disturbances.

### Change and civil disorder

All societies have adjustive mechanisms to maintain dynamic equilibrium under conditions of disturbance. But some disturbances, particularly conditions of unusual social change, may exceed the capacities of these adjustive mechanisms. When this occurs, social order begins to falter and the relations among people deteriorate. At this point the latent conflicts in the social structure may erupt into outbursts of civil disorder (see Tiryakian, 1967:69-97; Graham and Gurr, 1969; Fogelson, 1971; Short and Wolfgang, 1972; Connery, 1969; Gurr, 1970). These outbursts in turn often result in adjust-

ments to the arrangements of society, attempting to address grievances. Sometimes, however, these outbursts simply lead to increased levels of bureaucratic control over the existing arrangements of society. Latent tensions are repressed, and little effort is made to remedy the cause of the grievances. Unfortunately, the latter option occurs rather frequently in more complex societies. In less complex societies, civil disorders are effective in bringing grievances to the attention of and forcing responses from political elites (Silver, 1967:19). But redistribution and reorganization of the arrangements of society are easier in less complex societies than in more complex ones.

Examine more closely the impact of unstable rates of change in societies and the occurrence of civil disorders. As a rule in the twentieth century nation-states, relatively stable economic growth rates discourage civil disorders more than do wildly fluctuating rates of economic growth, such as those in pre-Nazi Germany. Fig. 4-9 illustrates the relation between various forms of civil disturbances and the fluctuation in economic growth. As the rate of economic growth begins to vary wildly from year to year, the proportionate incidence of civil distrubances dramatically increases.

Does this relation prove true in reality?

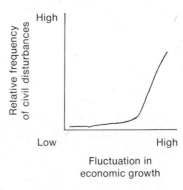

**Fig. 4-9.** Unstable economic growth and civil disturbances.

Fig. 4-10 shows the relation between fluctuations in economic growth and the proportionate occurrence of political revolts in 78 countries from 1948 to 1965. Similar patterns hold when comparing fluctuation in economic growth and political assassinations, guerrilla warfare, and sabotage. These patterns resemble that in Fig. 4-9.

### Change and bureaucratic control

In less complex societies, events of civil disturbances, such as those in Fig. 4-10, probably would force a political response to alleviate or to address grievances. However, in complex societies this is not likely, although still quite possible. Typically, complex societies respond to civil disturbances by drastically increasing social control. One such measure is martial law. Martial law is an extreme bureaucratic measure, designed to restore social order through extensive social control and social repression. Fig. 4-11 shows that, for the 78 countries illustrated in Fig. 4-10, declarations of martial law proportionately increase as the fluctuation in economic growth increases.

There is an alarming message in the data presented here. In less complex societies, civil disorders serve to make adjustments in those social arrangements responsible for the latent social tensions, to the extent that such adjustments are possible. But in more complex societies, particularly in the industrialized and industrializing nations,

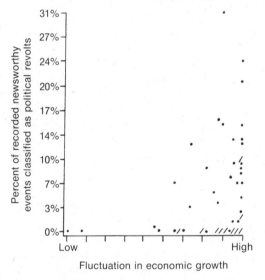

**Fig. 4-10.** Unstable economic growth and political revolts. To measure fluctuation in economic growth, variance in Standardized National Income across 18-year period from 1948 to 1965 was used. Standardized National Income is calculated by dividing each country's national income by its currency exchange rate for that year. This fraction is in turn divided by consumer price index for that year, multiplied by a constant (based on the consumer price index for the United States in 1953). Hence:

$$SNI = \frac{(NI/ER)}{CI * k}$$

where *SNI* is Standardized National Income for each country for each year; *NI*, national income for each year for each country; *ER,* currency exchange rate for each country for each year; *CI*, Consumer Price Index for each country for each year; *k*, U.S. Consumer Price Index, based on 1953 dollars.

Standardized National Income does not control for population change, because this factor should add to the instability we attempt to measure here.

Proportion of events derive from the Events Data Bank compiled by the Feierabends of San Diego State University. For each country, a series of events was recorded by year, from 1948 to 1965. The proportion of events reported represents that portion of all events (recorded for each country) classified as assassinations, guerrilla warfare, revolts, and sabotage. By calculating the proportion of events in this way, we avoid the obvious biases of differential rates of event reporting for various countries. The proportions do give a good reflection of the type of news events occurring in these 78 countries during the 18-year period.

Data bank used in compiling these graphs was prepared by Steven Thomas Seitz and Ronald William Duty in 1971.

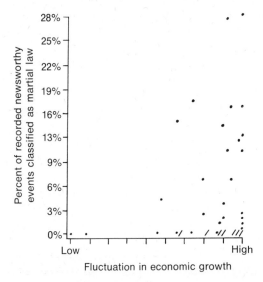

Fig. 4-11. Unstable economic growth and martial law. Incidence of martial law is proportion of all events classified as declarations of martial law reported for each country. Data from same sources as for Fig. 4-10.

the response is to secure equilibrium with greater levels of social control. Of course, there are examples where countries do attempt to make adjustments in the arrangements of society that led to latent conflicts. However, the trend is clearly toward maintaining existing arrangements through increased levels of bureaucratic control.

### Disorder and bureaucratic control— American style

Silver (1967:20) points out that systems of riotous demand and elite response largely are confined to preindustrial societies. And as noted above, popular unrest can disrupt severely the functional interdependencies on which the modern industrial order rests. Hence it should not be surprising that modern societies make more attempts to control the outbursts of popular unrest, even though the target of violence might be groups other than political elites. The history of social control in the United States amply illustrates this trend.

***Popular unrest in the United States.*** Before 1850 the United States was a preindustrial society. But during the past 125 years the United States has become the leading industrial nation in the world. During this period six major waves of violence have occurred in the United States (see Seitz, 1974). The first wave occurred during the 1850s and into the 1860s and was based on racial, ethnic, and religious group conflicts. The second, largely in the 1870s, again reflected racial and ethnic conflicts in the South after Reconstruction and problems of urban ethnic conflicts in the North. The third wave of violence, peaking in the late 1880s and early 1890s, marked sharp popular reaction to the economic depression. The fourth, from about 1915 into the early 1920s, continued emphasis on economic grievances, coupled with racial, ethnic, and religious conflicts. The fifth, peaking in the 1930s, reflected the economic depression and racial and ethnic group conflicts. The last wave occurred in the 1960s and illustrated a broad range of conflicts from economic and racial problems to protests over foreign policy.

A close examination of these waves discloses two rather surprising trends. First, as America moves into the twentieth century the waves of violence occur less frequently. Second, each wave of violence involves increased injury and death over the earlier waves of violence. Fig. 4-12 illustrates these two trends. The data are crude, but the pattern is obvious (see Seitz, 1974). Why do the waves of violence occur less frequently over time? And why are the later waves apparently more violent, as measured in the total number of deaths, injuries, and property destruction?

***Decreasing frequency of waves.*** Much of the change in frequency can be attributed to increases in social control. The urban police system in America emerged during the unrest of the 1850s. It became increasingly professionalized during the remaining part of the nineteenth century, con-

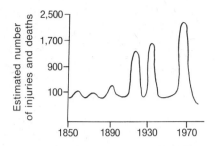

**Fig. 4-12.** Violence in United States. Data from news sources sampled at selected intervals from 1850 to 1975. Population size is not controlled because raw measure of death and injury is a better index of amount of control force needed to control disorders.

centrating more on social control and less on community service functions. The National Guard became an important agency for controlling civil strife in the late 1870s, and its utilization has increased dramatically since that time. Both the police and the guard expanded their control functions in the twentieth century, but the increasing severity of civil disorders required new and more elaborate mechanisms for social control.

In the 1930s new organizations were created to control civil disorders. The first was the Federal Bureau of Investigation (FBI), bringing considerable technical and some personnel assistance to local control forces across the nation. The second was the use of social welfare programs, such as Social Security and the National Labor Relations Board, to satisfy some of the grievances of those engaging in economic protest and to treat the poor as individuals, thereby minimizing organization among them (see Cloward and Piven, 1974:16-17).

The violence of the 1960s brought renewed efforts to maintain social order through bureaucratic organizations. President Johnson's Great Society programs served partly, even though unintentionally, to extend the control of welfare programs begun in the 1930s. But President Nixon added the largest impetus to increased

social control, largely through the Law Enforcement Assistance Administration (LEAA)(see Quinney, 1974:86-93, 105-110). Of all government agencies, its budget grew fastest, from $63 million in fiscal year 1969 to $1.75 billion in fiscal 1973 (Quinney, 1974:87). Much of the early work of LEAA provided money for purchasing riot-control weapons, electronic hardware, and other weapons for police use. Today the agency directs more of its attention to crime-control programs.

*Increased violence.* The waves of collective violence in the United States appear to become less frequent as bureaucratic mechanisms for social control proliferate in American society. At the same time, however, the more recent waves appear to be more severe than the earlier waves. Why? In part, the increasing severity results from the increased social tension accompanying rapid social change and growing complexity of the social order. And in part, the increased severity is simply a product of the larger numbers of people concentrated in our cities. But there are other reasons as well, and two of particular interest are the impact of increased social control and improved enforcement technology over the past 125 years. Like other complex societies, the conflicts inherent in our social order are governed by mechanisms of social control. But as these bureaucratic mechanisms become more extensive and more effective, the latent conflicts take longer to erupt. Social stresses and strains must reach increasingly higher levels of pressure before unrest erupts into civil disorder.

### Overview

Bureaucratic organizations help control civil disorder in complex societies. Functional interdependence requires a relatively stable social order. Although a variety of factors might disrupt social equilibrium, one of the most serious is rapid, unpredictable change, particularly in economic growth. To maintain social stability, complex societies must control the latent conflicts in society and reduce the impact of rapid, unpredictable change. To do so, complex societies use a variety of bureaucratic mechanisms, including martial law, professional control forces, and certain types of social welfare programs.

## CONCLUSION

All societies require coordination among their members. Coordination requires that interactions among people be predictable and the functional interdependencies among people in complex societies be maintained. Bureaucracies help maintain predictability in human interaction through the criminal law. And bureaucracies help maintain the level of social integration required in complex societies by civil law and civil procedure and controlling outbursts of popular unrest. One particularly important focus of civil law is the economic order. And one particularly important source of pressure toward social disorder is a major disruption in the economic order. Together, criminal law, civil law, and the control of civil disorder allow bureaucratic organizations to manage the social relations in complex societies.

## REFERENCES

Bakunin, M. *God and state.* New York: Dover Publications, Inc., 1970.

Beveridge, W. H. *The pillars of security and other war-time essays and addresses.* London: George Allen & Unwin Ltd., 1943.

Carson, R. B., Ingles, J., and McLaud, D. (Eds.). *Government in the American economy.* Lexington, Mass.: D. C. Heath & Co., 1973.

Cloward, R., and Piven, F. F. *The politics of turmoil.* New York: Random House, Inc., Vintage Books, 1974.

Connery, R. *Urban riots.* New York: Random House, Inc., Vintage Books, 1969.

Dahl, R. *Who governs?* New Haven, Conn.: Yale University Press, 1961.

Derthick, M. *Between state and nation.* Washington, D.C.: Brookings Institute, 1974.

Durkheim, E. *The division of labor in society.* New York: Free Press, 1964.

Flathman, R. *Political obligation.* New York: Atheneum Publishers, 1972.

Fogelson, R. *Violence as protest.* New York: Double & Co., Inc., Anchor Books, 1971.

Freud, S. *Civilization and its discontents.* New York: W. W. Norton & Co., Inc., 1961.

Galbraith, J. K. Market planning and the role of government. In R. Lora (Ed.), *America in the 60's.* New York: John Wiley & Sons, Inc., 1974.

Geertz, C. The impact of the concept of culture on the concept of man. In J. Platt (Ed.), *New views on the nature of man.* Chicago: University of Chicago Press, 1965.

Geiger, T. *On social order and mass society* (R. Mayntz, ed.). Chicago: University of Chicago Press, 1969.

Gellhorn, W., and Byse, C. *Administrative law* (6th ed.). Mineola, N.Y.: Foundation Press, Inc., 1974.

Gerth, H. H., and Mills, C. W. (Eds.). *From Max Weber.* New York: Oxford University Press, Inc. Galaxy Books, 1958.

Gluckman, M. *Politics, law and ritual in tribal society.* New York: New American Library, Inc., Mentor Books, 1968.

Gluckman, M. *The ideas in Barotse jurisprudence.* Manchester, England: Manchester University Press, 1972.

Graham, H. D., and Gurr, T. R. *Violence in America.* New York: New American Library, Inc., Signet Books, 1969.

Greenstone, J. D. *Labor in American politics.* New York: Alfred A. Knopf, Inc., 1969.

Gurr, T. R. *Why men rebel.* Princeton, N.J. Princeton University Press, 1970.

Henderson, W. O. *The industrial revolution in Europe.* New York: Quadrangle/New York Times Book Co., 1968.

Hicks, J. D. *The Populist revolt.* Lincoln, Neb.: University of Nebraska Press, 1961.

Hoebel, E. A. *The law of primitive man.* New York: Atheneum Publishers, 1968.

Keynes, J. M. *The general theory of employment, interest, and money.* New York: Harcourt Brace Jovanovich, Inc. 1935.

Mair, L. *Primitive government.* Baltimore: Penguin Books, Inc. 1962.

McKenzie, R. *On human ecology* (A. Hawley, ed.). Chicago: University of Chicago Press, 1968.

Mead, G. H. *Mind, self, society* (C. Morris, ed.). Chicago: University of Chicago Press, 1934.

Parsons, T. *The social system.* New York: Free Press, 1951.

Platt, A. M. *The child savers.* Chicago: University of Chicago Press, 1969.

Quinney, R. *Critique of legal order.* Boston: Little, Brown and Co., 1974.

Reagan, M. *The managed economy.* New York: Oxford University Press, Inc., 1963.

Rothman, D. J. *The discovery of the asylum.* Boston: Little, Brown and Co., 1971.

Samuelson, P. *Economics* (8th ed.). New York: McGraw-Hill Book Co., 1970.

Seitz, S. T. Social unrest and critical elections; periodicity in American history. Paper delivered at meeting of the American Political Science Association, 1974.

Sharfman, I. L. *The Interstate Commerce Commission.* New York: Commonwealth Fund, 1931.

Silver, A. The demand for order in civil society. In D. J. Bordua (Ed.), *The police.* New York: John Wiley & Sons, Inc., 1967.

Short, J. F., Jr., and Wolfgang, M. (Eds.). *Collective violence.* Chicago: Aldine Publishing Co., 1972.

Simmel, G. The metropolis and mental life. In K. Wolff (Ed.), *The sociology of Georg Simmel.* New York: Free Press, 1950.

Smith, A. The wealth of nations. In R. B. Carson, J. Ingles, and D. McLaud (Eds.), *Government in the American economy.* Lexington, Mass.: D. C. Heath & Co., 1973.

Tiryakian, E. A model of societal change and its lead indicators. In S. Klausner (Ed.), *The study of total societies.* New York: Doubleday & Co., Inc., Anchor Books, 1967.

# CHAPTER 5

# Bureaucracy and international relations

The industrial quest for raw materials has been a primary force in shaping international relations. The superpowers have created a military-technology complex that fosters a destructive political capitalism and converts international relations into a game of credibility chess. Bureaucratic organizations such as the multinational corporations and transnational political bodies have begun challenging the sovereignty of the nation-states.

## BUREAUCRACY AND THE NATION-STATE

All societies require social coordination to secure survival against the forces of nature, govern the relations among those in a society, and govern relations among societies. To accomplish these goals, complex societies rely on bureaucratic organization and sophisticated technology. Bureaucracy and technology have provided the foundations for two major developments in recent human history: the rise of the nation-state in the seventeenth century and the birth of industrialization in the eighteenth century. Taken together, the modern nation-state and the industrial machine have provided people with a means to brutally exploit the environment and to achieve unprecedented organizational control over the relations among people. These organizational controls include criminal law, civil law, internal security forces, and certain forms of welfare policies.

Through the nation-state and the industrial machine, bureaucratic organization and its attendant technology also have altered dramatically the relations among societies. The impact has been both indirect and direct. First, the industrial machine demands vast quantities of natural resources. To secure these resources, the nation-state has brought societies into frequent contact, which sometimes has escalated to dangerous conflict. Second, bureaucratic organizations exercise enormous control over the relations among those in a society. In so doing, they help fashion the contours of domestic policy. But nation-states do not exist in isolation from one another. On several important occasions, changes in domestic policies have altered the course of international relations. Third, more directly, bureaucratic organization and sophisticated technology provide new means for one nation-state to coordinate, control, and exploit its relations with other nation-states. The same bureaucratic organization and technology provides a foundation for alternatives to the nation-state.

These three issue imply complex connections between and among bureaucracy, technology, ecology, domestic policy, and foreign policy. What are these connections? What are the consequences for international relations?

## BUREAUCRACY, ECOLOGY, AND INTERNATIONAL RELATIONS

In complex societies, bureaucracies do far more than secure survival against the hostile forces of nature. In Chapter 3 we saw how bureaucracy and technology helped people overwhelm the ecosystem, allowing them to brutally exploit its resources. We saw that people have been shortsighted in their assaults on the environment. These assaults began in earnest with the industrial revolution. Bureaucratic organization made the industrial revolution possible and then made it possible to export industrialization from England to other countries in the world. Today the industrial machine is foreign to no country. Its demand for natural resources has expanded enormously throughout the twentieth century. This incredible demand quickly exhausted readily available supplies of raw materials, forcing people to expand the search for natural resources around the world and to intensify their exploitation. In turn, this extensive and intensive exploitation of limited resources has helped create a global ecocrisis.

To be sure, bureaucratic organization and sophisticated technology did not cause the demand for natural resources or the global ecocrisis. Ultimately, human decision makers are at fault. But bureaucratic organization and sophisticated technology made these decisions possible. In a sense, therefore, bureaucratic organization and sophisticated technology have helped aggravate old social problems and create new ones. Among these are the increased demand for natural resources and the global ecocrisis. The demand for natural resources is not unique to complex societies, but the intensive consumption of natural resources is unique, resulting largely from the industrial assault on nature and partly from the accumulation of political power found first in empires and then in nation-states. The global ecocrisis is a new problem. Even ancient empires could not exploit nature the way the industrial machine and the nation-state do.

### Demand for natural resources

Very few societies have all the raw materials necessary for survival and social amenities. The ancient Egyptians, for example, needed both lumber and stone. The great

pyramids of Egypt are testimonies to the power ancient Egypt exercised in transporting valuable stone from far places. It is also a testimony to the vanity of Egyptian power under the pharaohs. But other examples illustrate less vain efforts to acquire needed raw materials. Because of its short supply in various regions on every continent, salt has been an important raw material sought by numerous societies. To secure salt and other basic supplies for human existence, people must leave their territorial boundaries, often coming into contact with other societies in the process.

There is a simple point here. Desired raw materials are not distributed evenly across the world. In consequence, all but the most simple societies have looked elsewhere for certain raw materials, either taking them from neighbors who had these materials or trading goods abundant at home for goods abundant elsewhere. Nature does not equally distribute her wealth, so the task rests with people.

***Simple societies.*** Trade and welfare long have been two means of redistributing material resources from one society to another. One primitive form of warfare is the raid: parties of people who venture into hostile territory for desired resources and booty (see Ewers, 1967:327-344). Cities long have been the targets of raids, because materials and booty are concentrated there. One historian even attributes the fall of ancient Rome to German barbarians who murdered the Roman civilization through endless raids by unorganized bands of invaders (Piganiol, 1950). The legendary Viking raids are another example of brief warfare for materials and booty.

Less dramatic but far more extensive are the trade route among less complex societies (see Malinowski, 1961). Like raids and other primitive forms of warfare, trade helps to distribute desired resources from one society to another. Trade also helps preserve a peaceful equilibrium among these societies. Among relatively simple societies, trade involves far more than a market economy among societies coming into occasional contact with one another. Typically, trade relations rest on elaborate rites and myths coupled with peaceful competition over which group will be the more generous partner in the trade route (Malinowski, 1961; Mauss, 1967). Rites, myths, and the competition for prestige are subtle control mechanisms in less complex societies, checking the possible deterioration of economic barter into simple greed.

**Barter.** Less ritualized forms of exchange also occur among less complex societies. A primitive barter economy joined North Africa with peoples of the desert for centuries (see Bovill, 1968). Typically these barter routes joined peoples of vastly different cultures over terrain that made raids and other forms of warfare less profitable means of acquiring desired goods. Still, barter requires little social organization, save some idea of commodity equivalencies for exchange and some idea of the markets available. That is, to barter, different societies must know what other societies desire and how much they desire it. But the situation drastically changes when currency (money) becomes the medium for exchange. As we shall see later, currency increases the interdependence of societies, requiring considerably more social organization than a simple barter economy.

**Trade and empire.** The historical roots of empires lie in attempts by one society to extend political control over the political and economic life of another society. Invariably, empires grew to establish markets and to protect trade routes to important markets. Abundant examples of such trading empires exist, including the ancient Egyptian, Athenian, Persian, and Roman empires. Much the same can be said about the British, Belgian, French, Spanish, Dutch, and Portugese empires that emerged during the seventeenth and eighteenth centuries. Here, with a few exceptions, mercantilism became the driving

force toward empire. Except for the colonization of the Americas, these European governments had few territorial ambitions, as such, beyond securing trade routes and access to lucrative markets (Palmer and Colton, 1965:615).

Until 1875 even the European penetration of Africa remained relatively peaceful. At the turn of the eighteenth century, Napoleon opened Egypt to the world, and the Suez Canal eventually became an important trade link between Europe and the Far East. The English began minor colonization on the Cape of Southern Africa about 1815, but these efforts were closely tied to important English trade routes around the Cape of Africa. The third penetration of Africa came with the conquest of Algeria by the French after 1830, but again the penetration was closely linked to the growing trade routes around Africa (Banning, 1966:1-4).

**Imperialism.** Shortly after 1875 the penetration of Africa and Asia assumed a new form. By the end of the nineteenth century, the major European powers virtually had partitioned among themselves the vast continent of Africa. In part, the sudden change toward territorial acquisition was prompted by the increased needs for raw materials in the industrializing nations of Europe. Coupled with the growing strength of the nation-states, Europe found it easy to conquer the unindustrialized civilizations in Africa, taking from them needed raw materials and using them as ready markets for goods manufactured in Europe. In fact, between 1884 and 1898 European powers asserted sovereignty over most of the continent (Hargreaves, 1960:96-109). For economically, European life required the cotton, rubber, and petroleum of Africa (Palmer and Colton, 1965:618).

Clearly, the sudden territorial thrust into Africa, Asia, and South America had many roots, among them industrial, commercial and financial, scientific, political, and even religious and humanitarian (Palmer and

Colton, 1965:622). But the suddenness of the wave of imperialism that swept the globe can only be accounted for by the concentration of power in the nation-state, coupled with the vastly expanding demands of the growing industrial machine. Bureaucracy and technology provided the means for concentrating power in the nation-state, sustaining the industrial revolution and subsequently expanding the search for and means of acquiring needed raw materials. In fact, the very act of colonization brought the European bureaucracy into the underdeveloped nations of the world.

*The United States.* While Europe and Japan struggled for territory in other parts of the world, the United States turned westward, exploiting the vast resources of the North American continent. Throughout much of the nineteenth century, America's political contact with Europe and Asia was relatively limited, excepting trade in slaves and cotton, which abruptly declined with the Civil War. But in the twentieth century, America was drawn closer to the political problems abroad. Consequent to her participation in the First and Second World Wars, the United States became an international power. Subsequent American

involvement in Korea and Vietnam brought the United States into the thicket of post-colonial battles in Asia.

American military involvement in the struggles of Europe also changed her trade relations with other nations of the world. Fig. 5-1, *A,* illustrates the per capita growth of American trade (both imports and exports) from 1815 to 1973. The first jump in trade occurs with and following the First World War, but the major jump occurs during and after World War II. Fig. 5-1, *B,* illustrates the U.S. proportion of all world trade from the Civil War until 1973. The two trade peaks more clearly illustrate the impact of World War I and World War II on the United States trade position in the world market. The trough between the two World Wars indicates the impact of the Great Depression on the United States world trade position. Finally, note the continued decline in United States trade position from the late 1950s into the 1970s.

***Consequences.*** Nature has not distributed her wealth equally among societies. Consequently, people engage in warfare and trade to redistribute bounties. As we move from simple societies to the industrial nation-state, the scope of political interaction among nations increases accordingly.

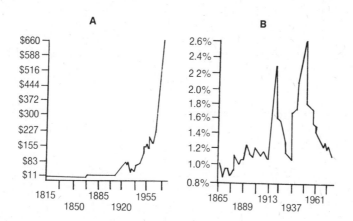

**Fig. 5-1.** United States trade. **A,** Per capita trade, 1815 to 1973, **B,** Percent of world trade, 1865 to 1973. Data from Inter-University Consortium for Political and Social Research, originally collected by Arthur Banks for *Cross-National Time-Series Archive.*

Through empires people attempt to secure control over the political and economic life of other societies, replacing earlier forms of raiding, barter, and trading rituals. With the early nation-state, trade routes were drastically expanded, and some colonization did occur, particularly in the Americas. But industrialization exaggerated the trend toward colonization; major industrial powers began asserting territorial sovereignty over vast sectors of the nonindustrial world. Similarly, industrialization increased the interdependence of nation-states through trade, because the vast demands of the industrial machine seldom could be satisfied by local resources alone and because new markets provided room for more industrial expansion at home. Fig. 5-2 illustrates the changing scope of interaction among societies, from the relatively low levels of rudimentary states, through the moderate interaction of empires, to the intensive interactions occasioned by industrial nation-states.

***Bureaucratization.*** The changing scope of interaction among societies requires greater levels of social organization, whether to conduct trade or war. Empires replaced the raids of unorganized bands with highly organized militaries. In turn these militaries required the organized mobilization of human and economic resources at home. Similarly, growing trade routes required increased coordination to protect existing routes while expanding these routes into new markets. To these factors the nation-

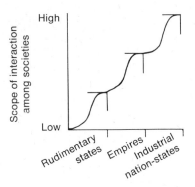

**Fig. 5-2.** Scope of interaction among societies.

state added the coordination necessary to concentrate the human and economic resources of millions of people in the hands of a single sovereign. Further, the industrial nation-state brought colonial bureaucracy to the underdeveloped regions of the world, helping the dominant foreign power mobilize natural resources for export and maintain sovereign control over the colony.

The years following World War II brought independence to many former colonies of the European powers. But the legacy of the colonial domination remained, reflected in the colonial nation's exports and relatively small militaries and their incredible lag behind developed nations of the world, measured by such factors as per capita gross national product (GNP) and energy consumption. Table 5-1 summarizes some of the important differences

**Table 5-1.** Comparison of bureaucratic states (1965)*

|  | COLONIAL | SEMIMODERN | MODERN | TOTAL |
|---|---|---|---|---|
| Number of countries | 37 | 46 | 30 | 113 |
| Energy consumption (kilograms per person) | 107 | 528 | 3,501 | 1,192 |
| GNP per capita | $120 | $313 | $1,513 | $568 |
| Defense spending per capita | $5 | $10 | $66 | $23 |
| Percent of GNP exports | 21 | 19 | 16 | 19 |
| Percent of population in the military | 0.5 | 0.8 | 1.2 | 0.8 |

*Data from Inter-University Consortium for Political and Social Research. Rudoph Rummell originally collected the raw data for *The Attribute of Nations Archive.* Monetary units have been converted to U.S. dollars.

between these colonial bureaucratic states (legacies of the colonial era), semimodern bureaucratic states, and modern bureaucratic states in 1965, twenty years after the end of World War II.

Several factors are readily apparent from Table 5-1. Energy consumption is highest in modern bureaucratic states, lowest in colonial bureaucratic states. Per capita GNP, per capita defense expenditures, and the total proportion of the population in the armed forces all follow the same pattern, with modern bureaucratic states scoring highest, semimodern bureaucratic states in between, and colonial bureaucratic states at the very bottom. On the other hand, exports account for higher percentages of the gross national product in colonial bureaucratic states than in either semimodern or modern bureaucratic states, consistent with the industrial demand for raw materials from these former colonies.

Compared with the industrial economies of the modern bureaucratic states in Table 5-1, the economies of the colonial bureaucratic states are underdeveloped. This is not particularly surprising, given the discussion above and in the preceding chapters. Still, the following points summarize the basic differences between the modern bureaucratic states and their former colonial possessions:

1. Industrialization increases the per capita consumption of energy.
2. Industrialization increases per capita wealth.
3. Industrialization increases per capita military expenditures, particularly among competing industrial nation-states.
4. Even after granting independence to their colonies, the industrialized nations continue to siphon vast amounts of natural resources from the less developed nations.
5. To protect their interests at home and abroad, industrial nations tend to

have a higher proportion of their citizenry in the military service.

## Global ecocrisis

In feeding the growing industrial machine, industrial bureaucratic societies have sharply altered the demands for natural resources across the world. In securing the desired raw materials, the industrial nation-states drastically altered the patterns of trade and warfare relations among societies. Less dramatically and less visibly, these same demands for natural resources have escalated ecological changes on this planet, perhaps creating a global ecocrisis that could end civilization as we know it today. A few examples will illustrate the scope and complexity of this potential global crisis.

*Examples.* We have seen that life on the earth is supported by a complex ecosystem. In turn, that ecosystem depends on ocean and air currents, evaporation and precipitation, cloud cover, heat absorption through the atmosphere, filtering of cosmic rays, and complex controls over normal radiation (Meadows et al., 1972; Study of Critical Environmental Problems, 1970). We have already seen how the industrial revolution upset the ecosystem, allowing people to brutally exploit its delicate balance. But the impact of industrialization might not stop here. Industrialization has led to enormous deforestations and rapid consumption of fossil fuels. The resulting increase in carbon dioxide, directly from fuel combustion and indirectly because the forests no longer are producing as much oxygen, could alter the balance between heat radiation trapped by the atmosphere and heat radiation escaping from the atmosphere. Carbon dioxide tends to hold heat radiation closer to the earth's surface, allowing less to escape from the atmosphere (Brown, 1974:132). If this process raises the earth's temperature by a couple degrees Celsius, it could melt the polar ice caps, flooding massive land areas and turning others into arid, unbearable deserts. Less dramatic, the available cardon dioxide might favor increased vegetation, although different in type and location. In turn, the "shifted" vegetation might alter the climatic conditions on an entire continent.

An opposite process might be happening with increasing global pollution. The industrial machine has dramatically increased the particulate count in the earth's atmosphere. These particulates tend to screen the sun's rays from the earth's surface. Most of us have seen an "orange" setting sun. The orange color is a product of particulates in the atmosphere, filtering out part of the sun's rays when seen by the observer. The increased air pollution resulting from industrialization might sufficiently decrease the amount of solar radiation reaching the earth that a new ice age could follow (Brown, 1974:132-133).

A third potential problem is a change in the protective ozone layer surrounding the earth. Jet aircraft, aerosol sprays, and other products of the industrial era might be depleting the ozone layer, allowing dangerous solar radiation to enter the earth's atmosphere. These particular solar rays are dangerous to both human and other life forms. Among other consequences, these particular solar rays might increase the incidence of skin cancer in people.

In all these cases, we are not quite sure about the ultimate impact technology and the industrial revolution could have on the global ecosystem. But the possibility of severly disrupting the basic conditions making life possible on this planet are quite clear.

**Consequences.** A global ecocrisis would require massive coordination among societies across the globe. However, the uncertainty surrounding the impact of industry and technology on the environment has allowed other matters, such as the demand for natural resources, to determine the contours of international relations. Only a crisis obvious to most nations and a crisis threatening all of them likely would spark coordinated efforts to remedy the damage people have wrought on their world. For the time being, however, scientific work continues, sponsored both by national and international organizations, that one day might leave a deeper impression on the contours of international relations than the limited impact we witness today.

### Overview

The industrial demand for scarce resources has increased drastically the scope and intensity of societal interactions, reflected in changing trade relations and general increases in military preparedness. In addition, the impact of industrialization and sophisticated technology one day might force humankind to face a global ecocatastrophe. Fig. 5-3 illustrates the impact of industrial bureaucratic society on people's relation to the environment and,

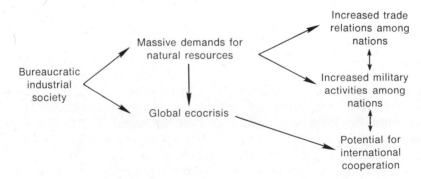

**Fig. 5-3.** Bureaucracy, environment, and international relations.

consequently, the relations among societies.

## BUREAUCRACY, DOMESTIC POLICY, AND INTERNATIONAL RELATIONS

For more than a century critics of industrial society have argued a relation between domestic policy and foreign policy. For example, Karl Marx thought he saw a strong relation between repression at home and expansion abroad. Similar accusations still are made today. Bertram Gross (1973: 290) argues that America has a managed society, ruled by warfare–welfare–industrial communications–police–bureaucracies. Even without suggesting these sinister motives, analysts do see some congruency between domestic and foreign policy, particularly when domestic policies are considered in light of their impacts on other nations (Pettman, 1975:41).

### Military-industrial complex

One focal point of the alleged congruency between domestic and foreign policies is the military-industrial complex in modern bureaucratic societies. Former President Eisenhower called it the legacy of World War II. In 1940, in contrast, American businessmen hardly were enthusiastic about converting to war production. Even though the steel industry operated at 54% capacity, steel executives feared being saddled with more excess productive capacity if they prepared for war and the war effort remained as small as in World War I (Barnet, 1973:35-36). But when the war effort began in earnest, the federal government provided attractive incentives to those companies that could marshal talent and facilities quickly. The largest corporations in America were the most prepared to do so (Barnet, 1973:36). By the end of World War II, big business in America had come to accept government military spending as a permanent force in the American economy (Barnet, 1973:37).

Does this military-industrial complex still exist today? What is its impact on domestic affairs? What is its impact on international relations?

*Manpower.* Does the military-industrial complex rest on the type of armed forces forged by Hitler before the Second World War? Fig. 5-4, *A*, illustrates the percentage of Americans in the military forces from 1815 to 1973. As expected, the high points of military personnel correspond to wartime, particularly the Civil War, the First World War, the Second World War, Korea, and Vietnam. In the twentieth century there is a definite trend toward proportion-

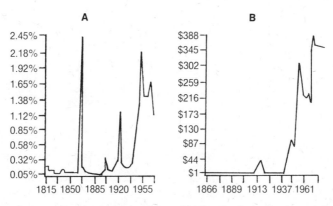

**Fig. 5-4.** United States military. **A,** Percentage of U.S. population in Armed Services, 1815 to 1973. **B,** Per capita defense expenditures, 1865 to 1973. Data from *Cross-National Time-Series Archive.*

ately larger military forces. But we have found this characteristic of industrial nations in general. As the Vietnam War wound down in 1973, the military employees returned to about 1.1% of the population, a figure roughly comparable with the military forces of modern bureaucratic states shown in Table 5-1.

*Military expenditures.* Does the military-industrial complex rest on military expenditures, apart from maintaining large armed forces? Per capita military expenditures in the United States are extremely high. In 1965, of all the nations in the world, the United States per capita expenditure for military purposes was the highest. In that year America spent an average of $266 per person, compared with an average of $66 for all modern bureaucratic states. Fig. 5-4, *B*, illustrates the per capita expenditures for military and defense purposes in the United States from 1865 to 1973. Note the sharp and sustained jump in per capita expenditures during and following the Second World War. Fig. 5-5 compares the United States and other countries of the world in terms of the percent of gross national product devoted to military purposes between 1961 and 1970. Again it is amply clear that the United

States devotes an enormous segment of its economy to military purposes.

*Contours of the military-industrial complex.* Look more closely at the contours of the United States, compared with other nations of the world in 1965, before the major Vietnam offensive. Table 5-2 compares the United States with 136 nations monitored that year. The United States differs from the world community in several respects:

1. Trade is a relatively small portion of the United States gross national product, even smaller than the percentage of GNP devoted to military expenditures.

2. Overall, United States government spending is considerably higher than the average world percentage of gross national product devoted to government expenditures.

3. Education accounts for a slightly larger share of total GNP in the United States than in the average nation. (Government expenditures on health and education combined are smaller than the percentage of GNP devoted to military expenditures.)

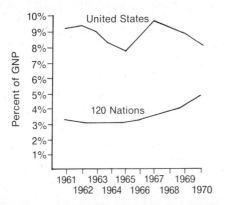

**Fig. 5-5.** Military expenditures as percent of gross national product, 1961 to 1970. Data from Inter-University Consortium for Political and Social Research; originally collected by U.S. Arms Control and Disarmament Agency.

**Table 5-2.** Comparison of the U.S. and 136 nations (1965)*

|  | UNITED STATES | 136 COUNTRIES |
|---|---|---|
| Trade (% GNP) | 7.3 | 46.9 |
| Government expenditures (% GNP) | 18.0 | 13.6 |
| Education expenditures (% GNP) | 5.3 | 3.5 |
| Health Expenditures (% GNP) | 1.8 | 2.1 |
| Defense expenditures (% GNP) | 7.6 | 3.7 |
| Percent of world's scientific authors | 41.7 | .9 |
| Percent working males in technology | 23.1 | 6.5 |

*Data from Inter-University Consortium for Political and Social Research. These data were originally collected by C. L. Taylor and M. C. Hudson, released under *World Handbook of Political and Social Indicators II: Aggregate Data Archive* U.S. figures are included in the averages for all 136 nations in 1965.

4. Public health expenditures represent a smaller proportion of GNP in the United States than in the average nation.
5. The United States contributes 41.7% of the world's total of scientific authors in the natural sciences.
6. A significant percentage of working American men are employed in technology, compared with the percentage of men employed in technology on the average for all 136 countries.

*Military-technology complex.* The data in Table 5-2 suggest that in the United States the term "military-industrial complex" is somewhat misleading. What the United States does have is a military-technology complex. There are several reasons why this term is more appropriate. First, the proportion of Americans in the armed forces is not unusually high for a modern bureaucratic state. Second, but expenditures per soldier are unusually high: $33,436 per soldier in 1972, compared with a worldwide average of $5,501.* Third,

---

*Data from Inter-University Consortium for Political and Social Research. Original data collected by R. L. Sivard and reported in *World Military and Social Expenditures, 1974.* New York: Institute for World Order, 1974.

large amounts of the cost per soldier go toward research and development contracts and the civilian employees of the Pentagon, numbering more than 1 million (see Ad Hoc Committee on the Economy and War, 1973:240-249; Adams, 1973:259-271). Fourth, the military-technology complex has created a technocratic class of workers, comprising almost one fourth of all male workers in the United States. Taken together, the technocracy and service sector of the American economy have grown dramatically since the end of the First World War. Fig. 5-6 illustrates the rapid growth of a work force employed in neither industry nor agriculture during the twentieth century in the United States. This shift in the American economy and work force helps explain the relatively modest role of trade in the United States gross national product.

### Impact on domestic affairs

A technocracy needs education. As Fig. 5-6, *A,* clearly shows, the proportion of the United States population enrolled in universities has risen sharply since the end of World War II. The rise begins with World War I, takes another upward turn after World War II, and really shoots upward after the Soviets launched Sputnik in 1957.

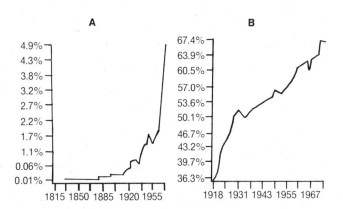

**Fig. 5-6.** Occupational structure in United States. **A,** Percent of population enrolled in universities, 1815 to 1973. **B,** Percent of work force not employed in agriculture or industry, 1918 to 1973. Data from *Cross-National Time-Series Archive.*

From this point, Americans entered a technology race, drastically changing the contours of American society.

The rise of a technocracy in the United States, with its impact on United States society, implies an astonishing conclusion about the military-technology complex. Before World War II, bureaucratic organization and technology helped people coordinate the arrangements of society. And they helped the industrial machine produce workers for its factories. But within the last generation the bureaucracy and technology of the military-technology complex have been a causal force in their own rights, reshaping American society in their image. How has America been transformed so quickly?

*Economic capitalism.* We typically think of a capitalist economic system as one in which private enterprise controls both production and distribution and consumers have free reign to determine what goods they wish to buy. But about a generation ago, Schumpeter proposed a different perspective on capitalism. He claimed that capitalism implies "creative destruction." That is, the capitalist machine keeps in motion by producing new consumer goods, new methods of production and transportation, new markets, and new forms of industrial organization. The shift in emphasis might appear to be subtle. But contrary to ordinary views of a capitalist economy, Schumpeter points out that capitalism does not thrive on simple price competition. Rather, capitalism thrives on new commodities, new technology, new supplies, and new types of organization (Schumpeter, 1962:83,84).

*Political capitalism.* Schumpeter (1962: 424) predicted the eventual conquest of capitalism by bureaucracy. In a sense he was right. But socialism (government control over production) did not appear in America in a version similar to that in Europe. Large corporations in the United States maintain considerable control over production and distribution in the economy. But the issue Schumpeter raises in his vision of capitalism is not the struggle between private and public ownership. As he sees it, capitalism was a source of incentive for rapid and massive change. Today, the military-technology complex has replaced the older form of economic capitalism with a political capitalism, with the government bureaucracy providing these incentives for rapid and massive change. Through a conservative multiplier effect, the military expenditures in the United States comprise between 18% and 19% of the entire economy. Hence, about one fifth of the economic potential of the United States rests with the military decision-making bureaucracies (Cypher, 1973:275).

How has the government managed to sustain political capitalism while assuming increasing control over the American economy through the military-technology complex? The obvious answer is the military subsidy of research and development in military technology. Quite often this subsidy takes on the following characteristics: (1) contracting companies are offered a fixed fee for the work; (2) the government assumes the risk involved in technological research; (3) cost overruns are absorbed by the government, not the contracting company. With this policy of no-risk, fixed-fee, plus cost-overrun contracts, the government has absorbed the risk of technological innovation while allowing political capitalism to continue the thrust toward massive change that Schumpeter thought would destroy economic capitalism, So, when economic capitalism did falter during the Great Depression, the military-technology complex became an innovative bureaucratic organization that helped replace it with political capitalism.

### Impact on international relations

Has this military-technology complex affected international relations? Remember that the military-technology complex has its roots in the institutions of the nation-state. It is not independent of the nation-state system. Consequently, the military-technology complex has aggravated the balance of power among existing nation-states. The problem is even more serious because these nation-states still operate in a global arena without an adequate international peace-keeping organization. With competition confined to nation-states, the military-technology complex within each superpower has sparked an escalated competition to develop more lethal and more costly forms of advanced weaponry and military technology. Nuclear escalation, developments in chemical and biological warfare, and developments in psychological warfare have brought the political capitalism of the world's military-technology complexes closer to destroying themselves and all human life on this planet.

***Image of power.*** The military-technology complex has given the bureaucracies of modern nation-states an image of power that feeds on its own vanity. Boulding (1961:115) suggests that the image determines current behavior and policy. The American image of herself as the "Number One Nation" helped lead her into the disastrous policies in Southeast Asia, even though intelligence reports from around the world (and some at home) indicated disastrous consequences from American policies in Vietnam. But the American bureaucracy did not heed warnings about the wisdom of its war in Vietnam (see Barnet, 1973; Stavins et al., 1971).

A former staff member of the National Security Council, Morton Halperin (1974: 11-12), cites a number of images shared by Washington bureaucrats, images that have shaped the contours of American relations with other countries. Among them are: (1) every nation falling to Communism increases the communist bloc power in its struggle against the Free World; (2) only the United States has the power, ability, responsibility, and right to maintain international order and defend the Free World from Communism; (3) the Third World is the battleground between Communism and the Free World; and (4) military strength is the primary basis of national security, and the United States must maintain military superiority over the Soviet Union.

The question is not whether these images are in themselves right or wrong. The problem is that they do guide bureaucratic decision making. And there is no international court of law through which to test the actions flowing from the images nations hold of themselves and others. Equally important, the image held by American military bureaucracies is shared widely around the world. The image of United States power and responsibility helped defeat the Swedish proposal to establish an agency to receive, investigate, and report on complaints of war crimes by the United States in Indochina (Report of the International Commission of Enquiry into United States Crimes in Indochina, 1972: vii).

### Overview

The military-technology complex of the post–World War II era has sparked an arms race of unprecedented proportions and unprecedented dangers. It is political capitalism in its purest form, preparing the way for continued revolution in military technology and perhaps sowing the seeds of its own destruction, either through annihilation of the human race or mutual restraint based on an understanding of the dangers implied by a continued escalation of military technology capabilities. In a sense, therefore, Schumpeter's prediction about economic capitalism is relevant to political capitalism: it carries within itself the seeds of its own destruction, for it must continue to revolutionize the standards of total military superiority. In the process, the superpowers develop even more efficient means of mass destruction and push people closer to either transnational organizations to control and defuse the arms race or the continued mobilization of society for developing new and better means of military overkill, while directing human talents from tasks that might prove more beneficial to mankind.

## BUREAUCRACY AND INTERNATIONAL RELATIONS

Bureaucratic organization has a direct impact on international relations in addition to its impact through the demand for natural resources, the growing ecocrisis, and the military-technology complex. Two issues are particularly relevant: the growth of multinational corporations and transnational organizations and changes in the conduct of warfare among nation-states. Both developments require advanced bureaucratic organizations and increasingly sophisticated technology.

### Multinational corporations and transnational organizations

Multinational corporations are companies incorporated under the national laws of one country, with subsidiaries incorporated under the national laws of other countries. Although the interests of multinational corporations are primarily economic, these goals cannot easily be separated from the political goals of nation-states. Henry Ford, for example, extracted major concessions from the British government when he threatened to close Ford factories in England. In short, there are conflicts between nation-states and multinational corporations. Transnational organizations also go beyond the older political organization of the nation-states. Those with avowedly political purposes, including the old League of Nations and the present United Nations, hold very little real power. But those with primarily economic ends have considerable influence over nation-states. Among these transnational organizations are the European Economic Community (Common Market) and, with less clout, the International Monetary Fund (IMF) and General Agreement on Trade and Tariffs (GATT).

***Technological foundations.*** Several factors have made the growth of multinational corporations and transnational organizations possible in the twentieth century. These include faster travel time; better communications systems; standardization of weights, measures, and consumer goods; more stable currency standards and more stable currency-exchange rates; and the increasing standardization of mass production and distribution procedures. As Drucker (1962:3) points out, the principle of mass production is a general bureaucratic means of organizing people to work together. In addition, the cybernetic revolution, particularly the use of large computers, has allowed the sending, receiving, storing, and processing of information needed to centralize, standardize, and manage operations as large as the General Motors multinational corporation (see Brown, 1974:146).

***Economic incentives.*** Why have these multinational corporations arisen? In a sense, the multinational corporation is another form of the bureaucratization of economic capitalism predicted by Schumpeter. These corporations come closer to the stabilization of production and distribution than do the military-technology complexes. Multinational corporations can circumvent various trade barriers, use the high technology developed in one area to exploit the resources in another, and even locate plants where labor, materials, capital, taxes, and stability produce higher margins of profit. Protecting profit margins is an integral part of multinational corporate decision making. Worldwide, these multinational corporations have more economic strength than many nation-states, and they tend to monopolize certain markets, prices, and production facilities.

The multinational corporations control a surprising amount of the economic activity across the globe. Consider, for example, General Motors, the second largest corporation in the United States. The corporation has assets of more than $21 billion, had sales of almost $36 billion in 1975, and employs almost three quarters of a million people in the United States and 21 other countries, plus a few other areas as well. In the 15 years from 1950 to 1965, the fixed assets of General Motors overseas rose from $180 million to $1.1 billion, a 600% increase (Barnet, 1973:195). By some estimates, the rate of international investment and output has grown twice as fast as the total world gross national product since 1950. By 1970, about 25% of all world market production was made through international corporations (*Monthly Review*, October and November 1969).

*Multinational corporations and the world community.* The interests of multinational corporations are not necessarily consistent with those of the nation-states. The economic potential of the multinational corporations requires many nation-states to actively consider their interests in policy making. War between two nations served by a multinational corporation, for example, could have a devastating impact on the corporation. Similarly, these multinational corporations require relatively stable social conditions, given the planning and coordination required by such large-scale organizations. Hence the multinationals have vested interests in guiding "appropriate" domestic and foreign policy among many nations of the world. Bribes to foreign officials and campaign contributions to particular political candidates are only two examples of the intrusion of multinational corporations on the older structure of the nation-states.

And there are other sources of conflict between the multinational corporations and the nation-states. These conflicts include a variety of problems, ranging from economic regulation, investment, taxation, and jurisdiction over disputes. As multinational corporations have grown in strength over the past generation, so has the body of transnational law within each nation-state. This transnational law attempts to regulate the activities of multinational corporations. But the nation-state is not a particularly appropriate forum for controlling activities of the multinationals. First, the transnational law governing multinationals in one country often differs from that governing multinationals in other countries. Second, the multinationals can use the promise of their economic potential to gain concessions from nation-states, thus forcing nation-states to compete for the attention and investments of the multinational corporations. In short, the multinational corporations have become a relatively new force in international relations.

**Transnational organizations.** Like the economic incentives for multinational corporations, the economic incentives for transnational organizations became increasingly apparent after World War II. From World War I through the Great Depression, various nation-states interfered with international commerce through high trade and tariff controls. By implication, the exercise of sovereignty by any one nation-state, particularly the larger ones, could drastically affect the commercial relations among nations. Consider, for example, the impact of the Smoot-Hawley Tariff of 1930, passed by the Congress of the United States. This act raised the value of gold on the international market, drastically affecting the currencies and trade positions of several countries around the world.

After World War II the international mood toward the gold standard began to change, making it possible to move toward the regulation of national currencies through transnational organizations. One attempt to do so was the International Monetary Fund (IMF). The International Monetary Fund seeks to curb national attempts to devaluate currency and to restrict the national use of currency exchange controls. But the IMF has not been able to control actions by major nation-states. Some agreements in the European Economic Community (Common Market) violate IMF regulations by fixing currency exchange rates among its members, allowing only slight fluctuations (2½%). And the unilateral decision by President Nixon in 1971 to devalue the American dollar and set it free from constant gold equivalencies, without even consulting the IMF, severely undermined the utility of the fund (see Steiner and Vagts, 1976:1141-1175).

*European economic community.* Perhaps the most ambitious transnational organization today is the European Economic Community. The EEC began operating in January 1958, seeking economic integration among several European nations. Of all the transnational organizations, this is the most comprehensive, complete with constitutional, executive, legislative, and judicial mechanisms to handle questions of economic sovereignty that arise among participating nations. Among its goals are the elimination of internal tariffs (patterned on the federal system among states in the United States), the establishment of a common customs union, and the establishment of common external tariffs (see Steiner and Vagts, 1976:1242-1420). Since its inception the EEC has developed a considerable body of law governing the activities of its member nation-states. Although observers do not agree on the eventual impact of the European Economic Community, the possibility does exist that one day the EEC will emerge as a United States of Europe.

**Implications.** Both the multinational corporations and the transnational organizations challenge the older sovereign claims of the nation-state. To date they have not replaced the nation-state. However, these large-scale organizations do transcend the boundaries of nation-states, attempting to achieve an integration among societies around the world that is difficult when nation-states claim complete sovereignty over their policy making and its impact on international relations.

### Bureaucracy and war

Bureaucratic organization also has affected dramatically the conduct of war. The natural history of warfare illustrates the enormous changes introduced by bureaucracy and technology. Compared with the modern military, raiding parties were unorganized, and their military strategy required that they live off the land as they raided and withdraw quickly once booty and resources were taken. With the ancient and preindustrial empires, military regimentation and supporting bureaucratic organizations at home made it possible to gain and maintain control over the political and economic institutions of other societies. With planning, mobilization of troops and resources at home, and administrative bureaucracies in the subject societies, empires became possible (see Otterbein, 1967:351-357).

Military strategy roughly can be divided into four general phases; raids, pre-Napoleonic empire-building, post-Napoleonic nation-state warfare, and credibility chess. Each level requires more bureaucratic organization and greater control over human and economic resources in a society, and each level implies greater levels of potential destruction to a person and property. Fig. 5-7 illustrates these two relations.

**1648 to 1789.** The military strategy permitting the growth of empires represents a major bureaucratic advance over unorganized raids. But the ancient empires of Egypt, Persia, Rome, and others lacked another bureaucratic advantage of more recent history: the nation-state itself. The nation-state represents an important advance over earlier forms of political organization, allowing greater consolidation of power through extensive bureaucratic organization. With the appearance of nation-

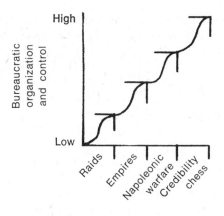 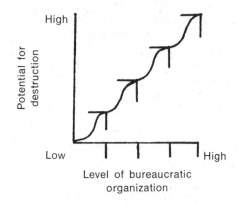

**Fig. 5-7.** Military strategy, bureaucratic organization, and destruction.

states in the seventeenth century, sovereigns could wage wars on other nation-states, based on assessments of the costs and gains to the sovereign, such as gain or loss of territory, fate of alliances, and changes in the prestige of any one nation-state. This was the classic age of power brokerage among nation-states. Military strategy was but one weapon in the arsenal of sovereign diplomacy, which also included intrigue, bargaining, and coalition formation among nation-states (Rapoport, 1968:18).

**Napoleon.** Napoleon brought an end to limited nation-state wars for limited objectives. The sovereigns of the early nation-states often relied on professional mercenaries. Napoleon replaced these with draftees, patriots who believed in the cause of their nation. Relying on this appeal to patriotism, Napoleon mobilized vast amounts of France's economic and human resources. No longer were nation-state wars limited by the resources of the king or emperor. And Napoleon introduced a change in tactics, attempting to annihilate the enemy and destroy its political structure as well (Rapoport, 1968:21). Eventually, of course, Napoleon was defeated, and for a century (1815 to 1914) the art of nation-state warfare incubated while Europe turned its attention to industrialization and

colonization. With the two World Wars of the twentieth century, the Napoleonic legacy reappeared.

**Clausewitz.** The importance of the Napoleonic legacy can be readily understood through the thoughts of Carl Von Clausewitz, a brilliant military strategist living through the Napoleonic transformation of warfare. Clausewitz saw war as a rational strategy, where one nation uses violence to compel another nation to do its will (Rapoport, 1968:21). Four tenets comprise his philosophy of international relations:

1. The state is a living entity with well-defined strivings, and it is endowed with intelligence to seek and examine means to its ends.
2. The state recognizes no higher authority.
3. The interests of states are always in conflict because all states seek to increase their power at the expense of others.
4. States resolve clashes of interests by imposing the will of one state on that of another (Rapoport, 1968:63).

*Impact.* We already have noted that "image" determines both bureaucratic conduct and foreign policy. Not surprising, the Clausewitz perspective took firm hold of bureaucrats in most nation-states of the twentieth century. Strategy became a permanent part of statecraft, where nations sought to control and mobilize the vast resources of their societies as quickly as possible to prepare for expected aggression from other nation-states. Our military-technology complex is one legacy of that image. The Clausewitz image had two important consequences for national security of bureaucracies around the world: it legitimized war as an expression of sovereign power, and it forced other nations into continued military preparedness. The legitimacy of war as an expression of sovereign power forms one important pillar of twentieth century Fascism. Benito Mussolini (1952:15, 23-24), Italian dictator and ally of Hitler during World War II, rejected peace as surrender and cowardice but extolled war as the people's seal of nobility.

**Post–World War II.** Napoleon brought the nation-states into an era of warfare that eventually produced Fascism and Naziism. So strong was the influence of nation-state sovereignty that even Lenin, while recognizing the importance of class over nation, still felt it necessary to keep control of the Russian revolutionary party in national, rather than international, hands. In many respects, World War II was the ultimate product of the Napoleonic legacy. The post –World War II era marks the beginning of another transition in international relations.

*Decline of the nation-state.* The most obvious change since World War II is the growing signs of decay in the nation-state as the ultimate source of sovereignty in the world. Certainly the United Nations has not usurped national sovereignty from the major powers. But transnational organizations, such as the European Economic Community, and military pacts, such as the North Atlantic Treaty Organization (NATO), the South East Asia Treaty Organization (SEATO), and the Warsaw Pact, clearly indicate a change toward organizations that transcend national claims to sovereignty. The same holds true if we ex-amine the growing importance of multinational corporations. Increasingly, these multinational corporations find themselves at odds with their host countries. We are, then, in an era of transition, slowly moving from the nation-state as the highest, most effective level of bureaucratic organization. Needless to say, however, the nation-state is far from withering away.

*Technology.* The United States ushered into the world the nuclear age, using two atomic bombs in Japan to end World War II. And the nuclear age drastically has altered the contours of potential warfare. Since the American use of the atomic bombs in 1945, all countries with the atomic or nuclear bomb have refrained from thermonuclear deployment, using conventional measures instead. But the real impact of the nuclear era has been on military strategy. We already have examined the military-technology complex and its impace on nuclear weaponry escalation.

A less obvious but critical consequence of the nuclear age has been the increased importance of "credibility" in military strategy. The bureaucracies of superpowers spend enormous amounts of time and energy on a game of "credibility chess." The game has two objectives: convince your opponent that you will use whatever strike capacity or second-strike capacity at your disposal, if conditions warrant, and convince the masses at home that the opponent will do the same. Nuclear destructive capacity has created a new role for propaganda tactics and "image-building," even more important than the conventional military tactics of yesteryear. The American military failure in Vietnam through conventional tactics only has escalated the importance of "credibility chess." Meanwhile, the game commands a large sector of total world gross national products, escalating the development of new weaponry and technologies to continue the revolution in sophisticated means of mass destruction.

## Summary

Bureaucratic organizations and their associated technologies have important direct impacts on international relations. First, they have made transnational organizations and multinational corporations possible. Both have helped undermine the status of the nation-state in the post–World War II era. At present, however, the nation-state is still the dominant political force in the world community. Further, bureaucratic organization and sophisticated technology have altered the course of warfare and military strategy among these nation-states. Technological developments, such as the atomic bomb and nuclear weapons, have fostered a military-technology complex, shifting military strategy to a curious form of credibility chess.

## CONCLUSION

Bureaucracies affect international relations both indirectly and directly. The demand for resources to feed the industrial machine helped spawn the imperialism of the late nineteenth century. The increased scope of interaction among societies, resulting from the quest for natural resources and new markets, greatly has expanded the scope and function of the nation-state bureaucracies, both for national security purposes and for the regulation of international commerce. And the same combination of nation-state bureaucracies supporting the industrial demand for natural resources slowly might turn this planet into an uninhabitable wasteland, an incidental by-product of a possible ecocatastrophe.

The decline of economic capitalism and the subsequent rise of political capitalism through the military-technology complex have drastically altered the course of domestic affairs and the course of international relations. Within a generation the military-technology complex has helped to create a technocracy within the American society. At the same time, the military-tech-

nology complexes among the superpowers carry seeds of their own destruction, for there are no inherent limits on this form of political capitalism that encourages technological revolution in the means of mass destruction, save mass destruction or the end of that political capitalism through bureaucratic controls that somehow limit the sovereign claims of the nation-state. Meanwhile, the military-technology complex feeds an image of national power than has worked against international political organizations with sufficient power to control the actions of sovereign nation-states.

On the other hand, bureaucracy and technology have made possible large-scale organizations that do transcend national boundaries. The interests of multinational corporations do not always parallel the interests of the host nation-states. When these interests conflict, the multinationals have not always lost the battle with the nation-state decision makers. Similarly, attempts have been made to establish transnational organizations. Few of these have been successful, although the European Economic Community might be an important exception to the weakness of transnational organizations in the post–World War II era.

In short, the post–World War II era pits two contradictory sets of forces against each other: those forces leading toward international organization and those forces maintaining the older form of the nation-state. The forces pushing toward international organization or transnational organization or multinational organizations include the industrial machine itself, the potential for a global ecocrisis, the possibility of global annihilation, and the very bureaucratic organization and technology that make supranational organizations possible. The forces helping to maintain the old nation-state system include the nation-state bureaucracy, the military-technology complex in each major nation-state, particularly as it competes with the military-technology complex in other nation-states, and the entrenched military strategy of "credibility chess," where propaganda manipulations and "image-building" help form those images that govern the conduct of both the masses at home and the national security bureaucracies. Short of a major global catastrophe, these forces will continue in opposition for some time to come.

## REFERENCES

Ad Hoc Committee on the Economy and War. Political power and military spending. In R. B. Carson, J. Ingles, and D. McLaud (Eds.), *Government in the American economy*. Lexington, Mass.: D. C. Heath & Co., 1973.

Adams, W. The military-industrial complex and the new nation-state. In R. B. Carson, J. Ingles, and D. McLaud (Eds.), *Government in the American economy*. Lexington, Mass.: D. C. Heath & Co., 1973.

Banning, E. The peaceful penetration of Africa. In R. F. Betts (Ed.), *The "scramble" for Africa*. Lexington, Mass.: D. C. Heath & Co., 1966.

Barnet, R. The roots of war. Baltimore: Penguin Books, Inc., 1973.

Boulding, K. *The image*. Ann Arbor, Mich.: Ann Arbor Paperbacks, 1961.

Bovill, E. W. *The golden trade of the Moors* (2nd ed.). London: Oxford University Press, 1968.

Brown, S. *New forces in world politics*. Washington, D.C.: Brookings Institute, 1974.

Cypher, J. M. The liberals discover militarism. In R. B. Carson, J. Ingles, and D. McLaud (Eds.), *Government in the American economy,* Lexington, Mass.: D. C. Heath & Co., 1973.

Drucker, P. *The new society*. New York: Harper & Row, Publishers, Torchbooks, 1962.

Ewers, J. Blackfoot raiding for horses and scalps. In P. Bohannan (Ed.), *Law and warfare*. New York: Doubleday & Co., Inc., Natural History Press, 1967.

Gross, B. Friendly fascism: a model for America. In F. Tugwell (Ed.), *Search for alternatives*. Cambridge, Mass.: Winthrop Publishers, Inc., 1973.

Halperin, M. *Bureaucratic politics and foreign policy*. Washington, D.C.: Brookings Institute, 1974.

Hargreaves, J. D. Towards a history of the partition of Africa. *Journal of African History,* 1960, *1,* 96-109.

Malinowski, B. *Argonauts of the western Pacific*. New York: E. P. Dutton & Co., Inc., 1961.

Mauss, M. *The gift*. New York: W. W. Norton & Co., Inc., 1967.

Meadows, D. H., Meadows, D., et al. *The limits to growth*. Washington, D.C.: Potomac Associates, 1972.

Mussolini, B. The doctrine of Fascism. In Department of Philosophy, University of Colorado (Ed.), *Readings on Fascism and national Socialism*. Chicago: Swallow Press, Inc., 1952.

Otterbein, K. The evolution of Zulu warfare. In P. Bohannan (Ed.), *Law and warfare*. New York: Doubleday & Co., Inc., Natural History Press, 1967.

Palmer, R. R., and Colton, J. *A history of the modern world* (3rd ed.). New York: Alfred A. Knopf, Inc., 1965.

Pettman, R. *Human behavior and world politics*. New York: St. Martin's Press, Inc., 1975.

Piganiol, A. The causes of the fall of the Roman Empire. *Journal of General Education,* 1950, *5.*

Rapoport, A. (Ed.), *Clausewitz on war*. New York: Penguin Books, Inc., 1968.

Report of the International Committee of Enquiry into United States crimes in Indochina. In F. Browning and D. Forman (Eds.), *The wasted nations*. New York: Harper & Row, Publishers, Colophon Books, 1972.

Shumpeter, J. *Capitalism, socialism, and democracy* (3rd ed.). New York: Harper & Row, Publishers, Torchbooks, 1962.

Stavins, R. Barnet, R., and Raskin, M. *Washington plans an aggressive war*. New York: Random House, Inc., Vintage Books, 1971.

Steiner, H. J., and Vagts, D. F. *Transnational legal problems*. Mineola, N.Y.: Foundation Press, Inc., 1976.

Study of Critical Environmental Problems. *Man's impact on the global environment*. Cambridge, Mass.: M.I.T. Press, 1970.

# PART TWO

# Microdynamics of bureaucracy

# CHAPTER 6

# Multiple bureaucracies

Fragmented power, specialized knowledge, and a diverse citizenry help create multiple bureaucracies in advanced bureaucratic states. These multiple bureaucracies exercise power over one another. Under certain necessary and sufficient conditions, communication increases the coordination among multiple bureaucracies. Applied to a case study of five criminal justice systems, these conditions help illuminate different degrees of coordination among 30 criminal justice agencies from five American cities.

## CONTEMPORARY BUREAUCRACIES

Bureaucracy is a special form of social organization that provides procedures for elaborating and administering substantive guidelines for structuring political action through the delegation and specialization of power and authority. Consequently, bureaucratic activity usually is perceived by policy makers and citizens as legitimate and authoritative only when these actions derive from duly established legal norms, rules, and constitutions; the procedures used for elaborating and administering policy fall within limits acceptable to policy makers and the citizenry; and bureaucracy uses the specialized knowledge needed to elaborate and administer policy appropriately. In all three respects, the authority of bureaucracy derives from sources external to it; seldom does the citizenry praise or worship bureaucracy for its own sake.

Consider the federal court system in the United States. The Supreme Court has unusual power, but much of that power derives from a cult of constitution worship (see Hartz, 1955:9). Routine decision making relies on a vast body of case law, legal arguments, and elaboration of various constitutional principles. Because this legal knowledge is so specialized, enormous amounts of time and effort are devoted to elaborating fine points of the law all but lost to the average citizen. However, this technical knowledge does not always insulate the Supreme Court from either policy makers or angry citizens. During the Roosevelt Administration, when the court continued to strike down social welfare programs designed to alleviate the national emergency, political pressures mounted for a bill changing the composition of the Supreme Court from nine to 15 members, allowing Roosevelt to appoint a majority more sympathetic with his policies. Although this "court-packing" bill did not become law, some members of the court began switching votes and others retired. A popular phrase of that era summarizes the situation nicely: "A switch in time saved nine."[*] More recently, popular disapproval of decisions from the Warren Court of the 1960s helped President Nixon alter the Court's composition to reflect more adequately the growing conservative mood in the United States in the late 1960s and early 1970s.

### Multiple bureaucracies

What happens because bureaucracy largely derives its authority from sources external to itself? Bureaucracy is vulner-

---

[*]For a discussion of the conflict between the constitutional cult and the turmoil of the New Deal, see Hartz (1955:281).

able to pressures from policy makers and the groups bureaucracy serves. Consequently, bureaucracies often attempt to protect themselves from these pressures. Less obvious but very important, as we shall see, the contours of bureaucratic organization often reflect fragmented policy-making procedures, specialized and fragmented bodies of knowledge, and the fragmented citizenry of complex societies. In short, as Fig. 6-1 illustrates, increased fragmentation among the sources from which bureaucracy derives its legitimacy tends to fragment bureaucratic organization as well. This is why in all advanced bureaucratic states there are multiple bureaucracies rather than a single, unified, bureaucratic organization. In turn, the existence of multiple bureaucracies creates another set of actors to which any individual bureaucracy might find it necessary to adjust.

*Fragmented policy making.* There is a storybook truth about democracy in the United States: power deliberately is fragmented. In Federalist Paper Number Ten, James Madison argued that a federal system of representation will help prevent tyranny of the majority by fragmenting the power a majority has at its disposal (Hamilton et al., 1961). Federalism does this by delegating power to representatives who might refine and enlarge the majority's will and by enlarging the size of each constituency to prevent one impassioned group from adversely affecting the rights of others. And to prevent political leaders' abuses of power, the Founding Fathers implemented a separation of powers doctrine, wherein the executive, legislative, and judiciary branches each checks the others.

An early observer of American democracy, Alexis de Tocqueville (1945:198) told his European readers that American citizens were taught from infancy to rely on their own efforts and to look on social authority with mistrust and anxiety. When they needed help, American citizens turned first to voluntary associations, not the state. According to de Tocqueville, these voluntary associations were needed to prevent the tyranny of a majority or the arbitrary power of political leaders (de Tocqueville, 1945:202). Madison and de Tocqueville took a pluralist view of American politics. That view has been a description of and prescription for American politics during the last two centuries. Robert Dahl (1967:24), a contemporary pluralist, points out that in both theory and practice American pluralism stands for multiple centers of power rather than a single center of sovereign power.* Here power is not "cleanly" divested or delegated. Rather, power is fragmented because these competing centers mutually restrain the exercise of power.

What is true of democracy in America is equally true of bureaucracy in America. The fragmentation of power in policy making readily extends to the fragmentation of policy elaboration and administration. The federal system distributes power among communities, states, and the nation. Corresponding to this fragmentation of power, bureaucracies can be found at the local, state, and national levels. Most of the 90,000 governments in the United States

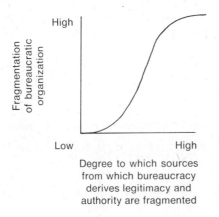

High

Fragmentation of bureaucratic organization

Low

Low                    High

Degree to which sources from which bureaucracy derives legitimacy and authority are fragmented

**Fig. 6-1.** Source of multiple bureaucracies.

*Arthur O. Lovejoy uses the term "counterpoise" rather than pluralism. See his *Reflections on Human Nature* (Baltimore: The Johns Hopkins Press, 1961, pp. 37-66).

have at least one attendant bureaucracy, and many of them have several bureaucracies. Similary, the separation of powers at the national, state, and local levels fragments power among the executive, legislative, and judicial branches of government. Each of these, in turn, often has its own bureaucracies. On some matters, such as budgeting, different branches of government have their own bureaucracies that help check the power of opposing branches. When the Office of Management and Budget gave the Presidency new power over the budgetary process, Congress had to respond by creating its own budgetary bureaucracy, thereby checking the growing power of the executive branch.

***Fragmented citizenry.*** In simple societies almost everyone shares the same conditions of existence. But in complex societies the people are fragmented into social groups and classes. This fragmentation has several consequences, the most important being the tendency of people from different parts of the social structure to develop unique sets of attitudes, experience unique social problems, share unique interests, and perhaps conflict with people from other groups and classes (see Durkheim, 1964:374; Mead, 1964:268; Mannheim, 1956:58-59; Marx and Engels, 1959). Typically, these groups and classes use bureaucratic organizations to advance and protect their interests. Historically, for example, laborers have made use of trade union bureaucracies when faced with continued low wages and poor working conditions. Farmers used farm organizations such as the Farmer's Union, National Farm Organization, and Farm Bureau when threatened by declining prices, high mortgages, rising transportation costs, and even government regulation. Similarly, business people have relied on a number of organizations, such as the National Association of Manufacturers and the Chamber of Commerce, to protect their economic interests against government intervention.

With industrialization came increased conflict among the groups and classes in complex societies. Karl Marx's ideas on class and class conflict summarized what many thought to be the inevitable class struggles of industrial society. However, another school of thought, commonly known as "corporatism," believed that the conflicting groups and classes could be harmoniously united by incorporating these groups and classes directly into the government, providing each functional representation in policy making, and distributing to each group or class sufficient power to reflect their importance in the state as a whole (see Kaiser, 1956; Mendes-France, 1963).

During the twentieth century several countries experimented with corporatism, among them the Salazar regime in Portugal, the Vichy regime in France, the Catholic regime in Austria, and the Fascist regime in Italy. In the latter case, Mussolini established a Ministry of Corporations, with himself as head. Descending the corporate hierarchy were the National Council of Corporations, the Central Corporative Committee, and finally, 22 corporations, formed to integrate functionally into government such groups as employers, workers, technicians, members of government, and agriculture. However, the bureaucracies representing different segments of the citizenry did not cooperate in a manner consistent with corporatist doctrine. Eventually, control over the corporatist state rested with the Fascist party. The party designated the officials of both worker and employer organizations and created a federation of worker and employer organizations from the national level down to the local level. The federation hierarchy began with the National Confederations, then the Federations, next the Provincial and Inter-Provincial Syndicates, and finally, the communal syndicates. Each of the communal syndicates included industry, agriculture, commerce, and credit and insurance.

Under Mussolini these corporations were supposed to collectively settle economic relations and fix prices for goods and services. To secure this type of bureaucratic hierarchy, however, Mussolini increasingly used dictatorial methods. Ultimately, the fragmented citizenry in Italy was united under the dictatorial control of the Fascist party, and the corporatist system came to reflect less and less the true economic structure of Italian society. Mussolini outlawed strikes, did not allow the workers to elect their syndicate directors, and then used the syndicates to impose wage cuts on the workers. In short, the apparent corporatist states achieved coordination only by ignoring the true conflicts in society and forcing cooperation through dictatorial policies (see Franck, 1935:355-368).

In the United States the fragmentation of power prevents many of these dictatorial policies and hence makes artificial corporatism less likely. In turn, however, Americans rely on a large number of bureaucracies to administer social problems. Hence Americans face a very real problem regarding the coordination and conflict among multiple bureaucracies.

*United States Department of Agriculture.* Consider one major bureaucracy in the United States today, The U.S. Department of Agriculture. The head of the Agriculture Department is a member of the President's Cabinet. On first inspection and given the original reasons for this department's creation, we might expect the Agriculture Department to elaborate and administer policy for the nation's farmers. The present Department of Agriculture was established in 1889, when Americans began their move into the nation's cities. But while America became a predominantly urban society, the Department of Agriculture continued to expand during the next 40 years. By 1935, for example, the department added the Rural Electrification Association (REA). Today 99% of rural homes have electricity, but the REA still

grows larger. So grows the department; its annual budget approximately $15 billion, it employs about 80,000 people and has one bureaucrat for every 34 farmers. Today the department lends more money than any other department of the federal government ($9 billion in 1977, much of it to the poor in communities with populations up to 50,000), builds more dams (2,000,000 to date), ranks among the top three agencies in publications, and operates most government food programs. With influential friends in Congress, the department continues to grow, even though many of its employees are underworked and much of its effort goes toward promoting itself or adding new agencies under its umbrella (House, 1977:1,12). Given the scope of its efforts, the department regularly overlaps or conflicts with a number of other government bureaucracies, including the Army Corps of Engineers, the Department of Housing and Urban Development, and the Department of Health, Education, and Welfare.

In theory, the strict corporatist state eliminates the duplication of function and competition for clientele that appears to characterize the Department of Agriculture. However, the practice of corporatism is seldom so successful without strong dictatorial policies forcing unified bureaucratic action. In the United States, where power is disjointed and where bureaucracies have some latitude for defining their own clientele, this duplication of function and competition for target clientele is the rule rather than the exception. In fact, this problem appears and reappears among all states governing a diverse citizenry.

*Fragmented knowledge.* Mazur (1968: 196) points out that knowledge is scientific "only when the people who know the theories know more about the real world than the people who don't know the theories." After examining the course catalog of any major university, one could amend Mazur's statement to read: knowledge is scientific only when the people who know the theories know more about *a small portion* of the real world than people who don't know the theories. Modern science produces empirical data and theory beyond the comprehension of the average person. In addition, today there is far more knowledge stored outside the human mind, in books and computerized data archives, than can be stored in a single human mind. To make use of the vast wealth of knowledge, people become better experts about smaller portions of the "real world." In short, knowledge is fragmented because specialized bodies of knowledge are seldom synthesized and modern scientific disciplines create communication barriers among one another. Like the blind men examining various parts of an elephant, scientists from different disciplines may look in similar places but see radically different things (see Kuhn, 1970).

What are the consequences of fragmented expertise? First, there is a huge communication gap between those knowing a specialized body of scientific knowledge and those unfamiliar with that knowledge (see Snow, 1962:81). Second, there is a tendency to refer technical matters to the "experts" (see Snow, 1962; Lowi et al., 1976). Third, there is an increased tendency to follow the advice of experts in policy making (see Snow, 1962; Lowi et al., 1976; Halberstam, 1973). Fourth, there are strong pressures toward increased technical expertise in bureaucracies. And fifth, because the "experts" do not always see problems in the same way, there is a trend toward multiple bureaucracies, each reflecting a particular technical perspective on a given problem.

Nowhere are these trends more apparent than in the military-technology complex of advanced industrial states. In his Harvard lectures of 1960, C. P. Snow warned about the scientific overlords in Great Britain during World War II (Snow, 1962; Halberstam, 1973). One year later the United States had a new President, whose administration was filled with bright technical experts who helped America become engaged in the Vietnam War. Not until late 1965 did President Johnson learn that the Defense Department had erred in its computer calculations about the war effort required in Vietnam and that the State Department had made much more realistic assessments about the situation years earlier (Halberstam, 1973:756). Unfortunately, as the war effort became increasingly unpopular, President Johnson and then President Nixon chose to listen to those bureaucratic experts who remained optimistic and told these policy makers what they wanted to hear. But unlike the near disaster in Great Britain during World War II that C. P. Snow spoke of in 1960, the consequences of Vietnam were disastrous for America's role in the world community.

The experience of Vietnam teaches some important lessons about bureaucracy and policy making. First, bureaucracies filled with technical experts are less vulnerable to pressures from policy makers, because the communications gap between experts and policy makers often affords the experts greater credibility than might be due. Second, the fragmentation of expertise and the proliferation of multiple bureaucracies reflecting different technical perspectives provide policy makers with a shopping list of expert opinions from which to choose, and more often than not, the policy makers choose to listen to those opinions most consistent with their own hopes and goals. Third, the relations among bureaucratic organizations might have a strong bearing on policy making. If, for example, then Secretary of State Dean Rusk aggressively had asserted the State Department concerns over Defense Department projections for Vietnam, Presidents Kennedy and Johnson might have received a more realistic and balanced assessment of the costs of United States intervention in Vietnam and a more realistic and balanced assessment of the consequences had the United States not intervened.

### Overview

Bureaucratic organization is a procedural device for elaborating and administering substantive guidelines to structure political action. But bureaucracy derives much of its legitimacy and authority from sources external to it. Because power, knowledge, and the citizenry are fragmented and hence bureaucracy derives legitimacy and authority from several sources, multiple bureaucracies are created. In turn a new problem emerges: the relations among multiple bureaucracies. In the sections that follow, we shall examine the relations among multiple bureaucracies in greater detail. In Part III of this book we shall return to the larger problem of fragmented bureaucratic organization in democratic societies.

Finally, we must note that bureaucratic agencies tend to stay alive once they have been created. Of those that do die, according to Kaufman (1976:64), their activities are either reassigned or undertaken by other organizations. Further, Kaufman observes that agencies are typically created in response to demand for service from mobilized sectors of society. These new functions are assigned to new agencies because of a general distrust of existing agencies and an apparent strategy to assure emphasis on the new program by making it the exclusive concern of a separate agency (Kaufman, 1976:66). Because bureaucracies are vulnerable to pressures from policy makers and from the citizens they serve, these organizations often engage in self-promotion and use expertise beyond the comprehension of policy makers and citizens for their self-preservation. This longevity, coupled with the trend toward creating new agencies for each new demand, has drastically increased the proliferation of bureaucratic agencies in the United States.

### POWER CHANNELS

Bureaucracy helps people coordinate human behavior to address various social problems. But what happens when power, knowledge, the citizenry, and bureaucratic organization are fragmented? Here the political environment contains several actors, including the policy makers from whom bureaucratic organizations receive the substantive guidelines they elaborate and administer, the target clientele to whom bureaucracies deliver their services, whether these clientele are inside or outside government, and multiple bureaucracies that might coordinate or compete with one another. With all these actors, how does any bureaucratic organization effectively pursue its goals?

Fortunately, there are ways to approach this problem systematically. A similar problem arises in the study of economic marketing, where manufacturers are linked to consumers through a series of distribution channels: a network linking procedures, distributors, and consumers. A similar power channel exists in the political environment, linking policy makers, policy administrators, and the target clientele for these services. Fig. 6-2, *A*, illustrates a very simple power channel system.

The existence of fragmented policymakers, clientele, and bureaucracy compounds this simple power channel in a number of ways. First, there are more channels linking policy makers and bureaucracy. Second, there are more channels linking the bureaucracy to target clientele. Third, a new set of channels is opened among multiple bureaucracies. Fig. 6-2, *B*, illustrates a more complex power channel.

### Target clientele

In Fig. 6-2, *B*, we have represented the target clientele of multiple bureaucracies by a set of overlapping circles. Ultimately, policy makers and policy administrators seek to resolve various social problems. Broadly defined, policy makers and mul-

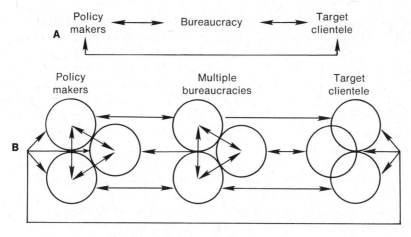

**Fig. 6-2. A,** Simple power channel. **B,** Complex power channel.

tiple bureaucracies do so by providing services to clientele, whether those services are law enforcement, economic regulation, welfare, or a host of other services commonly found in complex societies. However, very few social problems directly affect all members of society. More commonly, different problems affect different segments, given the diverse social stratification in complex societies. The overlapping circles in Fig. 6-2, *B,* suggest that these segments of the population might at times overlap; that is, the target clientele for one social problem might share members with the target clientele for other social problems.

Note, however, that the target clientele are not linked directly by power channels like those linking policy makers and multiple bureaucracies. For our purposes, we are interested in how the public is organized through administrative and legislative officers acting in its interests (Dewey, 1954:28). Dewey points out that multiple publics are born when the actions of particular individuals have extensive and enduring consequences for other people not immediately engaged in these actions (Dewey, 1954:27). According to Dewey, policy makers and policy administrators create publics by attending systematically

to consequences that flow from the activities of private individuals (Dewey, 1954: 16). Hence we have two criteria through which we can identify target clientele:

1. Target clientele are collections of individual citizens commonly affected by social problems arising from the actions of other individuals.
2. Target clientele are collections of individual citizens organized by policy makers and policy administrators in the process of attending existing social problems.

### Channel system

We have identified three basic components of the power channels in advanced bureaucratic states: policy makers, policy administrators, and target clientele. In turn, each of these components is related to the others by power channels: paths linking them together. Together these components and their interrelations comprise the realm of political action: the processes through which persons in advanced societies maintain or change the arrangements of society by coordinating human behavior in attending social problems. However, complex power channels make comprehensive and efficient coordination of political action rather difficult.

A power system suggests that policy makers, policy administrators, and target clientele are not isolated from one another. Although this point is rather obvious, it follows that the behavior of any one component in the channel system might have a profound impact on other components in the channel system. Such various directions of influence include (1) the impact of policy makers on one another; (2) the impact of policy makers on policy administrators and vice versa; (3) the impact of multiple bureaucracies on one another; (4) the impact of multiple bureaucracies on target clientele and vice versa; and (5) the impact of policy makers on target clientele and vice versa. In turn, each of these interactions might have subsequent consequences for other components of the channel system.

Power channels comprise a dynamic system among the various components. Although we will examine one portion of this channel system at a time, it is important to remember that the behavior in one portion of the system might affect other portions of the system and might be compounded by the simultaneous behaviors in other portions of the channel system. If we keep these matters in mind, we can get a more vivid picture of the problem of multiple bureaucracies in complex societies.

***Organization set.*** Multiple organizations emerge because power is disjointed, knowledge is specialized, and many social problems affect only certain segments of a society, thereby creating numerous target clientele. But why do power channels open among multiple bureaucracies? Some of the reasons include competition among multiple bureaucracies for scarce resources allocated by policy makers, particularly money; competition among multiple bureaucracies for similar target clientele, often a consequence of fragmented power and expertise; and the need to cooperate with other bureaucracies in providing more comprehensive service to target clientele. When power channels open among multiple bureaucracies, the behavior of any one member could have important consequences for other members in the set of organizations so linked. We shall call the interactions among multiple bureaucracies comprising the power channel an organization set (see Evan, 1969:73-88).

In practice, organization sets assume a variety of different forms. However, we can identify some of the basic forms that an organization set might take. The classic organization set is the hierarchy, with one bureaucracy at the pinnacle of a pyramid and other bureaucracies related to it through a formal chain of command. This is the model Mussolini tried to implement in Italy before World War II. A second model of an organization set is the coalition, where several bureaucracies are interconnected by a complex set of power channels linking all these multiple bureaucracies to one another. Another form of an organization set is the broken-channel model, where direct channels exist among some agencies, but no agency is related directly to all others and no agency is clearly superior to others by virtue of a formal chain of command. Fig. 6-3 illustrates each of these basic models. For a slightly different discussion of organization set models, see Evan (1969:73-88).

***Coordination.*** What purposes do power channels among agencies serve? Obviously, there are a number of specific purposes, including the gaining and sharing of information. But the basic purpose of power channels among agencies is to permit one agency to anticipate, monitor, alter, or adjust to the behavior of another agency, whether that adjustment results from competition for scarce resources, competition over target clientele, or efforts to deliver more comprehensive services to target clientele. To effectively pursue these goals, bureaucratic organizations must reduce the uncertainty and unpredictability of

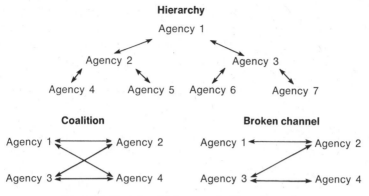

**Fig. 6-3.** Models of interorganization channels.

their environments. Similarly, for self-preservation bureaucratic organizations must reduce this uncertainty and unpredictability.

Suppose we compare similar court service programs, one implemented in a stable urban environment and the second in a rapidly changing urban environment. In the first city, program officials had relatively certain guarantees of further funding, understood the functions performed by other criminal justice agencies, and knew how their program was designed to resolve some specific long-standing social problems. In the second city, program officials had no guarantee of further funding, did not understand the functions served by other programs (partly because these programs changed so rapidly), and had no clear idea of how the program might contribute solutions to the myriad criminal justice problems facing the city. In the first case, the program was judged successful, but in the second case it was impossible to relate program activities to its formal goals.

If organizations flounder in changing environments, how can a bureaucracy make its environment more certain and predictable? Ultimately the organization must coordinate its efforts with other actors in the environment. That coordination can occur, as Lindblom (1965:3) points out, without a single dominant purpose, without formal rules prescribing agency interrelations,

and without a dominant coordinating agency. Lindblom calls this nonformal coordination "partisan mutual adjustment." Mutual adjustment among agencies is the process whereby one agency compensates for the actions of another, thereby helping protect its own stability and preserve its delivery of services in an effective and efficient manner. However minimal and however awkward, this mutual adjustment among agencies is a form of interagency coordination. Such coordination might result from competition as well as informal efforts toward cooperation. But how does this coordination come about? What is the implication of mutual adjustment among agencies?

## POWER AND COMMUNICATION

Power is a special relation among people or things interacting with one another (Lasswell and Kaplan, 1950:75). For our purposes it is the driving force behind partisan mutual adjustments. More specifically, one bureaucracy has power over another when agency X intervenes in the behavior of agency Y and agency X thereby increases the probability that agency Y will perform or refrain from performing a particular action, when compared with the probability that agency Y will perform or refrain from a particular action without the intervention of agency X (see Schopler, 1965:187; Dahl, 1976:25-41). More simply stated, power is the impact of the behavior of one agency on another. When agencies adjust to one another, there is a power relationship between and among them.

### Types of impact

Agencies might affect one another in a variety of ways. Although the most basic type of impact is brute force and violence, this seldom is used among agencies (Russell, 1938; Merriam, 1964). Instead, agencies use a variety of other means to influence the actions of other agencies, such as propaganda, authority, releasing incomplete information, and other more subtle means of influence, such as unilateral actions that effectively undermine the position of another agency, unless the second agency subsequently adjusts to the action taken by the first agency. A few years ago, for example, prosecuting attorneys began implementing a computerized Prosecutor Management Information System (PROMIS). The new system gave prosecutors much better control over the case flow in the courts. But other criminal justice agencies were quick to see the dangers of the new PROMIS system. In particular, other criminal justice agencies feared that they would lose control over court management because the prosecuting attorneys had a better system for monitoring and governing case flow. Consequently, judges and other criminal justice agencies began adopting versions of the PROMIS system for their own use, thereby balancing the advantage prosecutors created by implementing the PROMIS system.

### Communication

Apart from force, the primary medium for exercising power is communication. Communication requires a sender, messages, a transmitter capable of sending messages understandable by another, and a receiver capable of interpreting, or "decoding," messages coming in from another source. Agencies regularly seek to influence the behavior of other agencies through communication. Clearly, the messages can assume a variety of forms, including factual information and propaganda, and they can serve a variety of purposes, from communicating an order to altering subtly the image one agency holds of another. Quite frequently, then, the message is the medium of power among agencies linked by power channels.

*Organization sets.* Even in the hierarchy model we examined above, communication flows from the bottom of the pyramid to the top and from the top to the bottom. The real difference giving agencies at the top a power advantage over those at the bottom is the types of messages that flow among them. Under the system created by Mussolini, messages coming from agencies at the bottom of the pyramid supposedly contained factual information needed by the central agency. But messages sent from the supreme agency to those below it were commands—orders backed by the threat of sanction if the lower agency were to disobey.

In the coalition model and the broken-channel model, messages flowing in the power channels are more likely to contain factual information, perhaps propaganda, and perhaps suggestions for improving relations or improving the quality of comprehensive services to target clientele. Here the power advantage among agencies is less clear-cut. In one form of the coalition model, all agencies might have roughly equivalent power over one another. But regardless of the precise distribution of power advantage in either the coalition model or the broken-channel model, mutual adjustment occurs when the various agencies manage to maintain their power positions. If one agency gains a decisive advantage over others in the organization set, it then is in a position to secure the behaviors desired from other organizations in the set. In both situations some form of coordination occurs, although the coordination is more likely centralized and systematic when one agency exerts a decisive power advantage over others in the organization set.

**Coordination.** Communication makes coordination among bureaucracies possible because it provides a vehicle through which power relations might be exercised. Although communication provides the necessary or some necessary conditions for coordination, it is not sufficient in itself to guarantee coordination. Other factors influence the probability that coordination occurs. What are these factors?

*Hierarchy model.* In the hierarchy model of organization sets, one agency exercises power advantage over those below it. That power advantage is limited by contract, statute, or administrative law. Consequently, the relations among agencies are fairly well defined or fixed by formal arrangements. Here cooperation is supposed to follow the formal arrangements of agencies in the hierarchy, and the coordination of political action results from the integrating decisions made by the supreme agency. Of course, this is precisely what Mussolini attempted to accomplish with the corporatist state in Italy. As illustrated by Fig. 6-4, hierarchical power advantages established by formal arrangements such as contract, statute, or administrative law increase the extent of centralized coordination of services delivered by multiple bureaucracies.

*Coalition and broken-channel models.* If one of the agencies in an organization set gains a decisive power advantage over other agencies, the likelihood of centralized coordination increases accordingly. However, most coalition models and broken-channel models do not have one agency with a decisive power advantage over other agencies in the organization set. Still, coordination can emerge, but it is coordination that is less centralized, less systematic, and more likely a consequence of a dynamic balance of power among agencies in the organization set. For the coalition and broken-channel models, the problem of coordination centers more on how power is used for mutual adjustment than on which agency has the power advantage necessary to centralize coordination among agencies.

In both the coalition model and the broken-channel model, at least three purposes might describe the use of power in the organization set. First, agencies in the organization set might agree to respect the turf of other agencies, thereby respecting their claims to particular resources and particular clientele. In return, each agency expects other agencies to recognize its claims on resources and clientele. Second, agencies in the organization set might agree, for any number of reasons, to actively coordinate their activities, perhaps to pursue a more comprehensive delivery of services. In short, agencies in the organization set agree to facilitate the activities of one another. Third, the agencies in the organization set might actively compete with one another for scarce resources and target clientele. Here each agency must monitor the actions of its competitors closely to compensate for any changes in procedure or technique that could give one agency a competitive edge over others in the organization set.

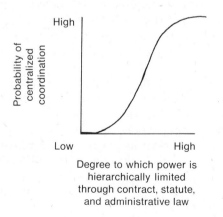

**Fig. 6-4.** Hierarchy and centralized coordination.

When agencies in the organization set agree to respect the turf of other agencies, they effectively accept the current balance of power among agencies. What is more, there is little further pressure toward increased coordination beyond the level achieved by the existing balance of power and resulting mutual adjustment. As agreements to maintain the current balance of power among agencies become increasingly binding on organizations in the set, the likelihood of more systematic coordination among agencies decreases accordingly.

If, on the other hand, agencies in the organization set agree to facilitate the activities of one another, this relation reverses. Agreements to facilitate the activities of other members of the organization set usually imply more systematic coordination and more comprehensive and uniform delivery of services from members of that organization set to target clientele.

The relation between competing agencies and coordination is less obvious. On first glance we might think that competition makes coordination impossible. To be sure, coordination does not result from open agreement to standardize the delivery of services to target clientele. But indirectly, coordination does emerge from competition among agencies for scarce resources and target clientele. Under conditions of competition in the organization set, each agency must seek information about its competitors and must seek to match any improvements made by one agency with similar improvements of its own. In economics this has been one primary consequence of capitalist competition. To prevent its competitors from gaining a power advantage, each agency in the market network seeks to match the technological developments of its competitors. As a result, capitalist competition has led to increased standardization of goods and services, increased standardization of production procedures, and increased standardization of the principles for organizing people to work

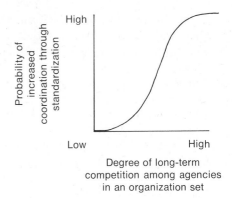

**Fig. 6-5.** Competition and standardization.

together, particularly the principle of mass production (Drucker, 1962:2-3).

The same tendency can be observed in public administration. Agencies competing with one another attempt to keep secret their operations and developments, while their competitors seek to discover these secrets. During the past decade, numerous examples of one federal agency spying on another have come to light, particularly in the areas of national security and domestic intelligence operations. Often the only secret left is the fact that the secrets of one agency are known to its competitors (Snow, 1962:65).

All told, competition tends to standardize the information, programs, and knowledge available to and used by competing agencies in an organization set. Like the mass standardization resulting from capitalist competition, agencies tend over time to pursue similar programs and to use similar knowledge to guarantee an equal footing with their competitors in the quest for scarce resources and target clientele. Fig. 6-5 illustrates the relation between long-term competition among agencies and the increased likelihood of coordination through standardization in the delivery of services to clientele.

## A CASE STUDY

Thus far we have examined a number of possible relations among multiple bu-

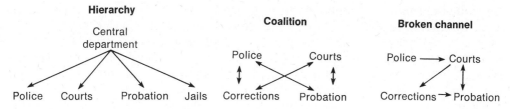

**Fig. 6-6.** Some organization sets in criminal justice.

reaucracies and the impact of these relations on coordination among multiple bureaucracies. Now examine a particular organization set to see how these relations and their impact on coordination help illuminate the real world.

### Criminal justice system

We typically think of criminal justice as a systematic, well-coordinated system for the delivery of justice to offenders. (Questions of effectiveness and efficiency are another matter.) The fact is, however, that the criminal justice system is an organization set that includes a police bureaucracy, a court bureaucracy, a corrections bureaucracy, and a variety of other agencies, depending on the community one examines. In some localities, for example, the probation office is a subsidiary agency of the courts; in others it is a subsidiary agency of corrections, and in still others it is an independent agency within the criminal justice organization set. Similarly, the public defender agency might be a subsidiary unit of the court or it might be an independent agency. In short, virtually every model of an organization set that one might imagine can be found in one or more criminal justice systems across the United States.

In some cities, the criminal justice system is organized like the hierarchical model, with a central agency coordinating the activities of the police, probation and corrections offices, prosecuting attorneys, public defenders, and judges. In other cities the various components of the criminal justice system form a coalition where each agency agrees to facilitate the activities of the other agencies. Alternately, a coalition of criminal justice agencies might agree to respect the turf of other agencies. Finally, there are a number of cities in which the various agencies of the criminal justice system follow a broken-channel model of an organization set. Here some criminal justice agencies have virtually no contact with other agencies. Fig. 6-6 illustrates three common examples of organization sets for the delivery of urban criminal justice.

In the first example a central agency coordinates the activities of the police, courts, and probation and corrections officers. In the second example each of the members of the coalition has roughly equal power advantages over the other agencies, and they either respect the turf of the other agencies or willingly facilitate the activities of the other agencies in the coalition. In the third example the courts have hierarchial control over probation but have little relation with corrections beyond referral of prisoners. Further, there is virtually no contact between the police and the corrections agency (the police have a detention facility, but either the state or county operates the jails), and there is only limited contact between the courts and the corrections agency and between the corrections and probation agencies.

Of course, these are only some of the examples of urban organization sets in criminal justice. Nor are these the most extreme examples to be found. In some communities, for example, the police and sheriff's departments openly battle for jurisdiction, often refusing even minimal cooperation. In other communities portions of the corrections services are under control of a probation department, other portions are under control of the state correctional agency, and still others are operated by the police. Sometimes these fragmented corrections services are coordinated through coalitions, but in many cases different agencies compete for court referrals.

### Punishment or treatment

There are multiple bureaucracies in urban criminal justice systems, and urban criminal justice systems assume a variety of different organization sets, including the hierarchical model, the coalition model, and the broken-channel model. These agencies of criminal justice do not always cooperate with one another. In fact, many urban criminal justice systems find agencies within the organization set competing with one another for scarce resources and target clientele.

One of the more interesting sources of competition among agencies of criminal justice is the basic assumptions about crime and the criminal. Some agencies emphasize the need for treatment and rehabilitation, while others emphasize the need for deterrence and punishment. C. Ray Jeffrey (1972:460) calls these two perspectives the positive school and the classical school. The positive school emphasizes that a criminal seldom has control over a criminal act, that crime is best understood as a psychological phenomenon and therefore should be treated as such. The classical school, in contrast, emphasizes an individual's responsibility for the crime, which is seen to be an act of free will; crime is a violation of the law, and punishment of the criminal is recommended as a deterrent.

The battle between proponents of punishment and proponents of treatment is important for several reasons. First, the battle helped multiply the number of bureaucratic agencies in criminal justice. Within the general area of corrections, for example, some agencies emphasize a basic punishment approach, while other agencies emphasize a treatment approach. Second, the battle helped fragment criminal justice, with officials at the local level often taking stands contrary to the positions of state and national officials in criminal justice. Third, when agencies within one organization set compete with one another because of differences in approach to matters of punishment and treatment, there is a tendency over time for one or the other perspective to win by increasing its share of local revenues and target clientele. Consequently, criminal justice at the local level tends to become standardized over time, with either punishment or treatment being the dominant approach to offenders by most agencies in the local criminal justice organization set. Fourth, because of disagreements among local, state, and national officials, the balance of power among criminal justice agencies at the local level sometimes is upset when state or national officials introduce new techniques or procedures for criminal justice at the local level.

### Five cities

We are going to examine the criminal justice system in five cities in the United States. Among the five cities, at least one had a version of the hierarchical model of organization sets, at least one had a coalition model with an agreement to facilitate the activities of other members of the organization set, still another had a coalition model with an agreement to respect the turf of other agencies, and at least one had a broken-channel model among the various agencies in criminal justice. In some of these cities, the battle over punishment and treatment has been settled; in others, the battle rages on. From these five cities we shall examine 30 agencies within the five criminal justice systems.* By so doing, some impressive evidence will illustrate our five propositions about communication and coordination:

A. Necessary conditions
   1. Communication makes coordination possible.
B. Sufficient conditions: hierarchical model
   1. The probability of centralized coordination increases as power is hierarchically limited through contract, statute, and administrative law.
C. Sufficient conditions: coalition and broken-channel model
   1. The probability of further systematic coordination decreases as agencies accept agreements to respect the turf of others.
   2. The probability of further systematic coordination increases with a willingness to facilitate other members of the organization set.
   3. The probability of coordination through standardization increases with long-term competition among agencies in an organization set.

***Communication and coordination.*** Does communication among agencies make coordination possible? Several hundred respondents from the 30 agencies in five cities were asked to assess the extent to which their agency communicated with a new court service program recently introduced into all five cities and the extent to which they felt their own agency could influence the behavior of the court service agency. Responses from each agency were averaged, and each agency was assigned the average response from members of that agency. Fig. 6-7, *A,* illustrates the results. As communication among agencies increases, the perceived ability to influence the decisions of another agency increase accordingly.

***Hierarchy and coordination.*** According to the argument above, agencies bound by contract, statute, or administrative law are more likely to coordinate their activities by virtue of the formal arrangements binding them together. Does this happen in criminal justice? Eleven of the 30 agencies interviewed were bound to the court service

*Data from the National Court Services Project, directed by W. Rhodes, T. Blomberg, and S. T. Seitz.

agency by contract or statute. However, the strength of these contractual or statutory ties had regular communication flowing in both directions, with the dominant agency more closely controlling the activities of the subordinate agency. Fig. 6-7, *B,* illustrates this trend.

***Mutual adjustment and coordination.*** The remaining 19 agencies were not bound directly to the court service program by either contract or statute. Among these 19 agencies, some agreed to respect the turf of the court service program, some competed with the program, and some agreed to facilitate its activities. Among those agencies respecting the turf of the court service program and those competing with it, there was only a modest flow of formal communication between the agency and the court service program. But among those agencies agreeing to facilitate the court service program, the formal flow of communication was quite substantial. As Fig. 6-7, *C,* illustrates, perceived facilitation among these agencies and the court service program increases directly with the perceived formal flow of information.

Agreements among agencies to facilitate the activities of one another should increase the likelihood of coordination among multiple bureaucracies. As Fig. 6-7, *D,* illustrates for the 19 agencies examined, facilitative agreements directly increase the perceived ability of one agency to influence the decisions of the court service program.

***Competition and coordination.*** Agencies sometimes compete for scarce resources and target clientele. Even among the 11 agencies tied to the court service program through formal contract or statute, some disagreed with the program's emphasis on rehabilitation, and the formal arrangements binding these agencies to the court service programs sometimes made these tensions worse, even though the agencies tried to fulfill their legal commitments. When competition is severe and when agencies are not bound to one another through formal arrangements, coordination is not the motive for gathering information about one's opposition. Rather, coordination through standardization results when competing agencies increasingly standardize their procedures and programs to equalize the perceived competitive edge that one agency might have on claims to scarce resources and target clientele. Does this happen among the 30 agencies examined?

Of the 30 agencies we monitored, seven ranked particularly low on facilitative relations with the court service program in

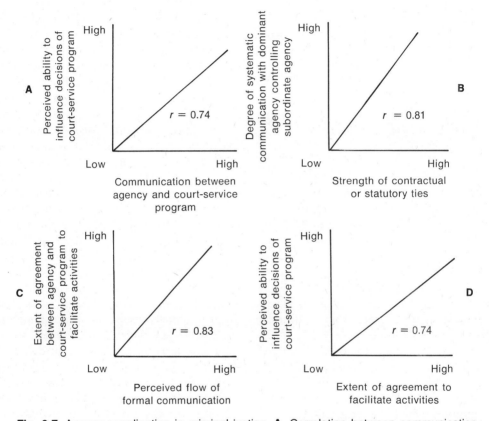

**Fig. 6-7.** Agency coordination in criminal justice. **A,** Correlation between communication and ability to influence decisions for 30 agencies is .74, significant beyond .01. Total communication is measured by flow of information from each agency to court service agency and from court service agency in each city back to various agencies interviewed. **B,** Correlation between strength of contractual or statutory ties and systematic communication and control of activities by dominant agency is .81 for 11 agencies, significant beyond .01. Strength of ties is based on average assessments by agency personnel about strength of contractual and statutory ties with court service agency. Systematic communication with control by dominant agency is assessed by equal sharing of information between agency and court service program, coupled with strength of command messages sent from dominant agency to subordinate agency. **C,** Correlation between perceived flow of information and agreement to facilitate activities for 19 agencies is .83, significant beyond .01 level. Facilitation is measured by average assessment of facilitative relations by respondents from an agency. **D,** Correlation is .74, significant beyond .01, for 19 agencies examined that do not have formal contractual or statutory ties with court service program.

their cities, while nine others ranked particularly high. Compare these two sets of agencies. The nonfacilitative agencies were extremely competitive with the court service program, while the facilitative agencies were not. Although the facilitative agencies felt they could influence the decisions of the court services program, the nonfacilitative agencies felt they could not influence the decisions of the court service program. Similarly, the facilitative agencies openly shared information with the court service program, while the nonfacilitative agencies described their relations with the court service program as more guarded and more deceptive.*

But two other differences between the facilitative and nonfacilitative agencies were particularly important. The court service program was a federally sponsored project with a heavy emphasis on treatment and rehabilitation. The nonfacilitative agencies strongly agreed that punishment was a better means of delivering criminal justice than rehabilitation. The opposite pattern emerges for the facilitative agencies. The facilitative agencies were found in cities with a strong emphasis on rehabilitation in criminal justice, while the competitive agencies were found in cities with a strong historical emphasis on punishment. After the court service program was implemented in the cities with a strong emphasis on punishment over rehabilitation, the competing agencies often brought complaints and charges against the court service program to policy makers and the public. Because of their relatively weak position in cities emphasizing punishment, the court service programs, once under public attack, began to tailor their programs more closely to the punishment

model used by the competing criminal justice agencies.

## CONCLUSION

Advanced bureaucratic states are characterized by multiple bureaucracies. These multiple bureaucracies are linked by complex power channels to policy makers, target clientele, and one another. Power channels among multiple bureaucracies allow communication and a means to exercise power over the decision making of other organizations in the organization set. Agencies bound together by statute, contract, or administrative law have formal channel linkages through which flow communication and formal commands, and these agencies are more likely to coordinate their activities as the strength of the formal arrangements increase. Agencies not bound by formal contract may either agree to respect the function of other agencies in the organization set, agree to facilitate the activities of other agencies, or openly compete with other agencies. Agencies that respect the jurisdictions of others are not likely to further increase the coordination among agencies. Agencies that agree to facilitate the activities of others in the organization set are more likely to increase the coordination within an organization set. Finally, agencies competing with one another tend over time to inadvertently increase the coordination of activities performed by members of the organization set, because competition tends to force agencies to standardize procedures and techniques so that another agency does not gain a competitive edge in the quest for scarce resources or target clientele.

## REFERENCES

Dahl, R. *Pluralist democracy in the United States.* Skokie, Ill.: Rand McNally & Co., 1967.

Dahl, *Modern political analysis* (3rd ed.). Englewood Cliffs, N.J.: Prentice-Hall, Inc., 1976.

Dewey, J. *The public and its problems.* Chicago: Swallow Press, Inc., 1954.

Drucker, P. *The new society.* New York: Harper & Row, Publishers, Torchbooks, 1962.

---

*All of the differences reported here are statistically significant beyond the .05 level, using a difference of means test to compare the group means and the standard deviations for each set of agencies with the other.

Durkheim, E. *The division of labor in society.* New York: Free Press, 1964.

Evan, W. M. Toward a theory of inter-organizational relations. In L. W. Stern (Ed.), *Distribution channels.* Boston: Houghton Mifflin Co., 1969.

Franck, L. R. Fascism and the corporate state. *Political Quarterly,* 1935, *6,* 355-368.

Halberstam, D. *The best and the brightest.* New York: Fawcett World Library, Crest Books, 1973.

Hamilton, A., Madison, J., and Jay, J. *The Federalist papers.* New York: New American Library, Inc., 1961.

Hartz, L. *The liberal tradition in America.* New York: Harcourt Brace and World, 1955.

House, K. E. Growing deadwood. *The Wall Street Journal,* April 12, 1977, pp. 1, 12.

Jeffrey, C. R. The historical development of criminology. In H. Mannheim (Ed.), *Pioneers in criminology* (2nd ed.). Montclair, N.J.: Patterson Smith Publishing Corp., 1972.

Kaiser, J. *Die Repraesentation Organisierter Interessen.* Berlin: Duncker & Humblot, 1956.

Kaufman, H. *Are government organizations immortal?* Washington, D.C.: Brookings Institute, 1976.

Kuhn, T. *The structure of scientific revolutions* (2nd ed.). Chicago: University of Chicago Press, 1970.

Lasswell, H. D., and Kaplan, A. *Power and society.* New Haven, Conn.: Yale University Press, 1950.

Lindblom, C. *The intelligence of democracy.* New York: Free Press, 1965.

Lovejoy, A. *Reflections on human nature.* Baltimore: The Johns Hopkins University Press, 1961.

Lowi, T., et al.: *Poliscide.* New York: Macmillan Inc., 1976.

Mannheim, K. *Ideology and Utopia.* New York: Harcourt Brace Jovanovich, Inc., Harvest Books, 1956.

Marx, K., and Engels, F. *Basic writings on politics and philosophy* (L. Feuer, ed.). New York: Doubleday & Co., Inc., Anchor Books, 1959.

Mazur, A. The littlest science. *American Sociologist,* 1968, *3,* 196.

Mead, G. H. *On social psychology* (A. Strauss, ed.). Chicago: University of Chicago Press, 1964.

Mendes-France, P. *A modern French republic* (A. Carter, trans.). New York: Hill & Wang, 1963.

Merriam, C. *Political power.* New York: Macmillan, Inc., Collier Books, 1964.

Russell, B. *Power.* New York: W. W. Norton & Co., Inc., 1938.

Schopler, J. Social power. In L. Berkowitz (Ed.), *Advances in experimental social psychology* (Vol. 2). New York: Academic Press, Inc., 1965.

Snow, C. P. *Science and government.* New York: New American Library, Inc., Mentor Books, 1962.

Tocqueville, A. de. *Democracy in America* (Vol. I). New York: Random House, Inc., Vintage Books, 1945.

# CHAPTER 7

# Bureaucratic leadership

The complexity and form of power channels limit the range of actions that might be taken by any channel component. Within these limits, however, leadership can alter power relations within a channel system. Merit and hereditary recruitment foster bureaucratic leadership, as do certain types of personnel policies. Patronage recruitment and some types of personnel policies impede bureaucratic leadership.

## POWER AND BUREAUCRACIES

The political environment of advanced bureaucratic states includes policy makers, multiple bureaucracies, and target clientele linked by a complex network of power channels through which power relations allow members of the channel system to alter behaviors of other members. Within this complex system a bureaucracy might be linked directly with policy makers, other bureaucracies, and target clientele. In turn each bureaucratic agency stands in a power relation with all other members of the channel system, either directly or indirectly. In Chapter 6 we examined three models of a channel system: the hierarchy, the coalition, and the broken-channel model. Further, within each of these models we saw a variety of power relations among members of the system.

What determines these power relations among members of the channel system? Actually, the question must be divided into three parts. First, what determines the channel system? Alternately, why does one model of the channel system tend to emerge rather than another? Second, how does the type of channel system influence the shaping and sharing of power among channel members? Third, within a given model of the channel system, what other factors influence the shaping and sharing of power among members of the channel system? We already have found answers to the first two questions in Chapter 6. Hence we will review briefly those answers here. The answer to the third question is rather complex. We will examine some answers in this chapter, more in Chapter 8, and still more in Part III of this book.

### Setting boundaries

In Chapter 6 we examined several factors that help determine the type of channel system found in a given political environment. Three factors were particularly important: the fragmentation of authority among policy makers, the fragmentation of society into multiple publics, and the fragmentation or specialization of knowledge. In turn each of these factors helps to transform bureaucratic organization into multiple bureaucracies. Consequently, advanced bureaucratic states tend to have highly complex power-channel systems, where power relations are multilateral, multidimensional, and represent a variety of motives and purposes (see McFarland, 1969:189). Like the United States, the Soviet Union has a complex channel system. Unlike the United States, the totalitarian party in the Soviet Union seeks to prevent the fragmentation of power among policy makers; hence the state organization in the Soviet Union more closely approximates the hierarchy model than does the United States (see Lippincott, 1965). However, it would be a mistake to assume that the Soviet channel system is a perfect example of the hierarchy model. Other factors, including multiple publics and specialized knowledge, tend to undermine the strict hierarchy sought by the totalitarian party. For example, Soviet industry demonstrates many characteristics of the coalition model often found in the United States, even though Soviet industry is state controlled (see McFarland, 1969:69).

In his discussion of pluralist power systems, Andrew McFarland (1969:31) argues that a power system is a system of social causation, and its complexity is a result of the number and variety of actors, the extent and occurrence of interdependencies, and the variability of these interdependencies over time. In sum, pluralist channel systems tend to emerge in political environments where authority is disjointed, knowledge is highly specialized, and the citizenry have diverse interests and problems.

How does the type of channel system influence the shaping and sharing of power among members of the channel system? Recall from Chapter 6 that power is a relation among people or things interacting with one another such that when actor X intervenes in the behavior of actor Y, actor X thereby increases the probability that actor Y will perform or refrain from performing a particular action, when compared with the probability that actor Y would perform or refrain from a particular action without the intervention of actor X. In pluralist channel systems, these power rela-

tions form a dynamic equilibrium. The notion of a "dynamic equilibrium" simply means that the actions of one member of the channel system likely will trigger other actions within the channel system. In turn, actions within the system might trigger a train of actions, involving or affecting all members in the channel system. Compare this effect with that produced when you drop a rock into a swimming pool. At first, ripples move outward from the point of impact. But when the ripples hit the edge of the pool, they bounce back toward the source of disturbance in the water. Fig. 7-1 illustrates this "ripple effect" within a complex distribution channel system.

The form this dynamic equilibrium takes is a consequence, in part, of the type of channel system operating in a given political environment. If actor X in Fig. 7-1 were the chief power holder in a command hierarchy, the impact of his or her actions would "ripple" downward through the hierarchy, without much probability that actors lower in the hierarchy might counteract the action of actor X. But if the channel system in Fig. 7-1 were a coalition model, then actor X can expect actions by other members of the coalition that "bounce back" to actor X, perhaps supporting the action, perhaps modifying the action, and perhaps attempting to prevent actor X from actions of a similar nature.

In pluralist power channels, power relations among actors seldom have isolated effects. Even the hierarchy model shaped by Mussolini in Italy triggered a variety of acts at the lowest levels of the command hierarchy in direct defiance of or resistance to orders issued from the top of the command

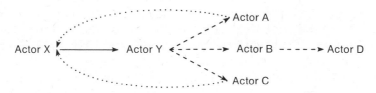

**Fig. 7-1.** Dynamic equilibrium in complex power channels.

hierarchy. In turn Mussolini continually had to counter these unexpected failures in the formal chain of command, often using very repressive measures to gain compliance. Generally speaking, in pluralist channels the power relations among two actors often are countered by other power relations embedded in the channel system. This "push and pull" of power relations takes an extreme form in pluralist systems, where authority, knowledge, and the public all are highly fragmented. In fact, as Fig. 7-2 suggests, the number of realistic alternatives available to any actor in a complex power channel decreases as the complexity of the channel system increases.

For example, consider the alternatives available to Richard Nixon when the Supreme Court ordered him to turn over tape recordings of Presidential conversations following the Watergate burglary and the attempt to cover up those involved in the planning and authorization of the burglary of the Democratic National Headquarters.

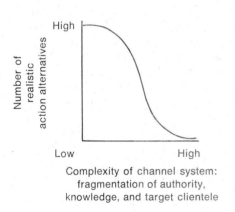

**Fig. 7-2.** Action alternatives in channel systems.

Had President Nixon ignored the court order, the power relation between Congress and the Presidency would have required immediate impeachment and conviction. The popular reaction to such a Presidential move would have jeopardized the reelection of a number of congressmen and senators, had Congress failed to act on impeachment. Regardless of his claims to power, Nixon found himself in a power channel that severely limited the alternatives open to him, once the Supreme Court had made its decision. Fig. 7-3 illustrates part of the complex channel system in which Nixon found himself.

### Leadership

The complexity (i.e., pluralism) and form (e.g., hierarchy, coalition, broken channel) of power channels establishes limits on alternatives available to each actor in the channel system. Although, for example, a broken-channel model helps us explain the limited alternatives available to Nixon after Watergate, it does not fully explain the course of events, particularly the relatively long time Nixon managed to remain in office after the initial disclosures about the conspiracy and subsequent cover-up. Other factors were involved in shaping power relations in this particular channel system. One of those factors is leadership.

Broadly defined, leadership implies unusual power—power above and beyond that inherent in the actor by virtue of position in the channel system (see McFarland, 1969:154; Lasswell and Kaplan, 1950: 152). Defined in this way, a leader may be an individual, a group of individuals, or an

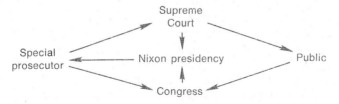

**Fig. 7-3.** Nixon and Watergate tapes.

organization. These distinctions are quite common to everyday language. We say, for example, that some politicians, some administrators, and some executives are "leaders." Similarly, we describe certain groups or social classes as "leaders." Finally, we often use "leader" to describe major companies, such as Standard Oil or IBM, or even a political party, such as the Bolsheviks in Russia. All these cases imply the presence of unusual power—something that makes these people, groups, and organizations stand apart from other people, groups, and organizations. Still there are some obvious differences among individuals as leaders, groups as leaders, and organizations as leaders.

*Individuals as leaders.* This view of leadership is the oldest and most universal. The focus on individuals implies two basic premises about leadership.

1. Individuals have unusual power because they have certain personal properties not widely distributed in society. Usually this means that an individual has personality traits that enhance personal power in relation to other people. In turn, it also means that this unusual power cannot be transferred or delegated to other people.

2. These unique individuals have an important impact on the course of human history.

At root, this is what the "great man" theory of history is all about: unique persons are the primary movers of human civilization (see White, 1949:234; Elwell and Malik, 1974). Lasswell and Kaplan (1950: 153) cite traits such as force of will, extent of knowledge, strength of conviction, self-sufficiency, certain moral or religious qualities, courage, pride, and strength (see also Lasswell, 1948; Freud, 1939). Using these traits, the individual demands deference from others. (For a classic statement of this viewpoint, see Cornford, 1945.)

*Group as leader.* The view associating leadership with certain social groups begins to emerge as societies become more complex. The focus on groups implies two basic premises about leadership.

1. Groups have unusual power because the group has certain unusual social properties not widely distributed among other groups in a society. Quite often these unusual social properties are a product of social position. And by implication this view suggests that social virtues or rewards are not distributed equally across the social structure.

2. These unusual groups have an important impact on the course of human history (see Mills, 1959:21; Benda, 1969; Arnold, 1969).

From this vantage point, leadership is not a product of personality traits but a product of moral and psychological training and the enjoyment of unusual social advantages, such as leisure and money (Mills, 1959:15). In a classic defense of aristocracy, Edmund Burke (1973:216-217) extols the leadership of those who are raised under privileged circumstances, allowed to read and reflect, and taught to embrace the highest virtues of civilization and to take a large view of people and social affairs (see also Lippincott, 1964). This natural aristocracy, according to Burke, elevates a nation from the despotism of its vulgar masses to the enlightened custody of a cultured elite.

*Organization as leader.* The view associating leadership with a principle of human organization is the most recent to emerge, and it commonly is used when discussing advanced bureaucratic states. The focus on organization implies two basic premises about leadership.

1. Organizations have unusual power because their principles of organization give them unusual advantage in pursuing certain courses of action. In the comparison of kinship, ecclesiastical authority, and bureaucratic organization in Part I, we found that bureaucratic organization had unusual advantages over the other two principles for structuring political action.

2. These unusual organizations have an important impact on the course of human history. In Chapters 3, 4, and 5 we examined the unusual impact of bureaucratic organization on modern history.

We all have heard the adage that "organizations don't act; men do." But the emphasis on principles of organization forces us to modify that adage. As we will see later, even personnel systems within bureaucratic organizations have an enormous impact on the power of an organization in a complex power channel. For an early example of this perspective, recall the work of Karl Marx. Marx (1959:136-137) saw individuals as personifications of economic categories—the embodiments of class interests and class relations. For Marx and Engels, the prime movers of history were not men but the principles of organization governing society during each historical epoch. For example, Marx and Engels (1959:12-13) argue that the bourgeois social organization requires continual revolt of productive forces against the conditions of production and property relations to increase production and exchange. For Marx, the bourgeoisie he saw in 1848 was not a collection of greedy capitalists. Rather, the bourgeoisie was a principle of human organization affecting the course of human history. In more recent times Peter Drucker (1962:4-5) has described the principle of mass production in a similar way. Both Marx and Drucker, among a host of others, both conservative and radical, point out that the structure of human organization is itself a source of leadership, or unusual power.

Of course, the principles of organization are not the only means through which organizations might be called "leaders" in modern society. The structure of Lenin's Bolshevik Party might help explain its success, but there are other factors involved as well, even apart from the strength of Lenin's personality. Two of these factors that help make organizations "leaders" are

the possession of information and the control over the meaning of that information. Information and the control over its meaning are extremely important for an adequate understanding of organizations in modern society. These two factors are discussed in considerable detail in Chapter 8.

## Power and leadership

In the remainder of this chapter we shall discuss bureaucratic leadership and especially the role of structuring principles within bureaucratic organizations as a means to enhance bureaucratic power within complex distribution channels. The discussion to follow freely draws from all three perspectives—the individual as leader, the group as leader, and the organization as leader—because it is virtually impossible to explain bureaucratic leadership in complex channel systems from one perspective alone. Further, bureaucratic leadership (or its absence) assumes a variety of different forms, with no one form being appropriate to all channel systems and all power relations within a given channel system. In Chapter 9 we will extend the discussion of bureaucratic leadership to the problem of management: the relation between bureaucratic leaders and the rank and file of a bureaucratic organization.

## INDIVIDUALS AND GROUPS

Bureaucracies are important actors in the dynamic power equilibrium characterizing complex power channels. The "push and pull" of power within the power channels sets limits on the alternative behaviors available to bureaucracies, just as it sets limits on the alternative behaviors available to other members of the power channel. While this dynamic equilibrium helps explain the behavior of members in the channel system, it is not a complete explanation. Other factors, among them leadership, affect channel behavior. In Part I we saw that bureaucracies provide procedures for elaborating and administering substantive guidelines for structuring political action through the delegation and specialization of authority. The concept of leadership applied to bureaucratic organizations suggests that within a complex channel system bureaucracies might acquire more power than that formally delegated to them. How does this happen?

### Recruitment

The first view of leadership outlined above suggests that individuals have unusual power because they have certain personal properties not widely distributed in society. And the second view of leadership suggests that groups have unusual power because the group has certain unusual social properties not widely shared by other groups in society. Both approaches can help us understand how bureaucracies acquire more power than that originally delegated to them. However, to use these two approaches to leadership, we first must discover how these unusual individuals and unusual groups become bureaucrats in the first place. How are bureaucrats recruited? Historically there have been three basic means to recruit bureaucrats: hereditary privilege; the spoils, or patronage, system; and the merit system. Both hereditary privilege and the merit system help recruit unusual individuals and unusual groups into bureaucratic positions. And by implication, these two recruitment systems tend to enhance the power of bureaucracies in distribution channels. In short, hereditary privilege and the merit system help create bureaucratic leadership, a situation where bureaucracies acquire more power in the channel system than that formally delegated to them. The spoils system tends to drain bureaucracy of its power. By making bureaucracy the tool of other members of the distribution channel system, the spoils (patronage) system of recruitment actually reduces the chance of bureaucratic leadership. Let us examine each of these recruitment systems more closely.

*Hereditary privilege.* Hereditary privilege suggests that individuals have a claim to bureaucratic posts by virtue of their class or social origins. Although this system of recruiting bureaucrats is seldom found after the nineteenth century, it was very important in intermediate bureaucratic states such as the European states of the Middle Ages. In fact, hereditary claims on the bureaucracy in European countries did not disintegrate until the seventeenth and eighteenth centuries. During the Middle Ages in Europe (and elsewhere), policy makers usually were determined by hereditary succession: the right to govern was the property of a particular royal family. In turn these hereditary monarchs would appoint bureaucrats to help administer their territories (see Rosenberg, 1958:6).

Slowly, however, these appointed bureaucrats managed to detach themselves from the royal court, preventing the prince or ruler from removing bureaucrats and appointing new ones. To do so, these bureaucrats required more power than that originally delegated with appointment. This unusual power emerged for two separate reasons. First, the bureaucrats used the power of office for their own ends (Rosenberg, 1958:6). Second, rulers often turned to the educated sectors of society for personnel, and these educated sectors already possessed social power apart from the offices given to them by the ruler. In short, bureaucracy became the property of a social aristocracy with sufficient power to remove the bureaucracy from control by the prince.

The Junkers, landed nobility of Prussia, were such an aristocracy with control over the bureaucracy. Rosenberg (1958:30) describes Junker leadership as a combination of large-scale land ownership and patrimonial possession of autocratic rights over local government offices. Eventually the Junkers became landlords, serf masters, entrepreneurs, estate managers, traders, church patrons, police chiefs, prosecutors, and judges. For a time, particularly with the absolutist rule of Frederick William I after 1660, the tide turned against the Junkers. But by 1799 the Junkers, together with a university-trained hierarchy of professional administrators had assumed considerable aristocratic control in Prussia through the state bureaucracy. Together these professional administrators and the Junkers became an organized, self-recruiting, and self-governing corporation with considerable political power (Rosenberg, 1958:200-202). As an exclusive political intelligentsia, this corporation determined policy and set standards for social welfare and other matters in the "public interest."

How does this hereditary privilege create unusual power in the bureaucracy and hence bureaucratic leadership by virtue of the group controlling the bureaucracy? First, hereditary privilege insulates the bureaucracy from intervention and control by a prince. Even though by law the Junker bureaucracy was an instrument of the king, its hereditary recruitment practices gave the Junkers an independent source of power, and the king or prince could not staff the bureaucracy as he saw fit. Second, hereditary privilege brings to bureaucratic positions a source of additional power not originally delegated to these positions by the prince. For the Junkers, their social and economic position in Prussian society brought additional power to their exercise of bureaucratic offices than was inherent in the bureaucratic position as such. In short, the power of the group controlling the bureaucracy through hereditary privilege added unusual power to the bureaucracy and hence gave it a leadership role in Prussian politics (see also Wiese, 1972).

***Spoils system.*** The roots of the spoils system for recruiting bureaucrats rests on two basic premises. First, there is a need to limit bureaucratic authority to that delegated, and the principle means to do so is to make tenure of office dependent on the wishes of those who delegate authority. Strong politi-cal leaders such as Frederick William I of Prussia, Louis XIV of France, and Peter the Great of Russia found it necessary to recruit men of ordinary social position into bureaucratic offices because this allowed making and unmaking of those chosen for bureaucratic appointments, prevented social groups from acquiring more state power, and permitted the prince to make the bureaucracy a personal tool (Rosenberg, 1958:67). Second, bureaucratic offices are the property of those in positions of policy making. This "property" thus became a source of patronage to reward individuals for past favors and to encourage future favors (Friedrich, 1937:10).

Of course, the patronage system assumes different forms, depending on whether policy makers are totalitarian or democratic. In the United States democracy helped create a peculiar form of patronage known as the spoils system. That system assumed traits similar to democratic procedures: (1) appointments primarily for political reasons, just as elections changed policy makers for political reasons, (2) the presumption that any person could discharge bureaucratic responsibilities, consistent with the democratic emphasis on the worth and dignity of each individual, and (3) the regular rotation of office holders, just as elections periodically are held to rotate policy makers (see Hoogenboom, 1968:4; see also Friedrich, 1937:14).

Friedrich dates the origin of the American spoils system to 1801, when President Adams frantically attempted to fill bureaucratic offices before the Federalists were turned from Presidential power. When Secretary of State Madison assumed office, some of President Adams' commissions had not been delivered, and Madison rescinded the appointments. The result was the famous *Marbury* v. *Madison* case taken before the Supreme Court. That suit, in addition to establishing the principle of judicial review, clearly revealed the extent to which bureaucratic offices were used as the spoils to support political parties (Friedrich, 1937:13). The second major event marking the growth of the American spoils tradition occurred in 1820 when Congress adopted a law, signed by President Monroe, which fixed the term of offices for federal officers to 4 years. These offices included district attorneys, marshals, customs officials, paymasters, and land office registers (see Bernard, 1885:35). Before the law of 1820, office tenure rested on good behavior in office. However, the law of 1820 made regular rotation of federal office holders possible. In turn this increased the amount of patronage available for distribution.

The events of 1801 and 1820 are milestones in the evolution of the spoils system in America. The system matured with the election of Andrew Jackson to the Presidency in 1828 and the formal Congressional debate that followed in 1832. Unlike his predecessors, President Jackson claimed the spoils system was democratic and that a standard of common moral decency was sufficient to qualify a person for bureaucratic office (Friedrich, 1937:14). Jackson matched words with deeds. Under the first six American Presidents, 73 people were removed from bureaucratic office, during a period of 40 years. During his first 9 months in office, Jackson removed 690 office holders (Bernard, 1885:25).

Like the *Marbury* v. *Madison* case in 1801, Jackson's activities brought the spoils system before public scrutiny. By the time of Jackson, however, the spoils system had become widespread, particularly in the urban states of the Northeast. The issue came before Congress in 1832, and during the debates Senator Marcy of New York defended the system with a phrase still known today: to the victor belong the spoils of the enemy. Acting this way, Marcy claimed, was totally consistent with competition for office. (See Bayard [1882] for a discussion of Daniel Webster's opposition to the spoils system.)

Recall that the Founding Fathers in the United States deliberately sought to fragment the power of policy makers, both through a separation of powers and a federal system of government. Hidden beneath the spoils system was a struggle for power and leadership in a political arena where power deliberately had been fragmented by framers of the Constitution. The bureaucracy was a prime target in the struggle for power. Both Congress and the political parties claimed property rights in the federal bureaucracy. With Congress dictating appointments to the federal bureaucracy, it could gain some control over the Presidency. At home the political parties often treated the nomination for Congress as patronage, for which successful candidates were expected to reward party regulars with jobs in the federal bureaucracy. The struggle became intense when factions within the political parties sought patronage and when the President himself sought control over the bureaucracy to enhance Presidential power. In fact, the battle over the bureaucracy was one motive for the Congressional impeachment efforts against Andrew Johnson after the assassination of President Lincoln. Fig. 7-4 illus-

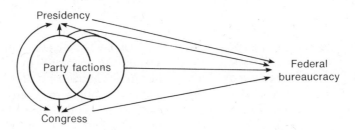

**Fig. 7-4.** Struggle for bureaucratic power.

trates the complexity of the struggle for bureaucratic power in America during much of the nineteenth century.

Under the spoils system the federal bureaucracy became a prize for other components in the power channel, particularly for competing policy makers. Consequently the bureaucracy did not exert much independent leadership in the channel system. Each of the contending forces in the political arena sought to place its people in the bureaucracy, both to reward service and to enhance power by guiding the bureaucracy. In short, the spoils system made it difficult for the bureaucracy in itself to gain power. Rather, it became the tool for enhancing the power of other actors under the spoils system.

**Merit system.** The final means of recruiting people into bureaucracies is based on the merit of applicants. Parliamentary reforms and increased technical sophistication led Great Britain to abandon the patronage system in the 1850s. But a generation or more would pass before America followed that example. Part of the reason why America lagged so far behind Great Britain lies in the struggle for power that was being waged in America. And part of the reason lies in the different rates of economic development. Great Britain industrialized sooner and faster than the United States. Trained competency in legal, pure sciences, and applied sciences became important credentials for bureaucratic office holders in an industrial era (Friedrich, 1937:14). As America became increasingly industrialized, the incompetency and graft of public servants became increasingly apparent to those within government and to the public. Jackson's universal qualifications for bureaucratic office simply did not square with the complex realities of an industrial age. Still, not until January of 1883, with the passage of the Pendleton Bill, did Congress adopt civil service reform and a merit system for appointment.

Debate on the Pendleton Bill began in December of 1881. During open debate, Senator Pendleton described the bill as a means to match appointment and promotion to qualifications objectively determined by open, fair, impartial, and competitive examination (Bernard, 1885:63). Today civil service in the United States rests on a merit system of recruitment, although there are some important exceptions (see U.S. Civil Service Commission, 1967:15-32). Several jobs excepted from the civil service law are classified into three categories by the Civil Service Commission: Schedule A jobs, Schedule B jobs, and Schedule C jobs. Schedule A employees are those for whom a competitive examination is not practical, such as student interns, part-time jobs in isolated areas, and other temporary jobs. Schedule B includes positions that require a qualifying exam but not a competitive examination. Schedule C jobs are the most important because these include top administrative jobs with a "policy-determining" character or jobs that have close and confidential working relations with top policy makers (see U.S. Civil Service Commission, 1967:24).

Other federal jobs are similarly excepted from the Civil Service System. Among these are Cabinet officers, federal judges, and prosecuting attorneys. During the Presidential campaign of 1976 Jimmy Carter promised to remove federal judges and prosecutors from the patronage system. However, the Carter administration faces considerable Congressional opposition. Currently, senators have a decisive voice over the appointment of 94 U.S. attorneys. In addition, the federal judiciary likely will be expanded by as many as 130 new district and appeals court judgeships—a 25% expansion. At the same time in 1977, about 30 positions were vacant. With stakes like this, even though smaller than those during the Pendleton debates from 1881 to 1883, it is no wonder that Congress opposes a challenge to the patronage system (see Miller, 1977).

### U.S. civil servants today

Who are the men and women employed in public administration in the United States today? Fig. 7-5 demonstrates some recruitment patterns for modern civil servants. Respondents employed in public administration were asked to identify the jobs held by their fathers. As can be seen, more than a quarter of those working in public administration today had fathers working in agriculture, fishing, and forestry. Fathers in manufacturing industries provide almost one fifth of our public administrators, and another quarter come from homes in which the father was employed in retail, wholesale, finance, insurance, real estate, and repair services. About 14% had fathers employed in public administration.

Table 7-1 summarizes personal and occupational characteristics of public administration employees, compared with all respondents in the general social survey taken in 1975. Public administration employees rank their jobs higher in prestige than does the average U.S. citizen, and they have more education than the average citizen. However, the education level for the fathers of public service employees is the same as the education level for fathers of the average respondent. Proportionately, there are more Republicans in the civil service than in the population as a whole. And there are more ideological conservatives in public administration than in the citizenry as a whole. As expected, public administration employees have a higher income than the average American worker.

### Knowledge and power

The merit system of recruitment emphasizes placing qualified personnel into jobs that often are classified by the functions to be performed by the office holder. Clearly, the emphasis in merit systems is on exploiting available knowledge and skills for technical tasks in bureaucracy that cannot adequately be performed by average people. Like Britain and America in the nineteenth century, developing countries in the twentieth century find it increasingly necessary to recruit competent, talented bureaucrats to carry out governmental duties, particularly if the country is attempting to use modern technology to encourage economic and social development (United Nations Technical Assistance Programme, 1961:34).

However, merit systems for bureaucratic recruitment introduce a new factor into the calculation of bureaucratic power and potential leadership: knowledge. Under a merit system, technical expertise often becomes a source of unusual power for a bureaucracy. This unusual power readily can be observed in agencies such as the Army Corps of Engineers, the Atomic Energy

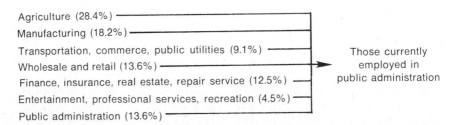

**Fig. 7-5.** Merit recruitment in United States. Data from General Social Survey, 1975, administered by National Opinion Research Center (NORC) and distributed by Roper Survey Center. Survey includes 1,490 respondents, of which 96 are employed in public administration.

Commission, and various local, state, and federal planning agencies. In developing countries the unusual power that bureaucracy acquires by virtue of technical knowledge poses a very serious problem. Often the mobilization of skill and knowledge for state purposes comes into conflict with the policy makers' needs to consolidate state power and authority (Pye, 1974). Policy makers in developing states require consid-

**Table 7-1.** Personal and occupational characteristics*

|  | ALL INDUSTRIES (1490) | PUBLIC ADMINISTRATION (96) |
|---|---|---|
| Occupational prestige (0-9) | 3.4 | 4.0 |
| Education (years) | 11.7 | 12.5 |
| Father's education (years) | 9.0 | 9.0 |
| Mother's education (years) | 9.5 | 9.8 |
| Spouse's education (years) | 11.8 | 12.2 |
| Religion: | | |
| Protestant | 65.5% | 67.7% |
| Catholic | 24.4% | 26.0% |
| Jewish | 1.5% | — |
| None | 7.6% | 6.3% |
| Other | 0.9% | — |
| Party identification: | | |
| Strong Democrat | 17.0% | 17.2% |
| Not very strong Democrat | 23.7% | 21.5% |
| Independent/Democrat | 14.3% | 12.9% |
| Independent | 14.3% | 14.0% |
| Independent/Republican | 08.3% | 14.0% |
| Not very strong Republican | 16.0% | 11.8% |
| Strong Republican | 6.3% | 8.6% |
| Political views: | | |
| Extreme liberal | 3.3% | 6.3% |
| Liberal | 12.8% | 12.6% |
| Slightly liberal | 14.0% | 9.5% |
| Moderate | 40.0% | 34.7% |
| Slightly conservative | 16.6% | 16.8% |
| Conservative | 10.7% | 11.6% |
| Extreme conservative | 2.5% | 8.4% |
| Income: | | |
| Under $1,000 | 2.4% | 3.2% |
| $1,000-2,999 | 6.9% | 1.1% |
| $3,000-3,999 | 6.0% | 4.3% |
| $4,000-4,999 | 5.1% | 6.4% |
| $5,000-5,999 | 5.1% | 4.3% |
| $6,000-6,999 | 5.2% | 4.3% |
| $7,000-7,999 | 4.1% | — |
| $8,000-9,999 | 9.5% | 12.8% |
| $10,000-14,999 | 24.5% | 29.8% |
| $15,000-19,999 | 14.1% | 22.3% |
| $20,000-24,999 | 7.9% | 4.3% |
| Over $25,000 | 9.1% | 7.4% |
| Job satisfaction: | | |
| Very satisfied | 54.2% | 59.5% |
| Moderately satisfied | 32.7% | 35.1% |
| Dissatisfied | 9.0% | 2.7% |
| Very dissatisfied | 4.1% | 2.7% |

*Data from the General Social Survey, administered by NORC and distributed by the Roper Survey Center.

erable control over the state bureaucracy, but the recruitment of persons with technical expertise tends to give the bureaucracy a power in its own right. Under these conditions we see the tensions between a spoils system and a merit system in sharp relief. The spoils system helps policy makers consolidate state power by using the bureaucracy as a tool for centralizing governmental control. But under a merit system the centralized government is itself fragmented by introducing into the government educated elites who are not always easily controlled by state policy makers.

### Overview

Certain individuals and groups of individuals dramatically can enhance the power of bureaucracies in complex distribution channels, well beyond the power formally delegated to those bureaucracies. The key to understanding the role of individuals and groups of individuals in bureaucratic leadership centers on the method used for recruiting men and women into bureaucratic office. Hereditary privilege and merit systems might foster bureaucratic leadership in complex channel systems by bringing into bureaucracies individuals or groups with unusual talent or social power not directly resulting from the bureaucracy itself. However, the spoils, or patronage, system is the negative face of bureaucratic leadership. This method of recruitment tends to remove extraordinary power from bureaucracy, making it an instrument for use by other components in the channel system. The spoils system inhibits leadership in bureaucracy by encouraging rapid turnover in personnel and making personal allegiance the prime qualification for appointment.

### ORGANIZATION STRUCTURE

The method of recruiting individuals and groups into bureaucratic office might foster or inhibit the growth of unusual bureaucratic power and hence bureaucratic leadership in complex channel systems.

But recruitment methods alone are insufficient to maintain bureaucratic leadership. Another factor focuses on the organization itself. Are there ways in which the structure of a bureaucratic organization encourages bureaucratic leadership? Why are some bureaucratic organizations more innovative than others? Why do some bureaucratic organizations seem to hold more power than others in complex distribution channels?

During the Nixon administration Henry Kissinger built his own bureaucratic elite while chairman of the National Security Council. With a smaller staff, Kissinger had greater impact on foreign policy than either the Secretary of State or the State Department. Eventually Kissinger assumed control of the State Department, but he often found it necessary to rely on his bureaucracy because many employees of the State Department did not favor Kissinger's brand of foreign policy diplomacy. Some segments of the State Department remained hostile to Kissinger throughout his tenure as Secretary of State. It is doubtful that Kissinger could have molded the State Department into an organization highly supportive of his personal diplomacy during the few years he held office. Is there something about the structure of the State Department or other bureaucratic agencies that inhibits leadership of the Kissinger variety?

Max Weber once argued that bureaucracy can be made to work for anyone who knows how to gain control over it. Because of its impersonal character and rationally ordered system of officials, a bureaucracy can work for anyone, so long as the top leaders are changed (Gerth and Mills, 1958:229). If Weber was right, why did Kissinger have so much trouble bringing the State Department to his point of view, even after he brought many of his own men into top positions in the department? If Weber was wrong, what did he overlook?

There are some bureaucratic organizations that conform to Weber's expectations.

Typically among these are military organizations and many modern business firms. What is more, these organizations often generate unusual power from within, moving talented individuals rapidly into positions of leadership. But there are other bureaucratic organizations, among them many subject to the United States Civil Service System, that do not conform to Weber's expectations (see Benedict et al.). Nor do these federal agencies generate unusual power from among the ranks with any systematic regularity. Are there ways in which the structure of a bureaucratic organization fosters or impedes bureaucratic leadership and the development of bureaucratic leadership?

### Personnel systems

Some bureaucratic organizations more readily adapt to changes in top leadership than others do. Other bureaucratic organizations more readily foster the development of bureaucratic leadership. Although there are a variety of reasons why this occurs, one critical variable is the personnel system: how an organization routinely exploits its personnel for service to the organization. Some personnel systems actively employ incentives to advance talented bureaucrats into top offices and to gain rapid compliance from rank and file to changing leadership. These personnel policies of a bureaucratic organization tend to encourage the development and deployment of bureaucratic leadership. Examine two extreme models of personnel systems in bureaucratic organizations to gain a better picture of the impact of these personnel policies on bureaucratic leadership.

*Lethargy model.* During each Presidential campaign, political observers warn candidates that the federal bureaucracy seems to have a life of its own, that it is difficult to change it from set paths, and that the cumbersome beast is not terribly innovative or adaptive. Even changes in top leadership within the bureaucracy seem to have few substantive results. There is some truth to

these charges, but the problem is not inherent in bureaucratic organizations as such. Seldom are such charges raised against major multinational corporations, which have bureaucratic organizations larger than many nations. Part of the problem dates from 1883, when Congress voted to remove the federal bureaucracy from the spoils system. At that time personnel policies were adopted that actually encouraged the type of lethargy we sometimes see in the federal bureaucracy today.

Three basic factors characterize personnel systems that encourage bureaucratic lethargy.

1. Personnel emphasis is on the position, not on the individual holding the job or occupying the office. Salaries and raises are more related to position than to the performance of individuals within these positions. In 1976, for example, 45,000 employees of the United States Department of Agriculture were eligible for merit pay increases. Of these, 44,956 received merit pay increases (House, 1977). Clearly, this is amazing for an agency that is overstaffed, underworked, and increasingly obsolete.

2. Advancement in grade or change from one level of appointment to another often is left to individual choice. There are few centrally administered incentives to rapidly advance talented officials. In fact, the system encourages work norms that discourage "rate busting" or "over achievement." Further, promotion usually is a result of demonstrating competency on qualifying examinations and other "objective criteria" rather than on the actual performance of the individual in his or her current position.

3. Retention of the individual in office is only related minimally to job performance, with a set minimum of job performance sufficient to guarantee tenure (see Benedict et al.:7).

How do these factors impede the development and deployment of bureaucratic leadership? First, new men and women appointed to top posts in these bureaucratic agencies have few incentives available directly to affect the job performance of individual bureaucrats. There are few centralized means for encouraging promotion and advancement of talented officials into higher job levels within the organization. Consequently, talent rises slower in these bureaucratic organizations than in business corporations such as the multinationals. Second, among bureaucrats security tends to replace achievement as the principal incentive for work. In turn this dampens the potential efforts of individuals within the bureaucracy and the bureaucracy as a whole. Finally, with set minimal standards for job performance, it becomes increasingly difficult to reward those who do outperform their colleagues, because performance is supposedly compared with a set standard rather than with the performance of others.

*Innovation model.* Unlike the lethargy model, some personnel systems actively encourage the development of talent within an organization and actively encourage personnel to adjust to changes of leadership. Among these bureaucratic organizations are certain military forces, modern corporations, and some public service agencies. How do these organizations differ from the previous model?

Three factors characterize the personnel systems of organizations falling under the innovation model.

1. Personnel emphasis is on the quality of an individual's job performance rather than on the position occupied. Here salaries and raises, among other incentives, are related directly to a person's relative rank with other employees in a work grade similar to his or her own.

2. Advancement in grade actively is encouraged by systematic, centralized efforts to continually compare the job performance of individuals and rapidly advance superior employees.

3. Retention of an individual depends more on relative job performance, when compared with his or her peers, than on meeting minimal job performance criteria (see Benedict et al.:8).

How does this type of personnel system encourage bureaucratic leadership in power channels? First, new men and women appointed to top posts in these bureaucracies have several incentives available to directly alter the job performance of individual bureaucrats and thereby change the overall course of the agency. Further, the systematic policy of worker review for advancement and reward by the centralized personnel rapidly moves talented people into better positions to exert influence on other components of the channel system. Second, the work incentive in these organizations centers more on achievement than on security. In turn this orientation injects a dynamic spirit into the bureaucracy. Finally, these bureaucratic organizations have a means to remove "deadwood" and demote unqualified personnel, enabling replacement with more productive staff.

*Value of each model.* Neither model is clearly superior under all circumstances or in all political environments. In some political environments the lethargy model helps prevent an independent bureaucracy from assuming unusual power in a complex channel system. In other environments policy makers need a personnel system that permits rapid reorientation of a bureaucracy in response to changing personnel in top positions in the bureaucracy. However, the same personnel system might encourage the growth of independent bureaucratic leadership, thereby fragmenting the state's power. Military coups in developing countries often involve the growth of an independent bureaucratic leadership in the military with power rivaling that of established policy makers.

**Comparisons**

The two models for personnel systems described here are extreme types. Different bureaucratic organizations might draw one or more principles from each system. Therefore it might be helpful to examine each of the three basic factors characterizing the lethargy and innovation models as separate dimensions of a personnel system. The three dimensions are allocation of rewards and incentives, centralized control of promotion and advancement, and the role of job performance in job tenure. In turn we shall relate each of these dimensions to the potential for bureaucratic leadership.

***Allocation of rewards and incentives.*** In the lethargy model, rewards and incentives are allocated to the position, not to the individual occupying a position. In the innovation model, rewards and incentives are allocated to individuals, based on their relative performance when compared with other individuals in similar positions. Suppose we draw a continuum connecting these two extremes and compare that continuum with the potential for bureaucratic leadership. Based on the discussion above, the potential for bureaucratic leadership should increase as we move along the continuum from incentives allocated to position to incentives allocated to individuals. Fig. 7-6 illustrates this relation.

The relation in Fig. 7-6 holds for several reasons. By rewarding equally everyone in the same position, neither merit nor substandard performance is recognized.

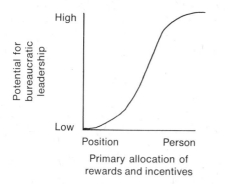

**Fig. 7-6.** Bureaucratic leadership and allocation of rewards and incentives.

Hence there is no incentive toward superior performance nor any incentive against inferior performance, except the incentive to meet minimal job performance criteria. Consequently, rewards allocated to positions tend to encourage group norms and individual expectations that focus on the smallest amount of work required by occupants of that position. By rewarding individual effort, we provide incentives for superior performance and disincentives for inadequate performance. Consequently, rewards allocated to individuals tend to encourage group norms and individual expectations that focus on achievement. Rewards and incentives allocated to individuals allow top office holders within the bureaucracy to change more quickly the course of an organization by rewarding those whose behavior more closely conforms to the changing expectations of leaders and by providing disincentives for those unwilling to change. The general spirit of achievement fostered by individual rewards and incentives creates a more dynamic atmosphere in the organization, paving the way for rapid change in organization goals as top office holders change or as new conditions require.

***Centralized control of promotion and advancement.*** In the lethargy model the individual has primary control over incentives for personal advancement in the organization. In the innovation model advancement and promotion are controlled centrally and are used systematically to promote talented personnel. From the discussion above, we should expect the potential for bureaucratic leadership in complex distribution channels to increase as we move from a fragmented incentive system for advancement to a centrally controlled system for advancement. Fig. 7-7 illustrates this relation.

The relation in Fig. 7-7 holds for several reasons. When incentives for advancement are left to the individual, the drive for personal advancement must derive from fac-

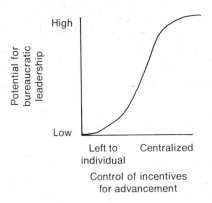

**Fig. 7-7.** Bureaucratic leadership and control of advancement.

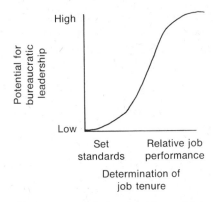

**Fig. 7-8.** Bureaucratic leadership and job performance and tenure.

tors extraneous to the work setting by and large, such as personality, family pressure, and so on. However, these incentives are neither systematic nor regularly distributed among members of a bureaucratic organization. Consequently, work norms actually might check an individual's drive for personal advancement. When incentives for advancement are controlled centrally and are used systematically to advance talented personnel, the work setting and organization structure provide additional systematic incentives for achievement. This means work norms more likely will favor advancement for meritorious performance, bringing talent higher into the bureaucracy and creating a more dynamic work situation in the organization. Centralized control over advancement gives new leaders added opportunities to promote personnel favorable to their policies. The advancement of highly talented individuals makes that talent available to the organization in its power relations with other members of the complex channel system.

**Job performance and job tenure.** In the lethargy model job tenure is determined by minimal job performance criteria. Here all an individual must do to maintain an appointment is meet established minimal criteria. In the innovation model job tenure is determined by the relative performance of each individual, when compared with others in the same work grade. From the discussion above, we should expect the potential for bureaucratic leadership to increase as we move along the continuum from minimal standards for job tenure to comparisons of relative job performance as a means of determining job tenure. Fig. 7-8 illustrates this relation.

The relation in Fig. 7-8 holds for several reasons. The minimal job expectations principle fosters values of security over achievement, both in terms of group norms and in terms of individual expectations. In turn, minimal job performance criteria help ensure the Peter Principle: people become frozen into job positions for which they are minimally competent but above which they are incompetent to rise. Judging job performance relative to that of other members of similar job positions fosters values of achievement and some competitiveness among members of the work group. Consequently, those who perform well at a given level may expect further promotion, while those who rise to the highest level of competency actually might face demotion or pressure to leave the organization. The comparative judgment of job performance allows top bureaucrats added flexibility over their organizations by permitting dismissal for substandard performance and thus opening new positions for recruiting more talented personnel. Al-

**Fig. 7-9.** Recruitment and personnel policies.

though competitive and perhaps aggravating to the individual in an organization, the comparative job performance criteria generally increase the work capacity of an organization, thereby contributing to its power position in a complex channel system.

**Recruitment and personnel policy**

It is possible to combine recruitment methods and personnel policies in a number of ways. Suppose we look at the spoils system of recruitment and the merit system of recruitment, on the one hand, and the lethargy model of personnel policies and the innovation model, on the other hand. Four combinations are possible: (1) spoils recruitment with a lethargy model of personnel policies, (2) spoils recruitment with an innovation model of personnel policies, (3) merit recruitment with a lethargy model of personnel policies, and (4) merit recruitment with an innovation model of personnel policies. These four combinations are illustrated in Fig. 7-9. Each of these combinations has a parallel in actual practice. Spoils with lethargy characterizes many of the federal bureaucracies during the nineteenth century, while merit with lethargy characterizes many federal agencies governed by the modern civil service system. Spoils with innovation often characterizes the bureaucracies in developing

countries, and merit with innovation commonly characterizes some military and many business organizations.

**CONCLUSION**

Bureaucratic leadership in complex power channels is a product of the individuals and groups recruited into bureaucratic organizations. Hereditary privilege enhances bureaucratic leadership by bringing to the occupants of bureaucratic office a social power not inherent in the office itself. In turn, hereditary control over the bureaucracy helps make it an independent actor in the political arena, often in direct conflict with other policy makers. The merit system brings in talented people with a knowledge advantage over many policy makers. That knowledge advantage, in turn, often encourages initiation and development of programs that might not be consistent with the desires or goals of policy makers (or target clientele). The spoils system, on the other hand, checks bureaucratic leadership by making the bureaucracy a tool dependent on the personal approval of other actors in the channel system.

The personnel structure of bureaucratic organizations also fosters or impedes bureaucratic leadership, depending on the form these personnel policies assume. Personnel policies can encourage a work atmosphere of security or they can encourage the advancement of talented personnel or they can leave advancement to factors at least partly extraneous to the organization itself. Further, personnel policies can grant flexibility to top bureaucrats in the organization or they can drastically limit the power of top bureaucrats to change the direction and goals of an organization.

## REFERENCES

Arnold, M. *Culture and anarchy.* Cambridge, England: Cambridge University Press, 1969.

Bayard, J. A. *Daniel Webster and the spoils system.* Oration at Dartmouth College, June 1882. New York: Civil Service Reform Association, 1882.

Benda, J. *The treason of the intellectuals* (R. Aldington, trans.). New York: W. W. Norton & Co., Inc., 1969.

Benedict, T. G., Buell, C. R., and Ellison, C. M. *Comparing career service systems.* Personnel Report No. 621. Chicago: Public Service Association, undated.

Bernard, G. S. *Civil service reform versus the spoils system.* New York: John B. Alden, Publisher, 1885.

Burke, E. An appeal from the new to the old Whigs. In L. E. Shaw (Ed.), *Modern competing ideologies.* Lexington, Mass.: D. C. Heath & Co., 1973.

Cornford, F. M. (Trans.). *The republic of Plato.* New York: Oxford University Press, Inc., 1945.

Drucker, P. *The new society.* New York: Harper & Row, Publishers, Torchbooks, 1962.

Elwell, E. A., and Malik, L. G. *Leadership: a new perspective.* New Delhi: R and K Publishing House, 1974.

Freud, S. *Moses and monotheism.* New York: Random House, Inc., Vintage Books, 1939.

Friedrich, C. J. The rise and decline of the spoils tradition. *Annals of the American Academy of Political and Social Science,* 1937, *189,* 10.

Gerth, H. H., and Mills, C. W. (Eds.). *From Max Weber.* New York: Oxford University Press, Inc., Galaxy Books, 1958.

Hoogenboom, A. *Outlawing the spoils.* Urbana, Ill.: University of Illinois Press, 1968.

House, K. E. Growing deadwood. *The Wall Street Journal,* April 12, 1977, p. 1.

Lasswell, H. D. *Power and personality.* New York: W. W. Norton & Co., Inc., 1948.

Lasswell, H. D., and Kaplan, A. *Power and society.* New Haven, Conn.: Yale University Press, 1950.

Lippincott, B. E. *Victorian critics of democracy.* New York: Farrar, Straus & Giroux, Inc., Octagon Books, 1964.

Lippincott, B. E. *Democracy's dilemma.* New York: Ronald Press Co., 1965.

Marx, K. Excerpts from *Capital.* In L. Feuer (Ed.), *Marx and Engels: Basic writings on politics and philosophy.* New York: Doubleday & Co., Inc., Anchor Books, 1959.

Marx, K., and Engels, F. The Communist manifesto. In L. Feuer (Ed.), *Basic writings on politics and philosophy.* New York: Doubleday & Co., Inc., Anchor Books, 1959.

McFarland, A. S. *Power and leadership in pluralist systems.* Stanford, Calif.: Stanford University Press, 1969.

Miller, N. The merit system vs. patronage. *The Wall Street Journal,* February 28, 1977, p. 12.

Mills, C. W. *The power elite.* New York: Oxford University Press, Inc., 1959.

Pye, L. *New approaches to personnel policy for development.* New York: Department of Economic and Social Affairs, United Nations, 1974.

Rosenberg, H. *Bureaucracy, aristocracy, and autocracy.* Cambridge, Mass.: Harvard University Press, 1958.

United Nations Technical Assistance Programme. *A handbook of public administration.* New York: Department of Economic and Social Affairs, United Nations, 1961.

U.S. Civil Service Commission. The Civil Service in the United States of America. In L. Fougere, *Civil service systems.* Brussels: International Institute of Administrative Sciences, 1967.

White, L. *The science of culture.* New York: Farrar, Straus & Giroux, Inc., 1949.

Wiese, W. *Der Staatsdienst in der Bundesrepublik Deutschland* (Chs. 2 and 6). Berlin: Hermann Lichterhand Verlag, 1972.

# CHAPTER 8

# Bureaucracy and cybernetics

In power channels and within organizations, different types of messages indicate different power relations between sender and receiver. The media of communication strongly correlate with the type of message, its range of meaning, and the amount of "noise" in the communication process. Communication creates images that determine how a message is evaluated and interpreted, thereby making possible the exercise of control through power channels and within bureaucracies.

## COMMUNICATION AND BEHAVIOR

We have seen that communication determines the shaping and sharing of power in complex power channels, and therefore we expect communication to determine the shaping and sharing of power among the members of a bureaucratic organization. Hence a study of communication will help explain bureaucratic behavior. What is communication? Communication is the interchange of information and meaning between a sender and a receiver through a common set of symbols (see Grabner and Rosenberg, 1969:228). These symbols might include the spoken or printed word, gestures, technical signs, and other codes.

How does communication affect the shaping and sharing of power? Recall that one actor has power over another when actor X intervenes in the behavior of actor Y, and actor X thereby increases the probability that actor Y will perform or refrain from performing a particular action, when compared with the probability that actor Y would perform or refrain from performing a particular action without the intervention

through which actor X seeks to affect the behavior of actor Y. The study of control through communication, ranging from mechanical control systems to organic control systems is termed cybernetics (see Weiner, 1961:11). For our purposes "cybernetics" is restricted to the study of communication as a device for shaping and sharing power, both within complex power channels and within a particular bureaucratic organization.

### Cybernetics

Our study of bureaucracy and cybernetics focuses on four basic questions. What are the communication systems that help determine the shaping and sharing of power? How accurately can symbols be transmitted in these systems? How precisely do symbols reflect the desired meaning? How effective are the received symbols in affecting behavior? (See Weaver, 1949:4) Fig. 8-1 illustrates the complex connections among these four questions of communication. In the diagram the arrows represent a communication channel between actor X and actor Y. Transmission noise refers to the problem of accurately transmitting symbols over a particular communication system. Encoding and Decoding noise refer to the problems of precisely communicating information and meaning through a chosen set of symbols, without omission or distortion.

### Behavior

Without communication, power relations between a bureaucracy and its environment and within a bureaucratic organiza-

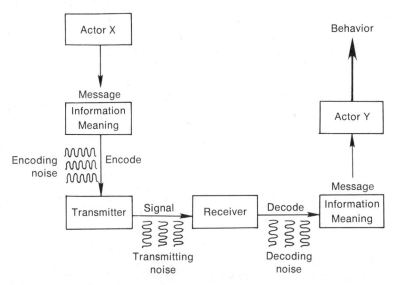

**Fig. 8-1.** Process of communication. Adapted from Weaver (1949:7); see also Guetzkow (1965:535) and Grabner and Rosenberg (1969:229).

tion either would not exist or would rest on brute force. As seen in Chapter 6, organizations adjust to one another through a complex exchange of communication. A similar process occurs among the members of an organization (Geutzkow, 1965:535). The key role of communication in explaining administrative behavior has long been noted. In 1938 Chester Barnard (1938:91), one of the fathers of modern administrative theory, pointed out that communication occupies a central place in organizational theory because the scope, extent, and structure of organizations reflect communication techniques. Similarly, Herbert Simon (1976:154) argues that communication techniques determine the way in which decision making is distributed throughout an organization. Walton (1963:46) maintains that communication is the most significant factor controlling organizational behavior.

Communication systems correspond to patterns of interaction between a bureaucracy and its environment and among members of a bureaucratic organization. Some communication systems correspond to the official organization charts, while other indicate the more spontaneous inter-

actions that emerge in work situations. As will be shown in the following discussion, the communication systems linking actors in complex power channels and actors within an organization create a variety of status relationships between the communicator and the recipients (see Pye, 1963:24). These status relationships are determined by the evaluation and interpretation of the message and by the observable response to it.

**COMMUNICATION SYSTEMS**

The cybernetic system in bureaucracies establishes power relations between a bureaucracy and its environment and among members of a bureaucratic organization. This cybernetic system is quite complex, for it includes a number of different cybernets: communication networks that provide channels for the exercise of power. The fact that these cybernets often overlap makes it difficult to isolate the effects of one cybernet, because the same two actors might assume different status relationships and use different means to evaluate, interpret, and respond to messages, depending on the cybernet. For example,

**Table 8-1.** Cybernets and the media of communication

| | SIMPLE COMMAND CYBERNETS | COMPLEX COMMAND CYBERNETS | SIMPLE EXPERTISE CYBERNETS | COMPLEX EXPERTISE CYBERNETS | GOSSIP CYBERNETS |
|---|---|---|---|---|---|
| Written | + | ++ | + | + | + |
| Mechanical | | | | ++ | |
| Oral | + | + | + | + | ++ |

+, Secondary medium or one of several media typically used in a given cybernet. ++, Dominant medium for the particular cybernet.

an incompetent supervisor has the authority to command a competent subordinate. Here the status relationship is reversed, and we can expect the incompetent supervisor to give considerable weight to the opinions of a competent subordinate.

To understand the exercise of power in complex channel systems and within complex organizations, we must closely examine the cybernets at work. We shall identify cybernets by the types of messages carried in the communication between sender and receiver. Three types of messages are particularly relevant here: commands, or the exercise of formal authority; expertise, or the use of specialized knowledge; and gossip, hearsay, small talk, and rumor (see Guetzkow, 1965:542-550; Grabner and Rosenberg, 1969:234-238). In addition, we shall examine three media of communication: written messages; mechanical messages, particularly those transmitted between person and computer; and interpersonal messages, particularly oral communication (Simon, 1976:157-164).

Generally speaking, each cybernet tends to rely more on one medium of communication than on others. However, the medium also tends to reflect the complexity of the power channel and the complexity of the bureaucratic organization. For example, the command cybernet in simple power channels and simple bureaucratic organizations might use oral and written communication equally often. But in more complex settings written communication is the primary medium. Similarly, in less technologically sophisticated bureaucracies the expertise cybernet may use both oral and written communication. In more technologically sophisticated bureaucracies, however, the expertise cybernets rely heavily on mechanical media for information storage and data processing. The gossip cybernet tends to rely more on oral communication and less on written or mechanical media. Table 8-1 illustrates the relations between cybernets and media of communication.

In power channel systems and within bureaucratic organizations these cybernets co-occur. One classic example of the relation among cybernets in bureaucratic organizations is found in the distinction between formal and informal systems of communication. The formal communication system (for example, a command cybernet) supposedly parallels the official structure of organization charts. The informal communication system (for example, a gossip cybernet) arises through the spontaneous interactions of people in work settings. According to Blau (1971:46), these informal relations and unofficial practices comprise patterns of activities and interactions not accounted for by the official structure and not the consequence of fortuitous personality differences.

Cybernets complement one another, but they might also work at cross purposes (see Cherry, 1957:29). When informal communication supplements formal communication channels, for example, it helps augment the power relations established by an official chain of command (see Simon, 1976:157; Blau and Meyer, 1971:50). However, when these cybernets work at cross purposes, the "informal" channels might modify or alter formal power relations. In some instances the formal and informal communication systems might directly conflict with one another. Alvin Gouldner (1954) describes a gypsum plant where a new plant manager sought to implement a strict hierarchy of command and discipline. Somewhat to the manager's surprise, strong informal ties among the workers led them to collectively resist the commands of management.

### Message content

We have identified three important types of message content: commands, expertise, and gossip. Command channels usually create the formal authority structure within power channels and within a bureaucratic organization. Command implies a power hierarchy where actors in subordinate positions accept as legitimate and binding the messages sent by superiors (see Guetzkow, 1965:543; Grabner and Rosenberg, 1969:234-235). In command cybernets the shaping and sharing of power is most apparent. Command cybernets imply that one agency or actor has sufficient power over another to influence regularly the behavior of other components in the channel system or other actors within the organization.

In Part I we saw that specialized knowledge is a characteristic of advanced bureaucratic organization. Expertise cybernets follow from this specialization of knowledge. Unlike command cybernets, the flow of expert information and interpretation may be vertical or horizontal, flowing in both directions between superiors and subordinates and in many directions among peers of an expertise work group (see Grabner and Rosenberg, 1969:235). And unlike command cybernets, expertise cybernets do not necessarily parallel formal organization charts. Expertise cybernets serve two basic functions: they help move information between superiors and subordinates (both directions) for use in decision

making, and they help move information among superiors or among subordinates for use in problem solving. The complexity of expertise cybernets reflects the demand for routine integration of specialized knowledge and the occasional need to apply technical knowledge and experience to nonroutine problems (see Guetzkow, 1965:543-546; Grabner and Rosenberg, 1969:235-236).

The final type of message is gossip. The gossip cybernet reflects a variety of interpersonal relations, ranging from friendship to respect and prestige (see Guetzkow, 1965:546-550; Grabner and Rosenberg, 1969:236-238). Gossip cybernets typically are broken channels: they do not link directly together all members of a channel system or all members of a bureaucratic organization (see Guetzkow, 1965:546). In fact, power channels and bureaucratic organizations often have a number of gossip cybernets, each connecting only a small portion of the actors in complex power channels and in complex organizations. Gossip cybernets establish power relations in several ways, among them communicating and reinforcing the expectations of others in the work environment, providing cues about appropriate and inappropriate activities, providing personal cues about other people in the work environment, establishing appropriate role models after which one should pattern his or her behavior, and providing access to secret or confidential information about the organization and its environment.

***Command cybernets.*** Command cybernets imply a hierarchy of power relations, whether between a bureaucracy and its environment or among the members of a bureaucracy. In Chapter 6 we saw that a command cybernet centralizes coordination in complex power channels. Similarly, a command cybernet centralizes coordination within a complex organization. In fact, Weber's model of bureaucratic organization concentrates almost exclusively on command cybernets. In addition to coordination, command cybernets typically foster the achievement of formal organizational goals, greater organizational effectiveness, and greater efficiency in achieving these goals, particularly when compared with gossip cybernets. Goal achievement, effectiveness, and efficiency all are basic to the rational action expected of bureaucratic organizations. For similar reasons, command cybernets usually imply set formal procedures for establishing and directing bureaucratic activities. Command cybernets rely on such procedures because they help make bureaucratic activities systematic and uniform. Further, command cybernets tend to limit the discretion exercised by subordinates in power channels and within complex organizations. Limiting discretion helps guarantee that bureaucratic activities are uniform and consistent across members of a work group.

Still, command cybernets do not exist in isolation from expertise cybernets and gossip cybernets. In turn, the extent to which command cybernets dominate the cybernetic system of power channels or complex organizations helps explain the degree of coordination, the emphasis on achievement of formal organizational goals, the emphasis on effectiveness, the emphasis on efficiency, the adherence to set procedures, and the degree of discretion found in a power channel or in a complex organization.

To examine empirically these relations, 562 respondents from 30 criminal justice agencies in five cities were asked to assess the extent of a particular command cybernet and to assess the resulting coordination, achievement of formal goals, degree of organizational effectiveness, degree of organizational efficiency, adherence to set procedures, and the degree of discretion. Fig. 8-2 presents the empirical findings.

***Expertise cybernets.*** Expertise cybernets allow bureaucratic organizations to synthesize and to apply the specialized knowledge

characteristic of bureaucracies. As we have seen in previous chapters, bureaucracies rely on an intellectual division of labor, allowing them to use vast amounts of specialized knowledge in solving both routine and nonroutine bureaucratic problems. We also saw in earlier chapters that expertise carries with it an aura of power: technical problems commonly are referred to the "experts" for solution or recommendation.

In well-organized bureaucracies and well-organized power channels, expertise cybernets usually supplement the impact of command cybernets. However, while command cybernets establish power relations directly by creating a formal hierarchy of authority, expertise cybernets establish power relations indirectly through the nature of expert knowledge. Thoman Kuhn (1970:4) argues that expert knowledge has two components: empirical observation and experience and an arbitrary element that helps form beliefs held by the experts in a given scientific community. Kuhn calls the entire constellation of beliefs, values, and techniques shared by a community of experts a "paradigm" (Kuhn, 1970:175). It is this paradigm that leads a community of experts to define problems in certain ways and to consider only those alternatives consistent with their viewpoints. Different scientific communities, however, focus on different matters, and professional communication across these groups often results in misunderstanding (Kuhn, 1970: 177).

The existence of expertise cybernets implies systematic deference to experts because certain bodies of expertise are perceived relevant to a particular problem and officials come to rely on the analysis and recommendations of experts. In turn, the impact of expertise cybernets follows from the notion of paradigms. With shared perspectives, beliefs, and techniques, expertise cybernets help foster coordination, the achievement of formal goals, and the perceived effectiveness of bureaucratic activ-

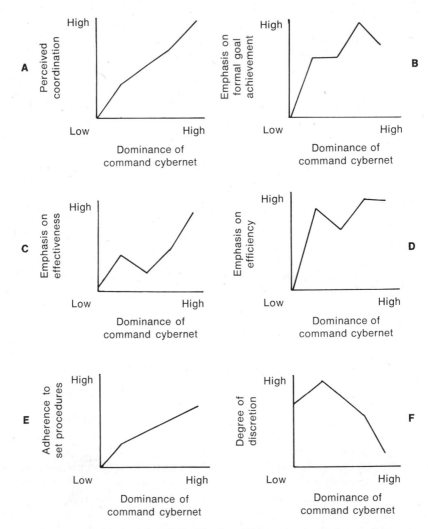

**Fig. 8-2.** Command cybernets in criminal justice. Responses to each question were coded on Likert scales. These scales range from strongly disagree (5) to strongly agree (1). Plots represent mean scale value for respondents in each Likert position on command cybernet question. Data from National Court Services Evaluation Project, conducted by William Rhodes, Thomas Blomberg, and Steven Thomas Seitz.

ity. Typically, bureaucratic agencies foster only one way of looking at a particular problem and rely on one body of expertise to address that problem.

While the command cybernet is concerned directly with organizational efficiency, the expertise cybernet often is concerned with routine and nonroutine problem solving. The distinction here is subtle.

Command cybernets are more concerned with identifying and employing the most efficient means to solve problems. Expertise cybernets are more concerned with the actual task of solving problems. Like the command cybernet, expertise cybernets tend to follow set procedures in solving problems, but unlike command cybernets, they often delegate more discretion to indi-

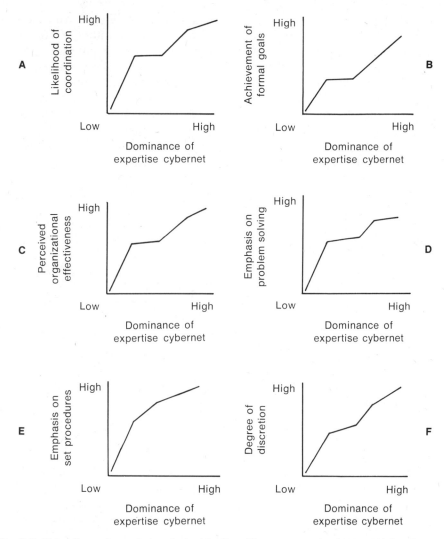

**Fig. 8-3.** Expertise cybernets in criminal justice. Figures represent mean plots of respondents for each category position on expertise cybernet question. Question responses were coded in Likert scales. Data from National Court Service Evaluation Project.

viduals than is typical under command cybernets. The additional discretion in expertise cybernets often reflects the trust and confidence that results from basic agreement on defining and resolving a problem.

To empirically examine the impact of expertise cybernets, the same 562 respondents from 30 criminal justice agencies in five cities were asked to assess the extent of a particular expertise cybernet and to assess the resulting coordination, achievement of formal goals, degree of organizational effectiveness, degree of emphasis on problem solving, adherence to set procedures, and the degree of discretion permitted. Fig. 8-3 presents the empirical findings. Once again the empirical results closely conform to our expectations.

***Gossip cybernets.*** Of the three types of message contents examined here, gossip cybernets are the most fragmented and least related to the formal activities of the bureaucratic organization. Unlike command and expertise cybernets, gossip cybernets seldom reflect set procedures or the formal organization charts. In turn gossip cybernets sometimes work at cross purposes to the command and expertise cybernets. This is particularly true when agencies in a power channel or members of an organization are linked primarily through gossip cybernets, without command or expertise cybernets helping to temper and to direct the impact of a gossip cybernet.

Lacking the structure and coherency brought to power channels and organizations by command and expertise cybernets, gossip cybernets may actually decrease coordination, decrease the emphasis on formal goals, and decrease organizational ef-

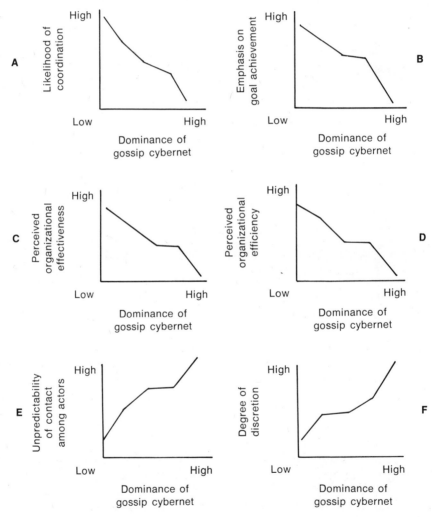

**Fig. 8-4.** Gossip cybernets in criminal justice. Figures represent mean plots of respondents for each Likert category on gossip cybernet question. Data from National Court Service Evaluation Project.

fectiveness and efficiency. These consequences are most likely to occur when the gossip cybernet is dominant in the cybernetic system and when there is considerable disagreement among members of a channel or among members of an organization. Unlike command and expertise cybernets, gossip cybernets produce rather unpredictable contact among actors. In turn, the exercise of power through gossip cybernets is neither regular nor systematic, particularly when compared with command and expertise cybernets. Further, when gossip cybernets are untempered by command and expertise cybernets, the amount of discretion available to any individual is quite high.

To empirically examine the impact of gossip cybernets, we again will analyze the responses from 562 bureaucrats from 30 criminal justice agencies in five cities. The respondents were asked to assess the dominance of a gossip cybernet unchecked by either command or expertise cybernets and to assess the resulting impact on coordination, the achievement of formal goals, the degree of organizational effectiveness, the degree of organizational efficiency, the unpredictability of communication, and the degree of discretion. Fig. 8-4 presents the empirical findings. Once again the results closely parallel our expectations.

### Media of communication

Earlier we identified three media of communication: written, mechanical, and interpersonal. Written communication refers to the flow of messages that take such forms as memoranda, letters, records, reports, manuals, and other printed forms (see Simon, 1976:157-162). Mechanical media involve the flow of messages between persons and machines, especially computerized information systems and computerized data processing systems. Interpersonal communication primarily involves oral communication, such as conversation, lectures, meetings, and tele-

phone conversations. Written and mechanical media differ from interpersonal media in two basic respects: written and mechanical communication are less subject to memory decay, distortion, and omission, and interpersonal communication often is far richer in content and meaning than either written or mechanical communication.

***Written communication.*** We tend to identify bureaucracy with paperwork, and for good reason. Written communication is essential to bureaucratic activity because it allows repetition in the very words used by the sender, and written documents can be reviewed as human memory requires (see Innis, 1968:47, 105). These might appear to be minor matters, but they are absolutely essential for the rational action pursued by more complex bureaucratic states. Describing the development of Roman bureaucracy, Innis (1968:47) observes that bureaucratic development depended on papyrus and then, given the brittleness of papyrus roles, the use of parchment. These media helped resolve the problems of administering a vast empire.

Following Innis, Marshall McLuhan (1964:86-87) argues that the written word permits continuity and uniformity of action. Because written communication allows verbatim repetition, the amount of diversity in interpretation is held to the ambiguity of language and the clarity of diction, without introducing the problems of bias introduced by oral communication and the biases of memory decay, omission, and distortion. In short, written messages maximize the continuity and uniformity of a message and maximize the regularity of its impact.

Given these qualities of written communication, it is particularly adapted to command cybernets. Here uniformity and continuity are extremely important. To be effective, commands must be uniformly understood and receivers must be able to refer back to messages they have forgotten. With

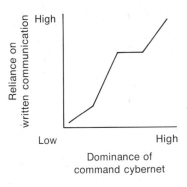

**Fig. 8-5.** Written communication and command cybernets in criminal justice. Question responses derive from 562 respondents in 30 criminal justice agencies in five cities. Figures plotted represent mean score of respondents for each Likert scale position on command cybernet question. Data from National Court Services Evaluation Project.

oral communication, on the other hand, commands are subject to the distortions introduced by oral repetition, omissions, and memory decay. Empirical data from criminal justice agencies confirm the relation between the dominance of command cybernets and written communication. As command cybernets become increasingly important tools for control over bureaucratic activity, the reliance on written communication increases accordingly. Fig. 8-5 illustrates the empirical data.

***Mechanical communication.*** The newest medium of communication in power channels and within complex organizations is the mechanical system for storing, retrieving, and processing information. Before the mechanical medium, the printed medium allowed people to accumulate far more knowledge than could be stored in a single human mind. But the increasing complexity of social problems and the demand for vast amounts of information in decision making requires the processing of an enormous amount of information in a relatively short time. For this purpose the written medium is not particularly appropriate, because it takes an enormous amount of

time to research literature and the knowledge extracted is likely to be dated. Further, information retrieved by reading is subject to memory decay and omission. In addition, if vast amounts of materials are reviewed, the reader might suffer something like a mental overload, thereby increasing the chance of cognitive distortion. Mechanical media help remedy these problems because an enormous amount of current information can be electronically stored and processed without unnecessary delays and without the problems of memory decay, distortion, and omission.

Although the computer age in bureaucratic activity has only just begun, the rapid conversion to computer systems in most complex bureaucratic organizations reflects the advantages of this medium over written communication. Simon points out that today's decision making is shared between human and computer components of a person-machine system (Simon, 1976: 292). The meaning of messages derived from mechanical media rest on the computer software programs used to process the data and the interpretations attached to the data by a group of experts. Once again we return to the importance of expertise paradigms in defining problems and establishing alternative recommendations for action. The information stored by mechanical devices cannot speak for itself, just as a statistic cannot speak for itself. Someone must compress this information in data processing and translate it for use by decision makers.

***Interpersonal communication.*** Of the three media discussed here, interpersonal communication is the richest in meaning but also the most subject to memory decay, omission, and distortion. In oral communication, for example, the eyes, ears, and brain act in busy cooperation, stimulating and supplementing one another (see Innis, 1968:105). Even in telephone conversations, voice intonation supplements the message of the spoken word. But the rich-

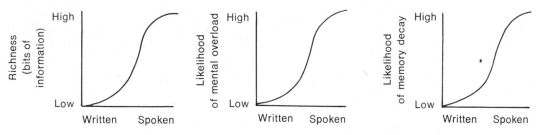

**Fig. 8-6.** Differences between written and spoken word.

ness of interpersonal communication is also its drawback. The human mind can absorb only a small fraction of the cues reaching it through the senses. In turn some of the information being transmitted is necessarily lost. Further, the selection of some cues over others may distort the meaning of a message being transmitted. And finally, memory decay makes the message subject to further omission and distortion.

Imagine a continuum from the written word to the spoken word. As we move along the continuum, information becomes richer per unit of time transmission. But the amount of noise or distortion also increases. Similarly, the rate of decay of information increases as we move from the written to the spoken word (see Grabner and Rosenberg, 1969:238-242). Fig. 8-6 illustrates some of the interesting differences between the written and spoken word.

The written word is subject to the ambiguities of language and expression. Mechanical media are subject to the programming and translation of experts. But interpersonal communication introduces even more room for differences of interpretation and ambiguity. The nature of meaning in interpersonal communication is tied intimately to the social process itself: the context in which messages are sent, the personal relationship of sender and receiver, and the expectations the sender and receiver hold prior to the delivery/reception of the message (see Mead, 1964:115-282). As interpersonal messages are repeated,

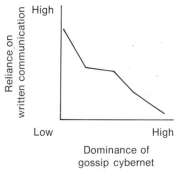

**Fig. 8-7.** Written word and gossip cybernets in criminal justice. From 30 criminal justice agencies in five cities, 562 respondents were asked to assess dominance of a gossip cybernet and resulting impact on written communication. Figures represent mean response scores for each Likert scale position on gossip cybernet question. Data from National Court Services Evaluation Project.

their meaning varies directly with the changes in context, relation between sender and receiver, and the expectations operating during the process of communication. Here continuity and uniformity are at their lowest points in the cybernetic system. Not only is the information likely to change with repetition, because of omission, distortion, forgetting, and decay, but the meaning of that information at least partly rests with the past experience of the receiver (see Boulding, 1961:6).

Gossip cybernets rely heavily on interpersonal media, particularly oral conversation. As gossip cybernets come to dominate a distribution channel or complex organization, the reliance on the spoken word increases accordingly. Conversely, as illustrated by the empirical data in Fig. 8-7, as a gossip cybernet comes to dominate both command and expertise cybernets, the reliance on written communication decreases accordingly.

## POWER AND CYBERNETICS

Messages carry information and cues about the meaning of that information. The accumulation of messages over a long time helps to create an image about people, activities, organizations, and what not (see Boulding, 1961:5). Long ago, for example, diplomats sent to foreign countries learned the need to build an image back home about the events, situations, and personalities in the country to which they were assigned. These images helped officials at home to see the problems abroad in ways similar to the diplomats. Without these images the diplomats found it difficult to influence the decisions of officials back home, because those in the home office could not see the problems in a manner consistent with the way the diplomats saw them. With these shared images, however, the diplomats found communication easier and found it more likely that they could influence the decisions of their leaders.

In an important respect, communication precedes the existence of a cybernetic system. Recall that cybernetics is the study of control through communication. Control is possible only if the receiver properly understands the message sent. Command cybernets, for example, imply the existence of an image of an authority hierarchy. Without that image the recipient of a command would not understand its true meaning and hence probably would not respond in a manner desired by the sender. Similarly, expertise cybernets presume an image of legitimate expertise. Even the gossip cybernet, in which one actor affects the behavior of another through informal messages, is impossible without some image

about the sender's credibility and the context to which a message refers. In short, communication helps establish mental images, which in turn make the control of behavior through communication possible (Boulding, 1961:6).

Communication helps determine the shaping and sharing of power in two ways. First, communication helps build images on which cybernets rest. For a command cybernet to operate, for example, actors must perceive an authority hierarchy. In this respect, as Thomas (1966) once noted, that which we perceive to be real is real in its consequences. Second, once a cybernet exists, communication reflects power relations where one actor seeks to affect the behavior of another by using the mental image held by the recipient of a message. Once a command cybernet exists, for example, a superior can issue an order to a subordinate and be relatively confident that the subordinate will act accordingly.

### Image building

Image building is the fundamental task facing a new bureaucratic organization. The same is true when a bureaucratic organization recruits new personnel. Control between a bureaucracy and its environment and control within a complex organization depend on mental images that make cybernets possible. If there is a formal hierarchy of authority, for example, it is important that all members of a power channel know about it immediately. Similarly, new recruits in an established organization must quickly acquire the prevailing images to ensure proper functioning of the command and expertise cybernets. These are not always easy tasks, and the problem can assume a variety of forms.

In India, for example, the central government built several new cities for the growing population, but people who moved to the new cities did not feel part of the new community. This lack of a common political identity had some serious implications.

Indian officials found it very difficult to establish an effective city administration for the delivery of public services, because the target clientele in the new city did not have an adequate mental image of the purpose or scope of the new administration. Only when common images of the city emerged, over several years, did the administrative crisis pass.

In another situation the management of an airplane factory once gave its employees a guided tour through a completed airplane. Workers were allowed to ask where their portion of the assembly belonged in the plane and what its functions were. Unexpectedly, production in the plant improved drastically after the tours because the workers had an image of how their efforts contributed to the overall production and of how they fit into the larger scheme of work at the plant.

When command or expertise cybernets are important for the proper functions of an organization, as they usually are, other members of a power channel and members of the organization must quickly learn the formal authority hierarchy and quickly discover the importance of available expertise. In the mid-1970s, for example, the federal government exported an innovative court service program to several cities in the United States, providing funds and technical assistance to get the program going. In some cities the new program was preceded by considerable planning, where other members of the power channel system were informed fully about the new program and how it fit into the larger scheme of criminal justice in that community. In other cities the new programs were introduced without this form of image building. In those cities that prepared a way for the new program, the problems of program implementation were minimal because the other members of the power channel knew what to expect from the new agency and knew what the agency expected of them. In the cities where image building did not

occur, the new programs faced long delays, bitter battles, gross inefficiency, and ineffectiveness, and some of them were even terminated when federal funds expired.

### Controlling noise

Apart from image building, another serious problem facing bureaucracies is the control of "noise" in the communication systems. This noise includes memory decay, omission, distortion, and the introduction of irrelevant messages into the cybernetic system. Two means of controlling noise follow from the discussion in the preceding section: (1) the use of written and mechanical media allows less distortion and memory decay than does oral communication; (2) gossip cybernets might be tempered by command and expertise cybernets. If desired, it is possible to drastically curtail a gossip cybernet. For example, workers could be physically isolated from one another, or conversation could be strictly forbidden. But the cost of these extreme measures outweighs the benefits gained. Some human interaction is essential in making the work setting more enjoyable, boosting morale, reducing turnover, and perhaps boosting productivity. In addition, gossip cybernets, properly tempered by command and expertise cybernets, actually can supplement command and expertise cybernets, particularly in the process of image building within an organization and within a power channel.

Other means for controlling omission and distortion in the bureaucratic cybernetic system are less apparent. Among these devices are redundancy, queuing, specialized languages, and feedback (see Grabner and Rosenberg, 1969:242-246).

***Redundancy.*** Redundancy means repetition. Under certain circumstances, redundancy might help a receiver properly understand a message being communicated. In addition, redundancy could serve as a check on the biases held by the receiver of a message. The English language, for example, is about 50% redundant, meaning that about half our letters and words are open to free choice, while the other half are fixed by the statistical structure of the language (Shannon and Weaver, 1949:13). There is an important reason for this. If language were completely nonredundant, the receiver would have to attend to every bit of information transmitted by the sender. But such a demand could exceed an individual's capacity to pay attention and absorb all the information bombarding his or her senses. Hence the chance for omission and distortion is very high. However, the redundancy of the English language makes it possible to compensate for bits of information lost by the receiver when the message is sent. This relation between redundancy and understanding is aptly caught by Harold Laski's comment that one should repeat a message three times for bright people, five for average people, and eight times for slow learners.

Redundancy also serves to check bias in the receiver. Cyert and March (1963:110) point out that departments in business organizations, such as the sales department and the accounting department, typically have filtering devices that bias the meaning of information at their disposal. In turn an organization must adapt to this biased information by providing counterbiases. Often this means that central decision makers gather estimates on the same problem from several different sources and then balance the biases through redundant information (see also Grabner and Rosenberg, 1969:245).

*Queuing.* Queuing is a device to order systematically the flow of information in a cybernetic system, thereby preventing an overload of information. Overloads increase the likelihood of omission and distortion because the human mind simply cannot absorb an infinite amount of information in a given time. Omission and distortion might be reduced by backlogging written communication, fixing certain times when par-

ticular information is relayed to the receiver, and sometimes bypassing those who need not be burdened with all the information that might be available at any given time. Clearly, command and expertise cybernets allow queuing more than gossip cybernets do. In turn, as the proverbial "rumor mill" implies, gossip cybernets might become overloaded and the flow of legitimate information severely impaired because of omission and distortion.

*Specialized language.* Specialized language, such as technical jargon or certain business jargons, also might help reduce omission and distortion in a cybernetic system. Specialized languages often are less ambiguous than ordinary language and admit of fever variations on the meaning attributed to a message. Typically these specialized languages and technical jargons help reduce the volume of communication as well, because they rely on symbolic codes and schemes for classifying information (see Grabner and Rosenberg, 1969: 244). Even when an organization does not adopt a specialized language deliberately, a specialized terminology provides greater clarity and greater efficiency of expression. For example, even a casual observer quickly can distinguish between an employee of the Department of State and an employee in the Department of Health, Education, and Welfare.

*Feedback.* Feedback is another means for controlling omissions and distortions in a cybernetic system. For our purposes feedback simply is a device through which the sender can verify that the receiver has received the message and understood its intended meaning (see Grabner and Rosenberg, 1969:245). Feedback devices can assume two basic forms: devices that verify the intended meaning of a communication and devices that allow the sender to monitor the behavior of the receiver, thereby permitting the sender to confirm that the resulting behavior is consistent with the message sent. Quite often feedback devices are built into the formal organizational structure, allowing superiors to confirm that commands have been received, understood, and acted on.

## CONCLUSION

Communication is the interchange of information and meaning between a sender and a receiver through a common set of symbols. In turn, a cybernetic system is one in which members of the system exercise control over others through communication. In power channels and within a bureaucratic organization, the cybernetic system includes a variety of cybernets, identified by the content of messages transmitted between sender and receiver. Three cybernets are particularly important: command cybernets, expertise cybernets, and gossip cybernets. We also have identified three important media for communication: written messages, mechanical messages, and interpersonal messages. Written messages are particularly important in the command cybernets of complex power channels and within complex organizations. The role of mechanical messages—person-machine interactions—is becoming increasingly important in expertise cybernets. Finally, the gossip cybernets tend to rely heavily on interpersonal communication, particularly the spoken word.

Cybernets have direct impact on coordination, the achievement of formal goals, organizational effectiveness, organizational efficiency, adherence to set procedures, communication for problem solving, the predictability of communication among actors, and the degree of discretion permitted to individual agencies in a power channel and individuals within an organization. While command and expertise cybernets usually complement one another, gossip cybernets can be counterproductive if left unchecked or untempered by command and expertise cybernets. Further, within these cybernets written and mechanical media are less subject to noise derived from omission, distortion, and memory decay and forgetting. Interpersonal media, on the other hand, are particularly susceptible to these problems, even though they are richer in meaning.

Communication helps determine the shaping and sharing of power within the power channel and within the organization by activating cybernets and providing a medium for a sender to alter the behavior of a receiver in a given cybernet. In turn, bureaucratic organizations face two important problems that arise from the nature of cybernetic systems: the need to build and foster images that activate appropriate cybernets and the need to control noise in the cybernets. Without cybernets, consistent power relations between a bureaucracy and its environment and among the members of an organization are virtually impossible. Without controlling for noise, the impact of a sender's message on a receiver in a cybernet might be diminished sharply.

## REFERENCES

Barnard, C. I. *The functions of the executive.* Cambridge, Mass.: Harvard University Press, 1938.

Blau, P. M., and Meyer, M. W. *Bureaucracy in modern society* (2nd ed.). New York: Random House, Inc., 1971.

Boulding, K. The image. Ann Arbor, Mich.: Ann Arbor Paperbacks, University of Michigan Press, 1961.

Cherry, C. *On human communication.* New York: Technology Press, Massachusetts Institute of Technology, 1957; John Wiley & Sons, Inc., 1957.

Cyert, R. M., and March, J. G. *A behavioral theory of the firm.* Englewood Cliffs, N.J.: Prentice-Hall, Inc., 1963.

Gouldner, A. W. *Patterns of industrial bureaucracy.* New York: Free Press, 1954.

Grabner, J. R., and Rosenberg, L. J. Communication in distribution channel systems. In L. Stern (Ed.), *Distribution channels.* Boston: Houghton Mifflin Co., 1969.

Guetzkow, H. Communication in organizations. In J. G. March (Ed.), *Handbook of organizations.* Skokie, Ill.: Rand McNally & Co., 1965.

Innis, H. *The bias of communication.* Toronto: University of Toronto Press, 1968.

Kuhn, T. *The structure of scientific revolutions* (2nd ed.). Chicago: University of Chicago Press, 1970.

McLuhan, M. *Understanding media*. New York: New American Library, Inc., Signet Books, 1964.

Mead, G. H. *On social psychology* (A. Strauss, ed.). Chicago: University of Chicago Press, 1964.

Pye, L. W. (Ed.). *Communications and political development*. Princeton, N.J.: Princeton University Press, 1963.

Shannon, C. E., and Weaver, W. *The mathematical theory of communication*. Urbana, Ill.: University of Illinois Press, 1949.

Simon, H. A. *Administrative behavior* (3rd ed.). New York: Free Press, 1976.

Thomas, W. I. *On social organization and social personality* (M. Janowitz, ed.). Chicago: University of Chicago Press, 1966.

Walton, E. A study of organizational communication systems. *Personnel Administration*, 1963, 26, 46.

Weaver, W. Recent contributions to the mathematical theory of communication. In C. E. Shannon and W. Weaver, *The mathematical theory of communication*. Urbana, Ill.: University of Illinois Press, 1949.

Weiner, N. *Cybernetics* (2nd ed.). Cambridge, Mass.: M.I.T. Press, 1961.

# CHAPTER 9

# Bureaucratic management

The management process shapes and shares power for the pursuit of organizational goals. To do so, it must balance stability with innovation. Seven policies encourage innovation, and six other policies encourage stability. Management motivates job performance by matching working conditions with personal needs and goals and by building influences conducive to goal achievement.

## DIMENSIONS OF MANAGEMENT

In the last three chapters we have closely examined the exercise of power between a bureaucracy and its environment and among the members of a bureaucracy. Why is this shaping and sharing of power so important? Power relationships are important because they determine the extent to which a bureaucracy effectively and efficiently can pursue its goals. These power relationships have an external and an internal dimension. Externally, the bureaucracy must achieve a desired impact on its target clientele. Internally, the bureaucracy must build collective intent among its members and secure the procedures for elaborating and administering its substantive guidelines (see Mohr, 1973:475). How do bureaucracies solve these problems?

Bureaucratic management is the process through which bureaucracies pursue these internal and external tasks (see Hersey and Blanchard, 1972:3). Clearly, management is more than a collection of supervisors in an organization. Similarly, management is not the equivalent of a hierarchy of author-

ity. Rather, management is the most important process for shaping and sharing power for the pursuit of organizational goals. In the language of Chapter 8, management is the principal function of the cybernetic system in bureaucracies.

### Management and power channels

Unlike the thermostat that automatically turns the furnace on when room temperature falls below a set minimum, a bureaucratic organization has no mechanical systems to make the necessary adjustments when the contours of power change in a power channel system. Instead, bureaucratic organizations must rely on human devices. The most obvious of these devices is management. Relative to the power channel, the process of management implies anticipation, monitoring, alternative planning, and compensating adjustments whenever changes in the power channel so demand. Drastic changes in a channel introduce uncertainty, perhaps disrupt the established procedures for elaborating and administering substantive guidelines, and perhaps impede the desired political action. To minimize uncertainty and its consequences, bureaucratic management might seek to maintain an equilibrium of power. Here every exercise of power is met by a countervailing exercise of power.

Sometimes, however, the push and pull of power in a channel system cannot restore balance or equilibrium. This is particularly likely when one component of the channel gains unusual power over other members. Here the old power relations are disrupted permanently, and new ones begin to replace the old "balance of power." We have abundant examples of these drastic upheavals. During the twentieth century, for example, corporate organizations gained extraordinary economic advantage over smaller enterprises through mergers and diversification. In the public arena, agency consolidations created huge bureaucratic monoliths that quickly absorbed the functions and clientele of numerous smaller agencies, many of them private. Compared with 50 years ago, for example, the power and scope of private charities drastically have been overshadowed by the public welfare agencies of today.

Under normal conditions bureaucratic management attempts to reduce uncertainty in the power channel by meeting one exercise of power with a countervailing exercise of power. By so doing, management helps secure both the internal and external tasks of an organization. But under conditions of radical change in the power channel, the tasks of management change accordingly. Radical change typically requires changes of procedures in elaborating and administering substantive guidelines. Quite often, radical change also might require changes in the desired political action. If these changes are to occur, bureaucratic management requires unusual power. One form of such unusual power is leadership.

**Leadership.** In Chapter 7 we saw that bureaucratic leadership is an important device for shaping and sharing power in complex channel systems. Leadership is an important tool in the process of management when it helps foster organizational goals under conditions of uncertainty or rapid change. Selznick (1976:573-574) summarizes three premises about bureaucratic leadership that are directly relevant to our dicsussion:

1. Leadership is a special activity that meets the needs of specific social situations.

2. Leadership is not necessarily identical with a formal hierarchy of command.
3. The need for leadership varies with both circumstance and situation.

From time to time the process of management requires leadership to cope with radical changes in the power channel. But at other times the task of management is less dramatic, for it focuses on the need to stabilize power relations in the channel system (see Sayles, 1962:62).

**Paradox of management.** Under stable conditions in the power channel, the function of management centers on those adjustive compensations necessary to maintain a balance of power, thereby securing organizational goals against potential changes in the channel system. Under conditions of radical change, the function of management centers on changing the procedures of an organization and perhaps its desired political action to ensure survival of the organization. Because leadership implies unusual power, it is more appropriate to the second condition (radical change) than to the first condition (stable conditions). Can the process of management incorporate the resources necessary for both functions?

There is a paradox in bureaucratic management. On the one hand, management must maintain stable operations in the pursuit of organizational goals. On the other hand, management must adapt to minor disturbances in the channel system and change operations when radical upheavals in the power channels so require. Quite often these processes occur simultaneously. Sayles (1962:62) argues that change is part of any administrative process, because a bureaucracy must identify where significant deviations are occurring and then either eliminate the instability or introduce long-term compensations for that instability.

**Management and organization goals.** A bureaucracy without management reduces the organization to an expendable tool at the mercy of other components in the power channel (Selznick, 1976:564). Without management—a dynamic process that allows adjustments to both short-run and long-run change—the procedures for elaborating and administering substantive guidelines likely will decay or become obsolete as the power relations in a channel system shift over time. Similarly, without management an organization faces modification or termination of its desired political action as power relations shift in the channel system. This is, of course, often the fate of organizations under the spoils system for recruitment. By implication, the process of management fosters organizational goals, even in the face of opposition, and helps maintain the organization itself, even though organizational goals may be sacrificed in the face of radical change.

Over time, enduring organizations build images of themselves, create and foster leadership and engage in actions that foster the continuity of organizational goals, and, if necessary, sacrifice these goals for the protection of the organization itself (Selznick, 1976:567-568). As Selznick (1976: 569-571) suggests, the organization becomes infused with a value beyond the simple requirements of an expendable tool.

What does it mean to say that an organization is "infused with value"? Clearly, the organization does not become a living entity with a will or existence of its own. The key lies in our discussion of image building in Chapter 8. An organization becomes "infused with value" when the members of that organization acquire a mental image of the organization, its meaning, and its purpose. Collective images make cybernets possible within an organization, make possible the collective intent necessary for the pursuit of organizational goals, and allow individuals to identify with the organization, making its protection and preservation a matter of personal concern. In turn, image building is another important function of management.

## Management and members of an organization

Image building is a fundamental task facing new organizations, and it is an important task when recruiting new people into an organization. As we saw in Chapter 8, control between a bureaucracy and its environment and control within a bureaucracy depend on the mental images that make cybernets possible. Without control through communication, the process of management cannot foster the collective intent necessary to secure procedures for elaborating and administering substantive guidelines and pursue the desired political action. Similarly, the process of management must control "noise," lest the desires and goals of individuals distort the collective intent necessary for achieving organizational goals.

Organizational goals are guides to action for the members of an organization (Mohr, 1973:477). In large organizations, as we shall see, it is virtually impossible to get all members of the organization to see organizational goals from a common perspective. Hence management faces two tasks in fostering the collective intent necessary for pursuing organizational goals:

1. Using the cybernetic system in bureaucracies, management must foster collective intent among as many employees of the organization as possible.

2. Using the cybernetic system, management must administratively coordinate different perspectives on organizational goals so that comprehensive administrative action is consistent with the image of organizational goals held by top administrative personnel.

White (1961:188, 190, 199) describes a medium sized metallurgical company in which the delegation of authority fostered in each division manager a loyalty to the autonomy, specialized goals, and ideological perspective of his department. Without managerial coordination, conflicts among departments erupted and decision making became more and more oriented to the internal disagreements over autonomy and goals. These chronic conflicts led to reassignments of responsibility and department reorganizations of some departments to help foster shared common goals for the company and an acceptance of the distinct role of each department. White's discussion is particularly helpful in illustrating the two tasks noted above. Given the nature of this company and its functions, particularly the distinction between research and development and production, it is extremely difficult to foster collective intent among all workers. In this case the conflicts were sharp, particularly because the production department wished to minimize the cost of production, while the research and development department wished to maximize quality and consistency. Hence the alternative strategy for fostering collective intent necessary for achieving the organizational objectives rested on continued attempts to coordinate department activities through reassignment, reorganization, and the administrative work of middle-level management.

### Maintenance and leadership

Within an organization, bureaucratic management must provide for three stages of image building and maintenance: building collective intent necessary to foster procedures for elaborating and administering substantive guidelines and pursuing desired political action, maintaing this collective intent, and adapting or modifying this collective intent as extraordinary events require. Managerial leadership is particularly relevant to the building and adapting phases. Because short-run and long-run changes are likely to occur during the history of an organization, the paradox of management appears here as well. Often the demands for adaptation occur simultaneously with the need to maintain collec-

tive intent. Clearly, the demands on management for adaptation and maintenance are not necessarily consistent. In fact, Blau (1960:41) argues that the methods and procedures for orderly performance and coordination sometimes impede initiative and creativity, and vice versa. On the one hand the process of management must encourage flexibility, inject new ideas into an organization, foster initiative, and permit innovation (see Dimock, 1959:121). On the other hand management must encourage regularity, routine, and stability to pursue effectively its established organizational goals.

### Overview

Management is a process of shaping and sharing power so that an organization can pursue its goals. In power channels the process of management must maintain existing power relations whenever possible or adapt to radical changes that are beyond the control of the management process. Internally the process of management must build the collective intent necessary for pursuing organizational goals, maintain that collective intent once formed, and adapt that collective intent when change requires. All these functions involve the exercise of power, primarily through cybernets that control behavior through various forms of communication. Further, the functions of management illustrate a fundamental paradox: the need for managerial leadership to adapt to radical changes in the power channel, build collective intent, and modify collective intent, and the need for managerial maintenance to counteract the exercise of power in channel systems and maintain collective intent among the members of an organization so that the pursuit of organizational goals is possible. And so we return to a question raised earlier: How can the process of management balance the need for leadership with the need for organizational stability?

## MANAGERIAL LEADERSHIP

Managerial leadership serves three basic functions: adapting to radical changes in the balance of power in power channels, building collective intent that fosters organizational goals within an organization, and adapting or modifying that collective intent as changes in the power channel require. How are these functions filled? What conditions are most conducive to managerial leadership?

### Recruitment

In Chapter 7 we saw that recruitment tends to enhance leadership potential in a bureaucracy if recruitment succeeds in bringing into an organization individuals or groups with unusual talent or unusual social resources. If recruitment is a means to bring vitality, initiative, flexibility, and innovation into a bureaucracy, we must answer two questions (see Dimock, 1959: 5). How are these special talents or social resources related to vitality, initiative, flexibility, and innovation? How are these special talents or social resources converted to power in a cybernetic system?

***Recruiting for change.*** At least two methods are appropriate for recruiting personnel who will foster vitality and change in an organization: recruit those with attitudes consistent with a desired change, and recruit those with strong ties to professional societies noted for innovation. The following example will illustrate how attitudes and ties to professional societies can foster vitality, initiative, and innovation and how these attitudes and professional ties might be converted to power in a cybernetic system.

Suppose you are the administrator of an old hospital where nursing care traditionally has been custodial and functional. Under this system the nurses, orderlies, and nursing assistants act as caretakers, with the custodial duties such as hygiene and distributing medicines functionally divided among the staff members. Recently the press has criticized your administration, comparing your nursing care unfavorably with the therapeutic or primary nursing used in a new hospital in another part of town. Under this system of nursing, the staff emphasizes personal relations with each patient, and one staff member performs all the nursing functions required by that patient. After examining the matter closely, you decide to implement therapeutic nursing in your hospital.

At this point two options are available. First, you may simply order the nurses, orderlies, and nursing assistants to attend training programs that will prepare them for therapeutic nursing. Once the training sessions are completed, you may then order immediate implementation of therapeutic nursing. Second, you may decide to implement the therapeutic nursing program gradually. To do so, you begin hiring nurses committed to therapeutic care. In addition you attempt to recruit nurses who have strong ties to professional societies that emphasize the virtues of therapeutic nursing. Further, you decide to concentrate your new recruits in a few wards and require the other staff members in these wards to attend training programs on therapeutic nursing. Once the training programs are complete, you immediately implement therapeutic nursing in wards where new recruits have been assigned.

Following the first strategy, you have no guarantee that the training programs have altered the attitudes of staff members toward nursing. In fact, the chances are good that considerable resistance to the new program will emerge among those who by habit and tradition have practiced under the custodial system. Further, chances are good that the program will not be implemented smoothly or quickly. In short, you have implemented a policy and must wait while attitudes become congruent with the policy. Meanwhile, bitterness, resentment, and resistance may decrease the efficiency and effectiveness of nursing care.

Following the second strategy, you have introduced a policy into wards where key personnel already share attitudes consistent with that policy. In addition you provide for the previous staff new recruits that serve as role models for proper therapeutic nursing. During conversations and in action, the new recruits can more readily justify and explain the new policy than can your formal command implementing that policy. Your new recruits serve as opinion leaders, smoothing the transition from custodial nursing to therapeutic nursing.

*Change.* There are a number of situations where management chooses to initiate planned change (Pearlin, 1962:325). In 1953 Kenneth Clark (1953:74) argued that the use of power to change behavior eventually compels compatible accommodation of attitudes. This is, of course, the logic of the first strategy for implementing therapeutic nursing. But power is more effective in reforming attitudes when supporting leadership accompanies the policies implementing a change in behavior (Pearlin, 1962:325). This is the logic of the second strategy for implementing therapeutic nursing. In a study of mental hospitals Pearlin (1962:332-334) found that registered nurses who were members of professional societies emphasizing treatment values were more supportive of the change to therapeutic nursing and that their behavior and attitudes served as a model on which their subordinates could pattern their own behavior under the new policy. Further, these key personnel helped reduce opposition to new policies, as long as opinions and policies were congruent.

*Expertise.* In the preceding paragraphs, we made passing reference to nurses with strong ties to professional societies. The role of professional memberships should not be discounted. Professionally active job occupants—those with regular ties to progressive professional societies—might introduce new ideas into a bureaucratic organization, many of which are directly re-

lated to reforming procedures for elaborating and administering the substantive guidelines for desired political action. Hage and Aiken (1967:508) point out that professional activities of staff members serve as communication links between an organization and its competitors and provide a source of new ideas and techniques.

Hage and Aiken raise another issue relevant to managerial leadership. Large numbers of occupational specialties in an organization act as a dynamic force for program change in the organization, because each group competes with the other in demonstrating the superiority of their ideas and techniques to central decision makers. When expertise cybernets complement command cybernets, the continued flow of competing ideas and techniques can produce a variety of programs and rapid programs change. As professional societies encourage new ideas and techniques, these competing professional groups will quickly introduce the ideas and techniques, argue their superiority, and urge program change or suggest that new programs be implemented. With these dynamic forces at work, an organization can experience rapid program development and change.

*Three roads to rapid change.* In the discussion thus far, we have identified three means through which recruitment dramatically can enhance managerial leadership and organizational change. Recruitment of personnel with attitudes supportive of a policy change can dramatically increase the rate of change once a new policy is implemented. Recruitment of personnel with strong ties to professional societies can rapidly increase the rate of program change in an organization. Recruitment of diverse professional specialities can rapidly increase the rate of program change in an organization. Fig. 9-1 illustrates each of these mechanisms.

**Managerial succession.** Most enduring organizations experience regular change of key authorities. In many smaller organiza-

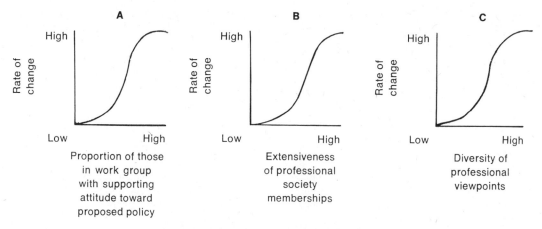

**Fig. 9-1.** Recruitment and program change.

tions the replacement or succession of these key authorities often produces instability, staff conflict, and lower morale because members of an organization tend to identify the organization with key personalities (see Grusky, 1960:105-115). In large organizations succession typically is more routine and less disruptive because increased bureaucratization provides a more rational basis for the succession of key authorities (Grusky, 1961:261-269; see also Kriesberg, 1962:355-359). In short, large organizations tend to divorce office from personality, while smaller organizations tend to fuse the two.

In smaller organizations the process of management is typically bound to the particular individuals holding kep positions of influence in the organization. When succession occurs in smaller organizations, the new authorities typically replace their immediate subordinates (see Grusky, 1961:267). These strategic replacements are part of a power struggle over the process of management. Controlling the management process, the new authorities can impress their personalities and wills on the organization.

Something quite different tends to occur in larger organizations. Here strategic replacements are minimal, but the average rate of succession among key personnel is higher in the larger organizations than in the smaller ones. This higher rate of succession helps larger organizations foster change by maintaining flexibility and injecting new ideas with the periodic change in key authorities. (Grusky, 1961:269). Nor is this repeated injection of new ideas random. The career patterns of top administrative authorities help foster succession of authorities and hence changes in the process of management within a large organization. Top administrators are typically itinerants: people with national reputations who advance by moving from one administrative position to another (Kriesberg, 1962:357). And once again, the ideas and techniques of confederates and competitors in the power channel might be carried from one organization to another. Through the command cybernet in bureaucracies and through the expertise cybernets, many of these ideas and techniques may change organizational behavior.

*Succession and change.* Managerial succession suggests two additional ways through which recruitment can enhance organizational change. In smaller organizations, where the collective image of an organization reflects the dominant personalities of a few key individuals, succession

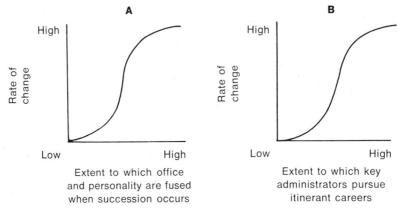

**Fig. 9-2.** Managerial succession and program change.

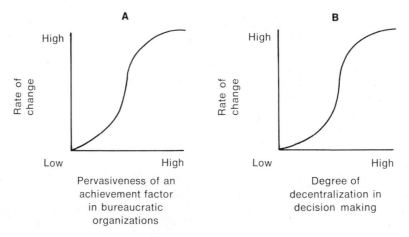

**Fig. 9-3.** Program change.

and strategic replacement alter the process of management to reflect the new personalities and different intentions. In larger organizations, where the key offices are divorced from individual personalities, rapid succession of itinerant authorities helps inject new ideas and techniques and helps one organization keep abreast of another. Fig. 9-2 illustrates each of these mechanisms.

**Personnel systems**

Two models of personnel systems were identified in Chapter 7. Of these, the innovation model is particularly appropriate to our discussion of managerial leadership. This model rests on an achievement motive. McClelland (1961) defined the achievement motive as a desire to perform to standards of excellence or a desire to succeed in competitive situations. A personnel system emphasizing achievement tends to motivate higher levels of work performance, brings more vitality into an organization, and fosters competitive pressures toward change and innovation. This achievement factor can permeate an organization, entering into the command, expertise, and gossip cybernets. In turn this pervasive emphasis on achievement provides a continual control over behavior, demanding higher levels of performance and more quality performance from agency personnel. Lawler (1973:22) concludes that achievement motivates behavior when the task to be performed is moderately challenging (about fifty-fifty chance of success); in competitive situations, where performance depends on an important skill; and in situations where performance feedback is given. While the achievement motive might bring vitality and innovation into an organization, it can be disruptive of stable procedures and can foster the intent of individuals over the collective intent necessary for pursuing organizational goals.

Personnel systems and other devices that foster achievement can introduce flexibility and the potential for rapid change into an organization. Fig. 9-3 illustrates the relation between an achievement motive and the potential for change.

### Decentralization

In their classic study of organizational change Coch and French (1948:512-532) found that decentralization of decision making in bureaucracies reduces the resistance to change among bureaucrats. More important, Hage and Aiken (1967:510) found that participation in decision making is directly related to program change in bureaucratic organizations. Apparently, decentralization fosters vitality and change by reducing the chances of a centralized veto, encouraging continued exchange of diverse opinions and perspectives, and giving several people a stake in the organizational goals and survival of an organization (see also Thompson, 1965:10-13).

Decentralization, it appears, is another source of organizational leadership. Maximizing diversity of opinion, decentralization might foster vitality and flexibility that reduces the resistance to change while promoting initiative and innovation. Fig. 9-3 illustrates decentralization as a tool for managerial leadership and change.

### MANAGERIAL MAINTENANCE

Managerial maintenance is the second side of management. Because no organization can survive without some stability in its work relations, the primary tasks of managerial maintenance are (1) maintaining the collective intent among organization members that is necessary for the pursuit of organizational goals and (2) maintaining a favorable balance of power in the power channel. Accomplishing these tasks gives bureaucratic organization its appearance of order and stability. To maintain stability, management must minimize the disturbances to patterned activity while maintaining adequate motivation among the members of an organization (see Chapple and Sayles, 1961:46-58).

### Attitudes

Working through bureaucratic cybernets, management must foster and maintain collective intent. But what is this collective intent? How does management foster and maintain it? Collective intent is not identical with commands issued by key officials. And we have seen that command alone is not sufficient to foster or maintain collective intent, because the behavior so ordered might be inconsistent with prevailing attitudes. In turn, resistance to policy helps reduce effectiveness and efficiency, at least until attitudes become more congruent with the expected behavior.

The key to collective intent and its maintenance lies in image building: how members of an organization acquire a mental image of their role in an organization and how that image somehow complements the mental image held by key authorities in the organization (Boulding, 1961:57). Here management faces a critical problem. The existence of several roles in an organization leads role occupants to see the organization in peculiar ways, colored by a set of perceptions, attitudes, and values (see Mannheim, 1936). Quite often these perceptions, attitudes, and values are inconsistent with the overall image of an organization and lead role occupants to behaviors inconsistent with organizational goals. If the behaviors of different units within an organization can be coordinated, collective intent is possible. If these resulting behaviors are not coordinated, the different perspectives, attitudes, and values are dysfunctional for the overall goals of the organization (see Evan, 1962:346-354).

Mead (1964:276) points out that individuals find it easiest to integrate their behaviors with that of others when they all are members of the same functional group: those individuals sharing common perspectives, attitudes, values, and purposes. Individuals find it most difficult to integrate their behaviors with those of others when these people are members of different functional groups: those individuals with widely separate perspectives, attitudes, values, and purposes. To remedy the problem of poor integration Mead (1964: 268) recommends reconstructions of particular social situations and modifications of social relationships to decrease the social distance between occupants of different roles in a complex social setting.

Mead's strategy is rather subtle. He does not propose a pep rally, such as that used by McDonald Corporation in training supervisors. And the strategy goes beyond management sessions where grievances are aired and where key officials supposedly reach some understanding of each other. Rather, Mead might propose manipulating the experience of supervisors so they interact with members of different functional groups, observe firsthand the activities and concerns of other functional groups, or rotate functional assignments on a periodic basis. Attitudes most conducive to collective intent arise from experiencing the diverse activities of an organization (see also Kuhn, 1970:187). Images of each functional group remain, but the experience of diverse activities helps supervisors to integrate these images and thus foster the

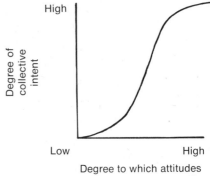

**Fig. 9-4.** Attitudes and collective intent.

collective intent and coordinated behavior necessary for pursuing organizational goals. Fig. 9-4 illustrates the impact of diverse experiences on fostering collective intent within an organization.

**Expertise**

In Chapter 8 we found that expertise cybernets often complement command cybernets. This occurs because complex organizations usually reflect a number of specialities, with considerable training required for each occupation and some degree of professional activity linking the organization to its environment (see Hage and Aiken, 1967:507). When these complex structures pursue organizational goals, power often is distributed widely across several decision makers (Zald, 1962: 336). In his study of five correctional institutions, for example, Zald (1962:335-345) found that delegation of authority tends to follow organizational complexity and the number of goals pursued.

Consider three forms of command cybernets outlined by Victor Vroom (1976:630-631): autocratic, consultative, and group decision making. In the first, a key administrator takes primary responsibility for a decision, at most seeking only information from subordinates. In the second, the key

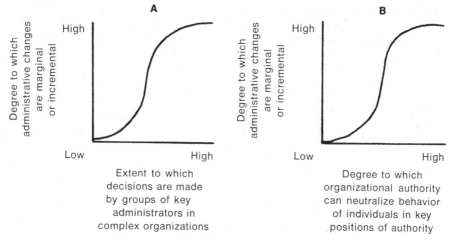

**Fig. 9-5.** Incremental administrative changes.

administrator consults with and seeks the opinion of subordinates before making a decision. In the third, the key administrator acts as a group chairman, and alternatives are generated and evaluated by a group of subordinate administrators. In complex organizations the complexity of issues, the range of alternatives, and the difficulty of evaluation often move decision making from an autocratic to a group form of decision making.

Group decision making tends to foster managerial maintenance. When issues and alternatives are evaluated by a group of key administrators, each administrator can explain the impact of various alternatives on his or her department, and each administrator can act as an advocate of the department's interest. Under these conditions the alternatives adopted are more likely to introduce marginal changes in procedure and desired political action and less likely to introduce sweeping changes. Fig. 9-5 illustrates the impact of shared decision making on the stability of a complex organization.

**Managerial succession**

Few large organizations can tolerate the disruptions of work routines and the power struggles that often accompany changes of management in smaller organizations. Managerial succession in larger organizations is, therefore, typically routinized so that the impact of changing personnel is minimized while there still is some room to absorb the new ideas and techniques brought to an organization from other organizations. Clearly, the balance between minimizing the impact of succession and maximizing the benefits from succession is crucial for complex organizations. Sometimes shake-ups do occur, and these radical changes often disrupt the stability of an enduring organization. Normally, however, the new ideas imported into an organization through itinerant administrators result in incremental or marginal changes that are absorbed readily by the bureaucratic organization (Galbraith, 1958:102). The extent to which an organization neutralizes the power of any key individual is directly related to incremental changes and hence to organizational stability. Fig. 9-5 illustrates this relation.

**Differentiation**

Differentiation is another managerial device for maintaining stability in large organizations. Differentiation is the division of an organization into several components along any of a number of dimensions, such as occupational, functional, geographical, and hierarchical (see Blau, 1970:201; Fesler, 1976;227-249). We have already seen that the formal structure of an organization tends to reflect the complexity of work carried out by that organization (see Blau, 1970:201-218; Udy, 1959:582-584). Among several others, Udy (1959:583-584) argues that there is a limit to the number of tasks to which any one person can give adequate attention during a set period. In turn this limit fixes the maximum number of subordinates that can be supervised effectively, depending on the number of tasks performed by each subordinate. The attention span required of a supervisor is therefore a composite of the number of tasks, the number of specialized operations simultaneously performed, and whether there is combined effort in the work process. If the required attention span exceeds a certain limit, the organization will likely develop three or more levels of authority for managing the organization. (Udy sets the attention span at five, beyond which an organization will develop three or more levels of authority.)

Blau (1970:212, 213) also points out that expanding organizations typically subdivide responsibilities to facilitate supervision by narrowing the span of control exercised by first-line supervisors. Here a curious problem emerges. On the one hand, structural differentiation creates homogeneous supervisory tasks for first-line supervisors. On the other hand, the same structural differentiation creates problems of coordination for supervisors at higher levels. While first-line supervisors take charge of larger numbers of people performing homogeneous tasks, the number of middle-management positions must expand to meet the demands for coordination at higher levels. Blau argues that the division of labor makes duties less complex, but the organizational structure more complex.

How does this differentiation contribute to organizational stability? First, the increased interdependency of units within the organization requires stable, routine coordination. Disturbances in any portion of this complex system will be transmitted throughout the organization because this complex interdependency usually implies that the work of one unit is essential for the continued work in another unit. Hence middle management must exert strong pressures to maintain routine coordination,

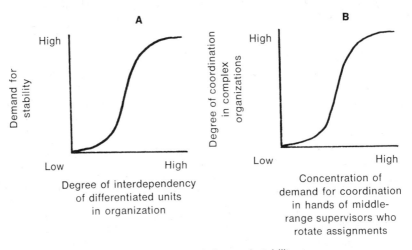

**Fig. 9-6.** Differentiation and stability.

lest operations in the entire organization be damaged. Second, when the task of co-ordination falls on middle management there are proportionately fewer people in the organization who must share the comprehensive organizational image necessary for pursuing organizational goals. Concentrating primarily on these middle-range supervisors, it is much easier to implement Mead's strategy for molding attitudes by shifting supervisory assignments so they can oversee different jobs and problems. These relations are illustrated in Fig. 9-6.

### Centralization

Earlier we saw that decentralization could foster administrative vitality and diversity. By the same token, however, that vitality and diversity might hamper organizational effectiveness and efficiency by undermining stability. The father of classical bureaucratic theory, Max Weber, (1947:334-340) argues that centralization is necessary for efficiency, precision, stability, and reliability.

In complex power channels, decentralization often is inadequate to pursue the desired political action embodied in organizational goals. According to Becker (1965: 37,39), the very fact that centralized power

enhances effectiveness and efficiency helps alter the stable self-balancing equilibrium of power in the power channel. Some organization will, during a given period, exercise its centralized power in the channel system. This prospect in turn requires other organizations to centralize power for meeting the challenge. In short, it is the power of managerial leadership that generates the need for centralization to stabilize an organization and the power channel of which it is a part. Suppose one organization centralizes power to regularize the work activity of the organization and neutralize the encroachment of other members in the channel system. By so doing, the organization begins to dominate the channel system it once sought to neutralize. Finally, these powerful managerial forces create a need for powerful management in other organizations, thereby creating a stalemate of managerial superpowers in the channel system (see Becker, 1965:43-44).

Managerial leadership might disrupt a power channel and thereby require other organizations to centralize power. When other members of the power channel have centralized power, the disruptive influence of managerial leadership can be neutral-

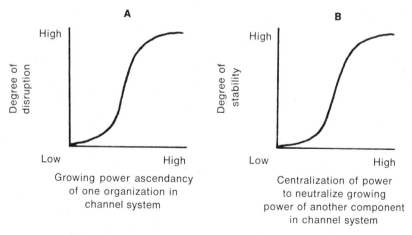

**Fig. 9-7.** Centralization and power channel stability.

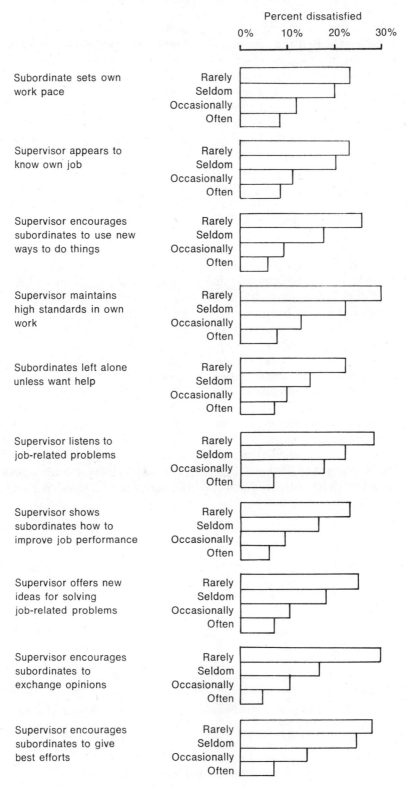

**Fig. 9-8.** Supervision and job dissatisfaction. Data from Institute for Social Research, Social Science Archive. Quality of Employment Study (1972-1973) was conducted by Robert P. Quinn, Thomas W. Magione, and Stanley E. Seashore.

ized and stability regained. Fig. 9-7 illustrates this process.

## Morale

The final managerial device for maintaining organizational stability is employee morale. Morale is critical to managerial maintenance because job satisfaction—how workers feel about their jobs—is bound intricately with such factors as absenteeism, turnover, and even strikes (see Lawler, 1973:43-44). We have explicitly excluded job performance from this list because the relation between job satisfaction and job performance is ambiguous. Lawler (1973:85) notes that job performance derives from efforts to obtain desired goals and outcomes, while satisfaction derives from the outcomes people actually obtain.

Morale can contribute to organizational stability, but the process of maintaining morale is rather complex. Two matters are particularly relevant: matching personal visions of the good life with working conditions and providing appropriate supervision for workers. Job satisfaction might be a means for improving the quality of life in society (see Gardner, 1968:25; Argyris, 1957). But in modern society it is much easier to recruit personnel with personal visions consistent with the out-

comes available from working than it is to alter working conditions to match personal vision. Hence the first task in building morale rests with recruitment. For example, most organizations avoid hiring people who are overqualified for a job, partly because the new employee probably will not be satisfied with the job.

Appropriate supervision can foster morale once an employee enters an organization. Although the matter is complex and varies from organization to organization, some trends in supervision tend to reduce job dissatisfaction.

Fig. 9-8 suggests a number of supervisory strategies for reducing job dissatisfaction. For example, the sample data indicates that a supervisor who lets subordinates set their own work pace has fewer dissatisfied employees than a supervisor who does not allow such flexibility. In many mass production organizations, of course, it is not feasible to allow the employee to set his or her own work pace. But from the data in Fig. 9-8, other strategies are available. For example, the supervisor might pay increased attention to discussions with employees over job-related problems. This strategy appears to reduce job dissatisfaction, as does the strategy of offering employees new ideas for solving job-related problems. From the wide array

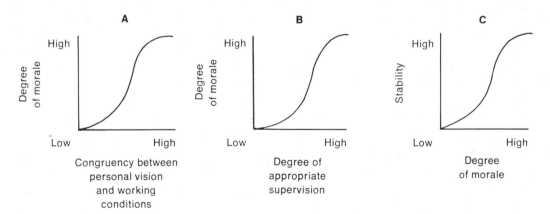

**Fig. 9-9.** Morale and organizational stability.

of options in Fig. 9-8, most organizations can implement at least some of these supervisory strategies for reducing job dissatisfaction.

In summary, morale can foster organizational stability by reducing absenteeism, employee turnover, and perhaps strikes. To foster morale, management must match personal visions of the good life with working conditions during recruitment and then provide a supervisory setting that encourages job satisfaction. Fig. 9-9 illustrates these relations.

## STABILITY AND CHANGE

In our discussion we have identified seven methods of fostering managerial leadership and six methods of fostering managerial maintenance. Undoubtedly other factors not discussed here contribute to managerial leadership and managerial maintenance. However, some interesting characteristics of the 13 factors help explain how the process of management balances the needs for leadership and the needs for stability. Each of the 13 factors is a gradient: decision makers can utilize each method with varying degrees of intensity. Eleven of the 13 factors may be pursued simultaneously. Only the centralization-decentralization dilemma requires that one be sacrificed in favor of the other. But even here there is a continuum between centralization and decentralization, and key decision makers can shift the distribution of power along this continuum as conditions require. At any time, the factors fostering managerial leadership and the factors fostering managerial maintenance comprise a dynamic system of checks and balances. When conditions require, decision makers can shift the system of checks and balances toward leadership or toward maintenance, thereby allowing the equilibrium to shift from time to time.

Now it should be clear why we look at management as a process rather than a collection of authorities. A process implies on-going operations. Whitehead (1929:174) observed that process is the growth and attainment of a final end. At the beginning of this chapter bureaucratic management was defined as the process through which bureaucracies pursue their internal and external goals. In Whitehead's terms, the organizational goals are the final end. In turn management reflects the growth and attainment aspects of Whitehead's formulation. Growth and attainment are dynamic matters, and so too is management.

## MOTIVATION

Management seeks to maintain organizational stability while making the changes necessitated by events in the channel system and developments in expert knowledge. But regardless of the managerial task at hand, key administrators face another problem: motivating the performance of their subordinates to maximize the effectiveness and efficiency of the organization. Without proper motivation an individual might perform at 20% to 30% of his or her ability and meet minimal job requirements, assuming that personnel and jobs are matched properly in the first place. Proper motivation can raise the level of performance to 80% or 90% of an employee's ability (Hersey and Blanchard, 1972:5). With discrepancies of this magnitude, motivation is a key problem that must be resolved through the management process.

Recruitment that adequately matches personnel and job does not solve the problem of motivation. Nor does the use of job training programs. In fact, some job training programs might generate unintended consequences that undermine employee motivation. In their study of job training programs Vincent and Keedy (1958:192-195) found that a majority of workers taking a job training program thought they had gained more working skill. However, only 39% of the respondents felt that the training program improved their productivity. Equally fascinating, 62% felt dissatisfied that job advancement did not follow training as fast as they had expected. For these workers the job training program appeared to be an incentive for advancement, not an incentive toward greater job performance.

### Motivation and behavior

Motivation is goal-directed behavior. For organizations, these goals somehow must be congruent with the overall goals of the organization. Where do these personal goals come from? How are these personal goals made congruent with the overall organizational goals? Ultimately, a theory of motivation is a theory of controlled behavior (see Lawler, 1973:5; Hersey and Blanchard, 1972:10-13). Only a theory of controlled behavior could account for goal-directed behavior among employees that simultaneously serves the larger organizational goals. In Chapter 8 we established the foundations for such a theory: cybernetics is the control of human behavior through communication.

***X and Y theories.*** Any control theory of human behavior implies some assumptions about human nature. McGregor (1960) proposed one classic dichotomy of managerial approaches to human nature. McGregor calls one perspective theory X and the other perspective theory Y. From the first perspective, people dislike work and avoid it when possible, thereby requiring management to coerce people to work toward organizational goals; but when work is necessary, the individual dislikes responsibility, has little ambition, prefers supervision over self-direction, and desires security (McGregor, 1960:33,34). From the second perspective, people like work if conditions are satisfying and thus will exercise self-direction and self-control in pursuing organizational objectives and derive satisfaction and self-actualization from work, accept responsibility, and exercise vitality and innovation in the work effort (McGregor, 1960:47-48).

Clearly, the implications of each theory suggest different control measures. If people really dislike work, the costs of not working must be kept very high (and this might well include minimizing welfare support) and the costs of poor performance must be maximized (the threat of job loss is one obvious technique). If, on the other hand, people have no natural aversion to work, administrators should concentrate on those working conditions that facilitate goal-directed behavior, self-control, self-direction, the willingness to accept responsibility, and the opportunity to exercise vitality and innovation in the work effort, so long as these are consistent with overall organizational goals.

Of course, there is something wrong with both images. They are too extreme, too certain about the cause of job performance and the promise of job performance. Work situations illustrate various combinations of both types: people who are motivated toward the higher levels of performance and people who avoid doing any more than is absolutely necessary to maintain job security. The diversity we see among people at work undermines the notion that there is one element of human nature governing an individual's approach to work.

***Human behavior.*** Our discussion of human behavior starts with this fundamental premise: there is no such thing as human nature independent of a social setting (Geertz, 1965:112). From this perspective we focus on the interaction of the human organism and its environment. Human behavior is a product of this interaction (see Etkin, 1967; Hinde, 1974). Let us schematically examine some of the major elements in this model of organism-environment interaction. The human organism has two systems of immediate relevance here.

First, the normal human organism has a complex system for receiving stimuli from the environment, which either activates the organism for response or inhibits the stimuli from activating the organism. We know that the senses receive far more stimuli from the environment than the nervous system can possibly handle. However, some of these stimuli do activate the organism for response, while others simply are shut off and not transferred to the nervous system for further processing. During sleep, for example, the body must minimize the stimuli reaching the central nervous system to allow rest. Even while awake we never become conscious of all the sensations impinging on the body, because we cannot absorb all these stimuli without overloading the central nervous system and thus transforming all stimuli into chaotic noise.

Second, the normal human organism has a complex neurosystem that integrates the drive states and past experiences, allowing an organism to reflect on alternatives before responding to particular stimuli (see Mead, 1964:115-198). Precisely what these drive states entail is open to question. Freud spoke of two fundamental drives: eros (love) and thanatos (death). Some behavioral biologists speak of sexual response capacities and aggressive response capacities. For convenience, suppose the drive states parallel Maslow's (1968) hierarchy of needs: physiological needs such as food, clothing, and shelter; safety or security; social needs such as the need for group ties and group acceptance; esteem or recognition; and self-actualization, or the need to maximize one's potential.

The complex neurosystem that integrates drive states and past experiences is the mechanism through which the mind pays attention to some stimuli from the environment but not others. Mead (1964: 139) suggests that attention implies a mechanism that allows us to select and order different stimuli, relate these stimuli to each other and to past experiences, and then to prepare an appropriate response. In addition, those drive states most dominant at any particular time will influence the stimuli selected and ordered by this mental mechanism.

From the environment, people receive the changing stimuli that activate the nervous system. (The drive states might also activate the nervous system to search out stimuli in the environment). As the nervous system receives environmental stimu-

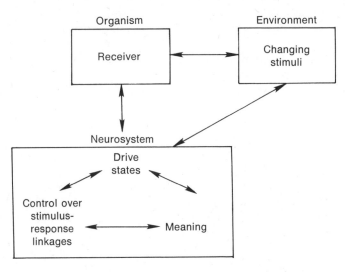

**Fig. 9-10.** Organism, environment and behavior.

li and activates responses, a "meaning" becomes attached to this package of stimulus and response. Meaning, Mead (1964:165) points out, is not a state of consciousness but the relation between a stimulus and a response as it occurs in the course of experience. In a concrete application of Mead's insight, McClelland (1951) discovered that individuals who experience pleasure or pain during a work task attach the "meaning" (in this case the sensation of pleasure or pain) to the cues present when the experience occurs. When the cues reappear, the feelings of pleasure or pain are reactivated. Most of us can easily recall such symbolic associations. A song might remind us of a past experience, an object might remind us of someone we once knew, and so on.

Although brief and simplified, our discussion of human behavior provides a background for a theory of controlled behavior. Fig. 9-10 illustrates our discussion of human behavior as a product of organism-environment interaction.

### Controlled behavior

In Chapter 8 we saw that communication helps build images (meaning) and allows cybernets to control behavior through further communication. These images are a set of control mechanisms—plans, recipes, rules, instructions—for the governing of behavior (Geertz, 1965:106-107). We have seen that an organization becomes "infused with value" when the members of that organization acquire a mental image of the organization, especially its meaning and its purpose. If images govern behavior, they must exist and be communicated to new recruits. We briefly discussed each of these matters in Chapter 8, so now let us examine the process of image building and image communication more closely.

*Image building.* Our diagram of human behavior in Fig. 9-10 suggests several propositions that help us understand image

building. The image is intimately associated with the interaction patterns of an organization (Mead, 1964:164). The meaning of an organization cannot be found in its organization charts or procedural handbooks. Rather, the meaning lies in how the charts and procedures are translated into action. Stated differently, meaning is experience (Mead, 1964:179).

The accumulated experiences in a given social process comprise a set of organized attitudes (Mead, 1964:187). The central nervous system stores experiences and constructs or reconstructs these experiences into a composite picture, or gestalt, of the organization (Mead:187-191). How attitudes are organized reflects the correspondence between drive states, ongoing experiences, and the range of responses available for any given communication. This might sound rather complex, but it simply means that our feelings about an organization are the product of how work experience reinforces or denies basic needs and how well our efforts produce the expected results (see Lawler, 1973:41-60).

The organization of attitudes is partly social or shared, because ongoing experience reflects the attitudes of others toward us and the expectations of others. Compare the private part of attitudes to "play" and the social part of attitudes to "games." During play we have broad discretion over stimuli and our responses. We may create stimuli almost at will (imagine a small child on a playground), and we may respond to these stimuli any way that suits our fancy. But when we play a game there are rules, and we must know what other people are going to do to partake in the game. Games require some form of social organization, reflected in the shared attitudes of the participants, so that the behavior of one individual calls out the appropriate behavior in another individual (see Mead, 1964:215-218).

Work is like a game. The ongoing experiences we accumulate tend to reflect the shared expectations of other people in the work setting. These expectations might be called the "rules of the game." These rules are social, and they help govern the behavior of individuals. These rules constitute the structure of social interaction in a work setting. Cybernets help maintain images by communicating to an individual that a rule has been broken and communicating to the individual the expected behavior under future circumstances (see Mead, 1964:223).

**Work setting.** Clearly, we cannot construct an organizational image like we build a machine. Nor, however, can we afford to ignore the problem of image building, particularly if the organizational image is a control mechanism for governing behavior. While we cannot create an organizational image, we can manipulate the conditions from which organizational images arise. Two factors are particularly important: the degree to which a job situation satisfies personal needs (the intrinsic quality of work) and the degree to which interpersonal influences conform to the collective intent necessary for the pursuit of organizational goals.

Although personal needs vary from individual to individual and within one individual over time, most individuals have one need or a set of needs that usually is dominant, such as the need for security or the need for esteem. Matching job requirements with personnel qualifications does not always guarantee that a job will meet personal needs. Rather, efforts must be made to match the intrinsic quality of jobs to the needs of personnel. This can be accomplished through job assessments and personality inventories. For job assessment we attempt to identify the types of gratifications inherent in high job performance. For personality inventories we examine the general psychological disposition of each employee. Factors that foster the satisfaction of personal needs include (1) the recruitment of professionals who can imple-

ment the ideas current in their professional societies, (2) the recruitment of itinerant administrators who move to further their own careers, (3) the pervasive achievement factor for those who seek challenge in a job, and even (4) differentiation, where workers at the lower levels can satisy their needs for security and workers at higher levels can satisfy their needs for esteem, self-development, and the like. In addition, extrinsic rewards might be attached to jobs to enhance the satisfaction of personal needs. Among the more obvious extrinsic rewards are promotion possibilities, pay incentives, and administrative recognition for job performance.

For convenience, we can divide interpersonal influences into two categories: supervisor-subordinate and peer influence. In Fig. 9-8 we saw a number of ways in which supervisory behavior can affect job morale. In addition, supervisors control extrinsic rewards and also might serve an instrumental role in fostering the intrinsic qualities of work. Hence the supervisor is in a unique position to maximize the degree to which the job situation satisfies the personal needs of subordinates (see Lawler, 1973, 171-197). The strong impact of peer influence on workers has been well known since the Western Electric studies in the 1930s (Roethlisberger and Dickson, 1939). Within different departments of Western Electric some groups had norms favoring high productivity, while other groups had norms minimizing productivity. Highly cohesive work groups have more power over individuals than do more loosely organized work groups (see Lawler, 1973: 194). If group norms are negative, cohesive groups will be detrimental to effectiveness and efficiency. If these norms are positive, cohesive groups can enhance productivity. Negative norms in turn are likely to develop with high job dissatisfaction and distrust of administrators (see Lawler and Cammann, 1972). Several factors contribute to positive peer influence, among them (1) the recruitment of personnel with attitudes supportive of a desired change, (2) fostering a pervasive achievement factor in the organization, (3) decentralization of decision making, (4) molding attitudes to reflect the collective intent necessary for pursuing organizational goals, (5) using group decision making, and (6) fostering morale.

## CONCLUSION

Management is a process for shaping and sharing power in the pursuit of organizational goals. Management must balance procedures for change with procedures for maintaining stability. Seven factors help inject vitality, flexibility, initiative, and innovation into a bureaucratic organization: (1) recruitment of personnel with attitudes supportive of desired policy changes, (2) recruitment of personnel with strong ties to professional societies, (3) recruitment of professionals from diverse occupational specialties, (4) change of key administrative officials when office and personality are fused, (5) recruitment of itinerant administrators when office is divorced from personality, (6) fostering a pervasive achievement factor in the organization, and (7) the decentralization of decision making. Six factors contribute to organizational stability: (1) molding attitudes to reflect the collective intent necessary for pursuing organizational goals, (2) using group decision making, (3) routinizing authority, (4) differentiating complex organizations, (5) centralizing power, and (6) fostering morale.

While maintaining a balance between leadership and stability, the process of management seeks to motivate employees toward high levels of job performance. It is not coincidental that many of the 13 factors we have used to explain the process of management also foster motivation or high job performance. Motivation is goal-directed behavior, and the primary task confronting management is the merging of personal goals and organizational goals. To do so, management must control behavior, directing it in ways congruent with the collective intent necessary for pursuing organizational goals. Indirectly, management must foster an organizational image through experience and communication in the organization. More directly, management must maximize the degree to which a job situation satisfies personal needs and must maximize the degree to which interpersonal influences conform with organizational goals. Overall, the process of bureaucratic management is the source of motivation in complex organizations.

## REFERENCES

Argyris, C. *Personality and organization.* New York: Harper & Row, Publishers, 1957.

Becker, J. F. Social integration and the power to manage. *Quarterly Review of Economics and Business,* 1965, *5,* 37-45.

Blau, P. *Initiative and bureaucracy.* Public Administration Review, 1960, *20,* 41.

Blau, P. A formal theory of differentiation in organizations. *American Sociological Review,* 1970, *35,* 201-218.

Boulding, K. *The image.* Ann Arbor, Mich.: Ann Arbor Paperbacks, 1961.

Chapple, E. D., and Sayles, L. R. *The measure of management.* New York: Macmillan, Inc., 1961.

Clark, K. Desegregation: an appraisal of the evidence. *Journal of Social Issues,* 1953, *9,* 74.

Coch, L., and French, J., Jr. Overcoming resistance to change. *Human Relations,* 1948, *1,* 512-532.

Dimock, M. E. *Administrative vitality.* New York: Harper & Row, Publishers, 1959.

Etkin, W. *Social behavior from fish to man.* Chicago: University of Chicago Press, 1967.

Evan, W. M. Role strain and the norm of reciprocity in research organizations. *American Journal of Sociology,* 1962, *68,* 346-354.

Fesler, J. W. The basic theoretical question: how to relate area and function. In R. T. Golembiewski, F. Gibson, and G. Y. Cornog (Eds.), *Public Administration* (3rd ed.). Skokie, Ill.: Rand McNally & Co., 1976.

Galbraith, J. K. *The affluent society.* Boston: Houghton Mifflin Co., 1958.

Gardner, J. W. *No easy victories.* New York: Harper & Row, Publishers, 1968.

Geertz, C. The impact of the concept of culture on the concept of man. In J. R. Platt (Ed.), *New views on the nature of man.* Chicago: University of Chicago Press, 1965.

Grusky, O. Administrative succession in formal organizations. *Social Forces,* 1960, *39,* 105-115.

Grusky, O. Corporate size, bureaucratization and managerial succession. *American Journal of Sociology,* 1961, *67,* 261-269.

Hage, J., and Aiken, M. Program change and organizational properties: a comparative analysis. *American Journal of Sociology,* 1967, *72,* 503-519.

Hersey, P., and Blanchard, K. H. *Management of organizational behavior* (2nd ed.). Englewood Cliffs, N.J.: Prentice-Hall, Inc., 1972.

Hinde, R. A. *Biological bases of human social behavior.* New York: McGraw-Hill Book Co., 1974.

Kriesberg, L. Careers, organization size and succession. *American Journal of Sociology,* 1962, *68,* 355-359.

Kuhn, T. *The structure of scientific revolutions* (2nd ed.). Chicago: University of Chicago Press, 1970.

Lawler, E. E. III. *Motivation in work organizations.* Monterey, Calif.: Brooks/Cole Publishing Co., 1973.

Lawler, E. E. III, and Cammann, C. What makes a work group successful? In A. Morrow (Ed.), *The failure of success.* New York: Amacom, 1972.

Mannheim, K. *Ideology and Utopia.* New York: Harcourt Brace Jovanovich, Inc., Harvest Books, 1936.

Maslow, A. H. *Toward a psychology of being.* New York: Van Nostrand Reinhold Co., 1968.

McClelland, D. C. Measuring motivation in phantasy: the achievement motive. In H. Guetzkow (Ed.), *Groups, leadership and men.* Pittsburgh: Carnegie Press, 1951.

McClelland, D. C. *The achieving society.* New York: Van Nostrand Reinhold Co., 1961.

McGregor, D. M. *The human side of enterprise.* New York: McGraw-Hill Book Co., 1960.

Mead, G. H. *On social psychology* (A. Strauss, ed.). Chicago: University of Chicago Press, 1964.

Mohr, L. B. The concept of organizational goal. *American Political Science Review,* 1973, *67,* 475, 477.

Pearlin, L. I. Sources of resistance to change in a mental hospital. *American Journal of Sociology,* 1962, *68,* 325, 332-334.

Roethlisberger, F., and Dickson, W. *Management and the worker.* Cambridge, Mass.: Harvard University Press, 1939.

Sayles, L. R. The change process in organizations: an applied anthropology analysis. *Human Organization,* 1962, *21,* 62.

Selznick, P. Leadership in administration. In R. T. Golembiewski, F. Gibson, and G. Y. Cornog (Eds.), *Public Administration* (3rd ed.). Skokie, Ill.: Rand McNally & Co., 1976.

Thompson, V. Bureaucracy and innovation. *Administrative Science Quarterly,* 1965, *10,* 10-13.

Udy, S. H., Jr. The structure of authority in non-industrial production organizations. *American Journal of Sociology,* 1959, *64,* 582-584.

Vincent, M. J., and Keedy, T. C., Jr. Employee training and industrial morale. *Sociology and Social Research,* 1958, *42,* 192-195.

Vroom, V. A new look at managerial decision making. In R. T. Golembiewski, F. Gibson, and G. Y. Cornog (Eds.), *Public Administration* (3rd ed.). Skokie, Ill.: Rand McNally & Co., 1976.

Weber, M. *The theory of social and economic organization* (T. Parsons, ed. and trans.). New York: Free Press, 1947.

White, H. Management conflict and sociometric structure. *American Journal of Sociology,* 1961, *67,* 188, 190, 199.

Whitehead, A. N. *Process and reality.* New York: Free Press, 1929.

Zald, M. N. Organizational control structure in five correctional institutions. *American Journal of Sociology,* 1962, *68,* 335-345.

# CHAPTER 10

# Bureaucratic decision making

The scope and frequency of choices available to bureaucratic decision makers generally are limited at each stage of the decision-making process. Available information and the ability to use that information also limit choices. Under normal conditions, decision making is the application of algorithmic or heuristic rules for making choices.

## MAKING DECISIONS

Decision making is a process of choice leading to action (see Simon, 1976:1). Decisions are possible only when choices are available. However, as the number of available choices increases, the resulting action becomes less predictable (see Wald, 1965: 36-37). Conversely, as the number of available choices decrease, the resulting action becomes more predictable (see Benn and Weinstein, 1973:320). Fig. 10-1 illustrates this relation.

No society or organization can permit unlimited choice, because the resulting action would be shapeless, ungovernable, and chaotic (see Geertz, 1965:108). Hence choices must be limited. Two vehicles for limiting choices are particularly important: controlling the scope of choices and controlling the frequency of choices. The scope of choices refers to the number of options available for choice. The frequency of choices refers to the number of times choices must be made. As we reduce the scope of choices, the number of action-alternatives decreases accordingly. In both cases, as illustrated in Figs. 10-1, *B* and 10-1, *C*, reducing the scope or frequency of choice increases the predictability of action.

## Stages

Throughout this book a number of methods and structures that limit bureaucratic choices have been examined (see Gerth and Mills, 1958:196). To systematically review some of the major vehicles for limiting bureaucratic choice, decision making can be divided into five categories: defining a problem, establishing alternatives, choosing among alternatives, implementing the chosen alternative, and evaluating the resulting action (see Lasswell, 1956). At each stage, the scope and frequency of choice are limited. However, bureaucratic organizations tend to have greater choice at some of these stages than others. Further, as will be seen, bureaucratic choice more often is restricted through limiting the scope of choice than through limiting the frequency of choice.

***Defining problems and establishing alternatives.*** In Chapter 2 we saw that most societies have adjustive mechanisms for absorbing usual disturbances arising within and outside the society. Among these adjustive mechanisms are devices for social control, devices for production, and devices governing intersociety relations. These adjustive mechanisms help comprise a dynamic equilibrium: a range of possible states that a society might experience without requiring radical social change.

*Normal disturbances.* Suppose, as illustrated in Fig. 10-2, the range of states a

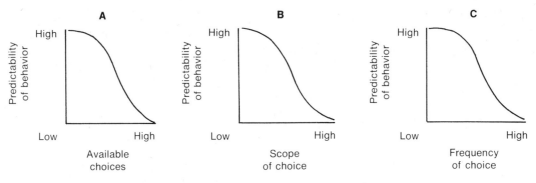

**Fig. 10-1.** Choice and predictable behavior.

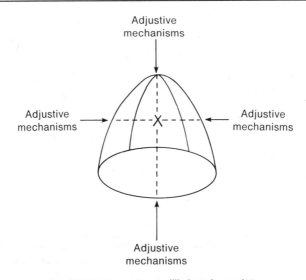

**Fig. 10-2.** Dynamic equilibrium in society.

society may experience is a "hat." At an imaginary point in the middle of this hat, all the adjustive mechanisms are in perfect balance. This point is the norm state for the given society. Normal disturbances will shift the balance away from this imaginary balance point, but the adjustive mechanisms will attempt to move the state of affairs closer to this norm state while making sure that the state of affairs does not slip beyond the borders of the hat itself.

Under normal conditions these adjustive mechanisms are linked together in a cybernetic system. One or more of the adjustive mechanisms becomes activated when in-

formation about the current state indicates movement from the norm state (the X in the center of the hat in Fig. 10-2)(see Vickers, 1970:148). Consider a simple case in which steady population growth requires increased production of food. Assuming increased production is possible or assuming that the needed food can be acquired elsewhere, actions will be taken to secure the needed food. In a market economy, for example, the increased demand for food might raise the price of food, thereby creating incentive for more food production because of increased profit.

The notion of dynamic equilibrium obscures two important aspects about available choices for decision making: the problem already is defined, once a norm state or goal exists; and the alternatives for addressing the problem are already established if adjustive mechanisms exist. In short, the existence of a dynamic equilibrium or the existence of a cybernetic control system suggests that the scope of choice in defining problems and elaborating alternatives has been restricted severely. Simply stated, when a society encounters disturbances, decision makers usually have an idea about what the problem is and what alternatives are available for addressing the problem.

Why is the scope of choice available to bureaucracy limited in the problem-defining stage and alternative-elaborating stage? In complex societies bureaucratic organizations provide the procedural devices through which existing adjustive mechanisms operate. Hence bureaucratic organizations form part of the dynamic equilibrium in complex societies, and they seldom are free to define new problems or to elaborate new alternatives. (The university may be an exception to this trend.) Bureaucratic organizations are components of complex power channels in which a dynamic equilibrium tends to govern the shaping and sharing of power among policy makers, policy administrators, and target clientele. Defining or redefining problems and elaborating new alternatives not only would upset the balance of power in a channel system but also would alter the channel system. Although such changes might occur, under normal circumstances there are strong pressures in the channel system against such changes.

*Radical disturbances.* Situations in which existing adjustive mechanisms could not absorb radical disturbances were discussed in Chapter 2. Under these conditions the scope of choice expands, allowing definitions of new problems and redefinitions of old problems and elaborating

new alternatives for addressing the problems defined. It was found that kinship, tradition, and ecclesiastical authority are too inflexible to allow radical change, whereas bureaucracy is more flexible. Expanding the argument in Chapter 2, it can now be seen that kinship, tradition, and ecclesiastical authority are not sufficiently flexible to allow choices at the first two stages of decision making: defining problems and elaborating alternatives.

Bureaucracy, democracy, and totalitarianism are more flexible devices for structuring political action because they divorce substance and procedure. In short, these devices allow choice in defining problems and elaborating alternatives when radical disturbances require such choices. Under conditions of radical change, policy making requires setting or devising a new norm state to which subsequent conditions may be compared and establishing alternatives for moving toward the ideal balance point and staying within an acceptable range of variation from that ideal norm state. Policy administration requires the elaboration of policy, or its translation into concrete programs, and the implementation, or carrying out, of these programs.

The distinction between policy making and policy administration often is clearer in theory than in practice. In highly complex societies, bureaucratic organizations often are asked to elaborate alternative approaches to a problem in addition to translating a policy into concrete programs and implementing those programs (see Long, 1954:22). Under conditions of radical change this trend is even more apparent. For example, new bureaucratic organizations typically are established to address emerging social problems (see Chapter 4). During their early histories these organizations have more choices available in elaborating alternative strategies than do the same organizations once policies are translated into programs and the programs are implemented. At this

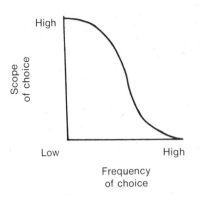

**Fig. 10-3.** Scope and frequency of choice.

point the agency becomes another component of the power channel, and its subsequent actions are checked by the dynamic equilibrium of that channel.

***Choosing among alternatives.*** This decision-making stage occurs with greater frequency than either the defining problems or elaborating alternatives stages. In Chapter 9, for example, the process of management was described as a recurring choice among techniques fostering stability and techniques fostering vitality and innovation. Compared with the first two stages, choosing among alternatives involves greater frequency of choice but smaller scope of choice. This relation, as illustrated in Fig. 10-3, generally holds across all five stages of decision making. When the frequency of choice increases, the scope of choice decreases. No society or organization can weather frequent choices that are wide in scope. Here we have a geometric, or multiplier, effect, in which frequent choices and wide scope of choices drastically decrease the predictability of action. In short, there is a need to limit one or the other, lest activity disintegrate into a chaos of pointless acts and exploding emotions.

*Power channels.* The scope of choice in a distribution generally is limited by the dynamic equilibrium among components of the channel and by the fragmentation of authority, knowledge, and target clientele that shape the channel system. While the number of realistic alternatives is diminished sharply, the frequency with which available alternatives are exercised is increased by the simultaneous choices of other components in the channel. Even with limited scope, the combination of choices that can be simultaneously made in a channel system are staggering. However, it is the uniqueness of limited choices made frequently and in different combinations that allows us to distinguish one Presidential administration from another, one itinerant administrator from another, and even one agency from its competitor.

Throughout Part II of this book, the role of leadership in complex power channels has been discussed. Recall that leadership implies unusual power. Two forms of leadership can be identified: leadership that expands the scope of choices available and leadership that expands the frequency with which choices are exercised. The first form of leadership is extraordinary, and its occurrence is something of a milestone in the history of people and organizations. The second is ordinary, but it is the type of unusual power that brings to power channels their dynamic equilibria, and it is the type of unusual power that typically enhances the pursuit of organizational goals. Fig. 10-4 illustrates the relation between each form of leadership and the impact on choice.

The discussion of choice and limiting choice also sheds additional light on the balance between managerial leadership and managerial maintenance discussed in Chapter 9. Techniques of managerial leadership either must contract the scope of choices available or decrease the frequency of choice. The curve in Fig. 10-5 helps illustrate the dynamic tension between managerial leadership and managerial maintenance. Point $B$ on the curve represents an imaginary minimum point where both the scope and frequency of choice have been limited. Points $A_1$ and $A_2$

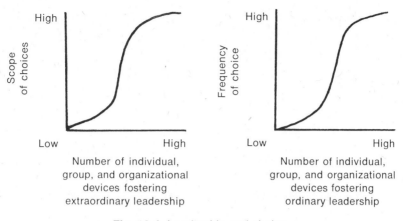

**Fig. 10-4.** Leadership and choice.

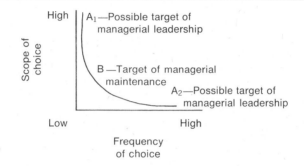

**Fig. 10-5.** Maintenance and leadership in management.

on the curve represent imaginary maxima where either the scope of choice is maximum ($A_1$) or the frequency of choice is maximum ($A_2$). In the process of management, managerial maintenance will attempt to pull the scope and frequency of choices toward point $B$, while managerial leadership will attempt to move toward one of the two extremes, depending on the stage of decision making involved. For example, if the bureaucratic organization is charged with elaborating alternatives to solve a social problem, then the movement will be toward $A_1$. If the organization wishes to maintain a favorable position in an existing power channel, it might wish to move toward $A_2$.

*Delegation and specialization of authority.* Bureaucratic organizations are procedural devices for structuring political ac-

tion through the delegation and specialization of authority. Both the delegation and specialization of authority suggest multiple decision makers. However, there is a key difference between the delegation of authority and the specialization of authority. When authority is delegated, several people are permitted to choose among available alternatives in solving problems (see Simon, 1976:154). Hence the delegation of authority increases the frequency of choice among bureaucratic personnel. When authority is specialized, different units within an organization are permitted to use a unique set of alternatives in solving problems. Hence the specialization of authority increases the scope of choice available to bureaucratic personnel. Fig. 10-6 illustrates these relations.

Increased frequency and scope of

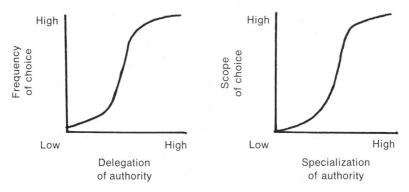

**Fig. 10-6.** Choice and delegation or specialization of authority.

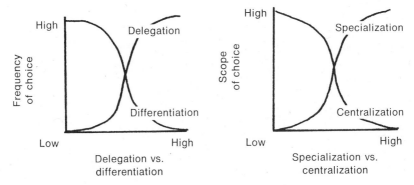

**Fig. 10-7.** Scope and frequency of choice in bureaucratic organizations.

choices reduce the predictability of action. By implication, therefore, the delegation and specialization of authority essential to bureaucratic organization tend to decrease the predictability of bureaucratic action. Clearly, there must be some mechanisms that counteract the impact of delegation and specialization on bureaucratic action. But what are those mechanisms? As discussed in Chapter 9, two mechanisms that are particularly important in counteracting the tendency toward expanding the frequency and scope of choice through the delegation and specialization of authority are the centralization of power and the differentiation of organization structure. Centralized power allows key administrators to limit drastically the alternatives available for problem solving. Differentiation concentrates the choice among alternatives in

proportionately few hands, thereby decreasing the frequency of choice exercised by organization personnel. Fig. 10-7 illustrates the countervailing forces of delegation and differentiation and of specialization and centralization.

*Implementation.* After an alternative is chosen, the next stage in decision making is implementing the chosen alternative. Of all decision processes in bureaucratic organizations, this often is least visible. However, choices at this stage are particularly important because they determine how a chosen alternative is translated into an operating program and how general rules are applied in particular cases. It is at this stage that the bulk of bureaucratic action occurs, particularly in public bureaucracies.

Suppose your community has an overcrowded jail and you decide to implement a release-on-recognizance program to ease the overcrowded conditions. The goals of this program are to release as many defendants as possible before arraignment and before trial, subject to community safety and a relative assurance that the defendants will appear for the scheduled court hearings. The program will reduce jail populations by moving defendants out of jail before arraignment, particularly if bail is set by a judge at arraignment, and by moving defendants out of jail while awaiting trial, particularly if they are too poor to post the required bail. You know that the program operates in several cities across the country, but you still face the concrete problems of implementing it in your community. Who should determine the eligibility for release? Several options exist, including law enforcement personnel, jailors, and even special recognizance technicians. Suppose you decide to let law enforcement personnel make the release decision. Should the release decision be made in the field at the time of arrest (field citation), or should the release be made at the station after booking (station citation)? Next, what criteria should be used to determine eligibility? And what should be done with marginal cases, where release eligibility is dubious? What should be done if a defendant fails to appear for a scheduled hearing?

Clearly, there is a broad scope of choices involved in translating a chosen alternative into an operating program. A high frequency of choices is involved when general rules are applied to particular cases. Consider the problem of law enforcement. There are virtually thousands of laws on the books, ranging from city and county ordinances to state statutes and federal laws. If all these laws were enforced rigidly, almost every adult in this country would have a criminal record. Even the most brutal totalitarian regimes known cannot enforce all the laws that might be relevant to a particular situation. Instead, policemen and prosecutors have at their disposal a grab bag of laws, any number of which might be applied to a particular situation, or policemen and prosecutors might choose not to apply any of them (see Edelman, 1967:44-72). Goldstein (1959-1960:543-594) cites a number of instances where police deliberately fail to enforce laws, such as trading enforcement for information from a narcotics suspect. Commenting on this discrepancy between rules and their implementation, Arnold (1962:151-152) notes that prosecuting attorneys are compelled to choose which laws will be enforced and which will be disregarded, given the limited resources.

How policies are translated into concrete programs and how general rules are applied to particular cases involves a rather wide scope of choices and a large frequency of choices. All implementation requires some degree of discretion. But some areas of bureaucratic activity, such as law enforcement, involve a high degree of discretion. We may value the ideals of equality before the law and the blindness of justice, but the problems of implementation make these ideals almost impossible to achieve. As discretion increases, both the scope and frequency of choice increase. And as the scope and frequency of choice increase during implementation, the conformity to ideals or goals decreases. Fig. 10-8 illustrates these two relations.

A bureaucratic organization faces serious problems if it cannot check the exercise of discretion. To do so the organization must find ways to limit the scope and frequency of choice when a policy is translated into concrete programs and when a general rule is applied to particular cases. The primary device for controlling or guiding the use of discretion is the organizational image. Recall that an organizational image is a set of plans, recipes, rules, and instructions for governing behavior. In short, the organizational image helps re-

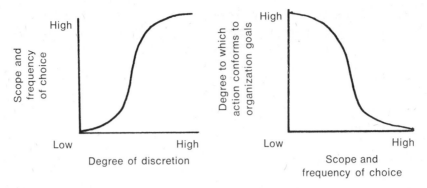

**Fig. 10-8.** Discretion, choice, and organizational goals.

duce the scope and frequency of choice among members of an organization, thereby making possible the collective intent necessary for pursuing organizational goals. In law enforcement, for example, key administrators communicate to patrolmen the types of laws that should be enforced and those that should be ignored. Further, depending on the style of law enforcement in a community, these same administrators communicate the degree to which laws should be uniformly enforced or the types of situations in which laws should be enforced or ignored. For example, many police departments will tolerate certain forms of gambling, prostitution, and pornography, so long as these activities are confined to specific areas of a community. If the activities spill out beyond the specific areas, then the relevant laws will be enforced accordingly. Once these expectations are communicated to patrolmen, they are enforced through various cybernets in the organization.

***Evaluation.*** The final stage of decision making is evaluation. Whether explicitly or implicitly, all decision processes involve some form of evaluation. Evaluation determines whether previous choices have been adequate to address the problem at hand and whether the decision cycle should begin again. If the actions resulting from choices at each of the first four stages are judged inadequate relative to the desired

results, then the decision cycle must begin anew. The impact of evaluation can be modest or dramatic, depending on what we evaluate. If we evaluate the degree to which decisions approximate set goals, then the impact of evaluation is relatively modest. At best, it triggers a new search for better solutions. However, if we evaluate goals, then the impact of evaluation can be quite dramatic. Questioning the value of a goal may reopen choices at the problem-defining stage and the alternative-elaborating stage. In bureaucratic decision making, evaluation usually centers on the means chosen to achieve goals. Only rarely does evaluation raise the larger issue of the value or worthiness of ends being pursued.

Bureaucratic organizations tend to persist for long periods, once they have been established (see Chapter 4). There are three reasons for this. First, the organizational goal becomes a vested interest of the organization, some policy makers, and some target clientele. In a political system in which power is greatly fragmented, this often is sufficient cause to continue a particular bureaucratic activity. Second, bureaucratic organizations seldom undertake the radical form of evaluation that subjects its goals to scrutiny and judgment. Third, even when required to do such assessment, bureaucratic organizations can easily muster reasons why the goal is important and worthy of continued support.

In the following section, we will examine more closely the limits of radical evaluation.

## Overview

Decision making implies choice, but increased scope and frequency of choice imply unpredictable action. In bureaucratic decision making it is essential that the number of choices and the frequency of choices be limited so that bureaucratic action can be regular, stable, continuous, and uniform. Choices in defining problems and elaborating alternatives typically are limited by existing dynamic equilibria in power channels. Only when radical disturbances occur are choices required at these two stages of decision making. Extraordinary leadership expands the scope of choices, while ordinary leadership expands the frequency of choices. The delegation of authority increases the frequency of choices in bureaucratic decision making, and the specialization of authority expands the scope of choices. Management techniques such as centralization of power and differentiation of the organizational structure help check this expanding scope and frequency of choice. Discretion expands the frequency and scope of choice, but the organizational image helps check the exercise of discretion. Evaluation typically centers on the means chosen in the pursuit of goals, not on the goals themselves. In turn the concentration on means rather than ends tends to limit the scope and frequency of choices when the decision cycle is reactivated.

## INFORMATION AND CHOICE

At each stage of the decision cycle, a variety of factors helps limit the scope and frequency of choices available to bureaucratic decision makers. Without these limits bureaucratic action would become too unpredictable, irregular, and inconsistent. However, even when choices are available, other factors limit the scope and frequency of choice. Two factors particularly relevant here are the amount of information available and the ability to utilize available information. Each factor imposes some critical limits on bureaucratic action.

## Available information

Less than a generation ago, the information needed to guide even routine choices in bureaucratic organizations was sorely inadequate. Available information often was out of date, and much more data was needed to make reasonable and timely decisions. Modern computer technology has helped remedy some of the more pressing problems of the past generation, but it has not resolved a larger problem: making comprehensive assessments of available choices. Making comprehensive assessments of available choices involves two dimensions: defining and ordering the values to be maximized and selecting the most appropriate methods for maximizing these values.

There is a simple vehicle for distinguishing the first dimension of comprehensive assessment from the second. When we discuss questions of value or when we attempt to order values from least to most important, we soon discover that there are no universally accepted criteria for defining and ordering values (see Mannheim, 1936:57). However, once we agree that one value is more important than another or once we agree that we should maximize "freedom" before "equality," then we have criteria for judging how well we have achieved our goals. Hence the process for comprehensively assessing questions of value is quite distinct from the process of comprehensively assessing questions of fact (see Simon, 1976:56). The first process requires normative judgment; the second process requires empirical research.

***Questions of value.*** Bureaucratic organizations seldom undertake comprehensive assessments of value. Nor do most bureaucratic organizations choose the values they seek to maximize. These tasks fall to other procedural devices for structuring political action, particularly democracy and totalitarianism (see Simon, 1976:57). Of course, we have seen a number of examples where bureaucracy might be involved in the assessment and choice of values. However, this is not the primary function of a bureaucratic organization, and a bureaucratic organization seldom undertakes this function without the guidance of democratic or totalitarian devices. We shall return to this matter in Part III.

Under normal conditions the questions of value have been resolved by procedural devices apart from bureaucratic organization. Once resolved, the chosen values are reflected in organizational goals: what a bureaucratic organization attempts to accomplish. As was seen in Chapter 9, the process of image building infuses an organization with value, activates cybernets that make possible the collective intent necessary for the pursuit of organizational goals, and allows an individual to identify with an organization, making its goals and its preservation a matter of personal concern.

***Questions of fact.*** The problem of available information becomes critically important when assessing questions of fact. Here decision making involves a matching of means to ends and a choice among competing means to best achieve the stated ends or goals (see Lindblom, 1959:83). A comprehensive assessment of questions of fact would require solutions to several problems (see also Lindblom, 1959:81):

1. Values or goals must be clarified.
2. All possible methods for translating a policy into concrete programs must be elaborated.
3. The impact of each program must be examined carefully and thoroughly.
4. The relative impacts of each program must be compared with the impact of other possible programs.

5. The application of general rules to specific cases must be fully examined, all possible points of "slippage" noted, and all necessary precautions taken to ensure regularity and uniformity.
6. All extraneous factors that might alter the impact of a program or the application of general rules to specific cases must be examined, and appropriate control over these extraneous factors must be implemented.
7. The programs and application of rules to particular cases must be monitored closely so that fluctuations or failure to achieve maximum results can be corrected.

The story is told of a Greek philosopher named Cratylus who, having resolved never to speak anything of which he was not completely sure, was reduced to wagging his finger and never spoke again. The same would be true of bureaucratic action if all seven issues above were religiously solved. If these seven criteria are the guidelines for rational action, then rational action simply is impossible. On the one hand the necessary information for such comprehensive assessments simply is not available. To presume, for example, that we can anticipate and correct the impact of extraneous factors on concrete programs is to claim nothing short of onmiscience in our knowledge of social causation. On the other hand, virtually all bureaucratic attention would be devoted to solving these seven problems, and hence action would be limited to this eternal cycle of assessment and evaluation.

### Utilizing information

Lindblom (1965:137-143) argues that comprehensive decision making virtually is impossible because we lack the necessary information and we lack the ability to use all available information. Several years ago, for example, the Hungarian government implemented a comprehensive production plan requiring plants to produce fixed amounts of any given product and allowing very little variation from the fixed target. Plant officials would be sanctioned if they did not achieve the fixed quota. In one rubber plant production could not be tuned as finely as that required by the comprehensive plan. Hence when production appeared to exceed the quota for a given month, plant officials would decrease the amount of air injected into the rubber during processing. When production appeared to fall short of the quota, officials would increase the amount of air injected into the rubber. Using these techniques the volume of rubber produced fell within acceptable limits, but the variations in quality were severe.

*Limits of comprehensive decision making.* Lindblom (1965:138-143) cites several reasons why comprehensive decision making seldom is pursued: (1) total comprehensiveness at all stages of action is beyond a person's mechanical or intellectual abilities; (2) information seldom is adequate for comprehensive assessments of available choices; (3) the cost of comprehensive assessments is prohibitive; (4) planning failures drastically increase the cost, information, and intellectual demands needed to correct the failures; (5) questions of fact often are mixed with questions of value; (6) too many factors are indeterminate, hence comprehensiveness is undermined; (7) comprehensiveness cannot reflect the diverse forms in which problems might arise.

*Too many choices.* Comprehensive decision making expands both the scope and frequency of choices. We already have seen that the simultaneous expansion of both the scope and frequency of choice drastically reduces the predictability and regularity of action. Weaver (1949:12) compares the expansion of choice to the concept of "entropy" in physics. Entropy implies randomness, or lack of order. Within an organization the scope and frequency of

choice involved in comprehensive decision making increase the entropy of complex organizations. That is, increased choice increases the randomness of communication, which in turn impairs the organizational image, hinders development of the collective intent necessary for the pursuit of goals, increases the amount of choice, and decreases the effectiveness of cybernets as control devices. In short, there is an unexpected consequence that derives from increasing choice through comprehensive decision making: it reduces the chance that an organization will become "infused with value."

### Bureaucratic action

The available information and the ability to utilize information help shape the contours of bureaucratic action. No bureaucratic organization can find or attempt to find optimal solutions for *all* problems requiring choice (see Simon, 1976:272). Rational behavior cannot be defined simply in terms of maximizing a goal or set of goals. Rather, rationality is relative to available information, clarity of goals, and the limits imposed on available choices (Simon, 1976:241). Simon substitutes the term "satisficing" behavior for rational behavior in bureaucratic organizations. Satisficing behavior differs from purely rational behavior in that rational decision making seeks an optimal or maximal solution, while satisficing decision making seeks a choice that is simply "good enough," and rational decision making requires a comprehensive picture of the real world, while satisficing decision making simplifies the picture of the real world to limit choice (Simon, 1976).

What are the implications of this form of decision making? Clearly, satisficing behavior helps reduce the scope and frequency of choices and thereby helps an organization pursue its goals by allowing an "infusion of value" to occur. In addition, limiting the scope and frequency of choice

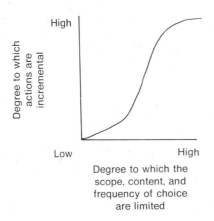

**Fig. 10-9.** Choice and incrementalism.

also limits the range of possible organizational behaviors, thereby increasing regularity, consistency, and predictability. Lindblom (1965:148) calls this type of bureaucratic action incrementalism.

Three conditions favor incremental action: (1) the scope of choices is limited drastically, (2) available choices are only marginally different from the existing state of affairs, or (3) the frequency of choices is determined by problems as they appear, not by the style of decision making itself. Compared with satisficing styles, for example, an optimizing style of decision making fosters frequency of choice in a search for optimal solutions to a given problem. As Fig. 10-9 illustrates, incremental action results from limiting the scope, content, and frequency of choices.

**HOW DECISIONS ARE MADE**

In the preceding discussion, how the choices available to decision makers are limited and the consequences of limiting or expanding the choices available to decision makers were examined. A third problem of decision making is how decisions are made. (Analysis of this problem follows the discussion of human behavior in Chapter 9.) Recall that the human organism may be viewed as a complex information-processing system with devices for receiving and attending to stimuli from the environment and a neurosystem that in-tegrates past experiences and drive states and allows control over the linkage between stimulus and response (see Newell et al., 1958:151-166). Further, recall that the integration of past experiences and drive states helps produce images—control mechanisms, plans, recipes, rules, or instructions—for governing behavior.

Suppose we compare these images to a computer program. The program must tell the computer (in this case, the neurosystem) how to read or interpret the incoming data (what the stimuli mean) and how to process or analyze the data (determine what responses are appropriate to the stimuli). Like simulation computer programs, the central nervous system has a mechanism for delaying responses to stimuli so that we may review past responses and match or rematch responses to stimuli. Hence we may test out various completions of an act (various combinations of stimuli and responses) before acting (see Mead, 1964:177-179). Like a computer program, the central nervous system follows a set of "rules" in matching stimulus and response. These rules are part of the image governing behavior. Unlike a computer program, however, the central nervous system has a mechanism that allows a change of program as well as a mechanism for using "rules" to solve problems. Examine each of these mechanisms more closely.

**Program changes**

In Chapter 9 we saw that meaning arises through experience, particularly in the process of matching responses to environmental stimuli. The child, for example, does not instinctively know the meaning of a milk bottle, but it does not take the child long to learn that the milk bottle means food. The central nervous system stores these experiences and constructs a composite picture of the world from these experiences. Sometimes, and these occasions are rare, the composite picture of the world is reconstructed through the mechanisms that allow us to select and order stimuli, relate these stimuli to one another and to past experiences, and prepare an appropriate response to a given situation. When this reconstruction occurs, the human mind has changed its "program," or image, for interpreting stimuli and preparing appropriate responses.

The notion that images can change is not new. Kuhn, for example, argues that scientific communities share paradigms (images): constellations of beliefs, values, and techniques. On rare occasions a scientific community will experience a revolution in paradigms when a new paradigm supplants an older one. Kuhn (1970:123) points out that these revolutions take large portions of past experience and transform them into a new bundle of experience.

These radical transformations of the way we view the world about us are not limited to scientific communities. Occasionally religious conversion will sweep thousands into a new way of looking at life and death. One particularly interesting example of such major image change occurs when a student from a small rural community attends college in a diverse metropolitan environment. Often such students undergo identity crises in which their outlook on life, the things they value, the morality that governs their behavior, and the interpretations of their past experiences are transformed radically. When such identity crises occur, the accumulated experiences do not change, but the meaning of those experiences changes. In Chapter 9 we saw that experience is a fusion of fact and value; when this package of accumulated experience is inadequate in a new environment, there is a good chance that the package is overhauled, so that a new fusion of facts and values permits behaviors more consistent with the expectations of others in the new environment.

At a less dramatic level, the same process occurs when an organization attempts to change its image. If successful, the old recipes, plans, rules, and instructions carried in the mind that govern behavior are replaced by a new set of control mechanisms. As was seen in Chapter 9, such changes often provoke considerable resistance because the change in image literally requires people to let the old organizational image disintegrate and replace it with a new "infused value." Gerber, for example, used to advertise "Babies are our business, our only business." Currently they advertise "Babies are our business." This change followed a declining birth rate, which forced Gerber to diversify. When the company marketed a new brand of peanut butter, many consumers felt that the product was not an "adult" food. Gerber advertising attempted to capture the preteen market for peanut butter, because the old organizational image carried by consumers could not easily be displaced, without jeopardizing their older markets, by the fact of their diversification into other products.

A change in image is most likely to occur when radical disturbances force consideration of questions of value. Existing images cannot handle these problems because the questions of value open for assessment and judgment are the very values on which these images rest. When we assess questions of value, we invite innovations or radical transformations of the meaning our images provide (see Tiryakian, 1967: 83). Images include mental pictures about human nature, the relations among people, and the purposes people pursue (see Seitz, 1973:8). When fundamental images change, so does the composite picture of all dimensions of life.*

---

*Changes in images occur infrequently. That they do occur indicates some important aspects about the knowledge on which images rest. The world is too vast and too complex for the mind to develop a complete factual and theoretical picture of that world. Sense experience and our interpretation of that experience are neither neutral nor unbiased. Two corollaries follow: our mental images of the world or of an organization are biased and partial, and knowledge deriving from experience is not necessarily additive or cumulative (see Seitz, 1972:13).

## Using programs

While questions of value might trigger massive transformations of the images governing behavior, questions of fact usually rely on these images for guidelines in making decisions. It is at this stage that computer problem-solving programs more clearly parallel the process of human decision making. Images help us choose among alternatives, help us translate policy into concrete programs, and help us apply general rules to particular cases. Similarly, problem-solving programs search among alternatives, translate alternatives into symbolic solutions, and help apply general rules to particular cases. When playing chess, for example, neither the computer nor the human mind can project alternatives much beyond five possible moves at one time. In fact, the actual number of possible moves taken five deep (projecting ahead five turns) is about 100 million million (Newell et al., 1959:13-20). Clearly, considering all these alternatives is beyond both human and mechanical ability. Instead of projecting all possible alternatives, we tend to rely on rules of thumb when playing chess. One such rule is development: attempt to make a move that maximizes the number of moves available on the next turn. Computers can be programmed to use this same rule of thumb for chess playing.

Two broad types of rules guide decision making by both persons and machines. One type of rule determines an exact solution to the problem at hand. Multivariate statistical formulas are obvious examples of this type of rule. Another type of rule aids in solving a problem, but it cannot provide an exact or unique solution. Rules of thumb, such as development in chess, are obvious examples of this type of rule. Technically, rules that provide exact solutions are algorithmic rules, and rules that guide choice but do not provide definite solutions are heuristic rules.

*Algorithms.* Earlier we spoke of the difference between satisficing and rational behavior. Satisficing behavior uses heuristic rules; rational behavior uses algorithms. In those limited situations in which a search for optimal solutions is possible, algorithms typically are used. Algorithmic rules suggest that if two or more people apply the same algorithm to a given problem, each will come up with the same choice (see Taylor, 1965:73). Since World War II the use of algorithms in decision making has become increasingly important. Two schools are particularly important: rational-man modeling and operations research.

*Rational-man modeling.* The use of rational modeling falls under a number of different terms, among them social-choice theory, public-choice theory, and game theory. These algorithms posit a basic economic assumption about human motives: an individual or group will attempt to maximize personal utility or minimize personal disutility. Rational behavior is the continued attempt to maximize utility, whether that be defined as pleasure, economic gain, or whatever. Von Neumann and Morgenstern (1953:31) describe this algorithm as the mathematically complete principles defining "rational behavior" and derive from them the general characteristics of "rational behavior" (see also Arrow, 1951).

Suppose Jack and John are the only two employees who handle problem cases in a social welfare agency. During the regular 8-hour day each of them handles four cases, although they know they could handle six cases a day if necessary. Because of the caseload in recent years, both Jack and John have been working overtime, processing one additional case each day. For the overtime work, each man receives $20. A new supervisor takes charge of the unit and, although realizing that forcing the men to handle five cases during regular hours will reduce morale throughout the unit, decides that something must be done

John

| | Accepts | Rejects |
|---|---|---|
| Accepts | John loses $5<br>Jack loses $5 | John loses $20<br>Jack gains $10 |
| Rejects | John gains $10<br>Jack loses $20 | John loses $20<br>Jack loses $20 |

Jack (row label)

**Fig. 10-10.** Payoff matrix.

about the overtime situation. Hence the supervisor forbids overtime and threatens to hire a parttime employee to process the additional two cases a day, at a cost of $30, $10 below the current cost of overtime paid to Jack and John. However, the supervisor offers to pay an incentive of $30 a day if one or both of the men agree to handle the additional two cases during regular hours. If Jack and John refuse the incentive, each will lose $20 a day in overtime pay. If Jack or John accepts the incentive offer and the other refuses, one will lose the $20 in overtime but the other will earn an extra $30, $10 more than he made with overtime. If both men accept, each will earn $15, but their overall loss will be $5 because the overtime pay originally was $20 per person. Fig. 10-10 summarizes the possible payoff matrix.

Here we find an apparent dilemma (often referred to as the prisoner's dilemma [see Brams, 1976:83]). Jack would like to see John reject the incentive offer, so that he could accept it and gain an extra $10. But John would like to see Jack reject the offer, so that he could accept it and gain an extra $10. If both reject the offer, they lost the $20 in overtime. If both accept, the losses are held to $5 a piece. What is the most rational strategy for each to follow? Clearly, the supervisor was very shrewd, because the optimal strategy for both men is to accept the incentive offer, thereby minimizing their losses. In turn this maintains the productivity of the special problems unit, but it also reduces the

cost and avoids the need to add an additional person. (Because each man has a chance to gain from the arrangement if the other refuses, the supervisor also might avoid part of the hostility for introducing the new rules. However, hostility is not part of the calculus at hand.)

Clearly, this is only one of a variety of examples that could be used to illustrate rational-choice theory. If all people behaved according to the motive of minimizing losses and maximizing gains, then the theory could have widespread utility in management. However, the assumptions about rational human behavior are not always adequate. Hence this algorithm might not produce the desired consequences. Years ago administrators attempted to use a price-per-item incentive system to increase worker productivity. In strict economic terms the incentive systems should have motivated superior performance among employees. However, the results were quite mixed. In several plant divisions strong social norms developed that sharply curtailed the productivity of individuals within a group, keeping individual work close to a group norm. Only those who did not respond to the sanctions of the group were motivated by the economic incentives.

*Operations research.* As its name suggests, operations research is a set of algorithms that helps solve problems of operation through scientific management. Using models of real-life situations, these algorithms attempt to define optimal

**Table 10-1.** Auditing short and long forms (IRS)

| | TOTAL WORKDAYS AVAILABLE | REQUIREMENTS PER SHORT FORM | REQUIREMENTS PER LONG FORM |
|---|---|---|---|
| Computer programming | 2 | .05 | .25 |
| Secretarial service | 2 | .05 | .05 |
| Auditor time | 10 | .20 | .50 |

choices for decision making (see Hillier and Lieberman, 1974:3, 4). Two particularly important algorithms for operations research are linear programming and queuing theory. Linear programming attempts to identify an optimal operations strategy, given certain constraints or limits in available capacity or resources. Queuing theory is a mathematical algorithm used to optimize scheduling and has been used widely in such areas as airport arrivals and departures and car dispatch and call assignment in police departments. Let us look at an example of linear programming in bureaucratic decision making.

Suppose you are the supervisor at a regional Internal Revenue Service office. April 15 has come and gone, and now you are going to concentrate your staff on auditing. You have ten auditors, two secretaries, and two computer programmers. You know that on the average each audit of a short form produces $100 over cost in added tax revenues and each audit of a long form produces $300 over cost in added tax revenues. The problem is, how many short and long forms should be audited each day? Each short-form audit requires about .05 workdays of computer-programming time, .05 workdays of secretarial time, and .20 workdays of auditor time. Each long-form audit requires about .25 workdays of computer-programming time, .05 workdays of secretarial time, and .50 workdays of auditor time. To maximize the amount of additional tax revenue your audits produce, how should you distribute the work load between short and long forms and still remain within your secretarial, programming, and auditing capac-

ity? Table 10-1 summarizes the constraints on your decision.

From Table 10-1 we know that the total number of short and long forms cannot exceed 2 workdays of computer programming for any given 8-hour shift, the total number of short and long forms cannot exceed 2 workdays of secretarial service, and the total number of short and long forms audited each day cannot exceed 10 workdays of auditor time. These are the constraints surrounding the decision. In addition, you want to maximize the profit from each day's auditing, and each short-form audit produces an average of $100, while each long-form audit produces an average of $300. Finally, you know that the public would start cheating on their taxes next year if you audit all short or all long forms, so you decide to audit at least one of each type per day.

Subject to the constraints in Table 10-1 and the additional constraint that you must audit at least one long and one short form each day, you wish to maximize the equation

Profit = $100 (number of short forms) + $300 (number of long forms)

Although computer programs can solve problems like this, it is sufficiently simple to solve by hand.

1. The amount of secretarial service available limits the total number of forms processed a day to 40, regardless of whether they are long or short, because the time required for each type of form is equivalent.

2. The maximum number of short forms that the auditors can do is 47 (this

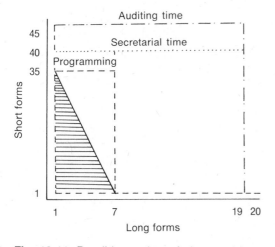

**Fig. 10-11.** Possible number of short and long forms that can be audited per day. Shaded portion represents only combinations of short and long forms permissible, assuming at least one of each within computer programming, secretarial, and auditing workday constraints.

leaves time for at least one long form), and the maximum number of long forms the auditors can do is 19 (again leaving time for at least one short form).

3. The available computer programming time allows a maximum of seven long forms (again leaving time for a short form) or a maximum of 35 short forms (leaving some time for one long form). These constraints are sketched in Fig. 10-11.

Now all we must do is locate the one point in the triangle where the profit from auditing is maximized. Because we are limited to between one and seven long forms, we have only seven equations to review. (The number of short forms for each number of long forms can be calculated by finding out how many short forms the available computer programming will allow. From the diagram it can be seen that the other two constraints—secretarial and auditor time—are well beyond the triangle and hence will not in this case need to be included in the calculation of the number

of short forms.) The seven profit figures are:

$$Profit = \$100(35) + \$300(1) = \$3,800$$
$$Profit = \$100(30) + \$300(2) = \$3,600$$
$$Profit = \$100(25) + \$300(3) = \$3,400$$
$$Profit = \$100(20) + \$300(4) = \$3,200$$
$$Profit = \$100(15) + \$300(5) = \$3,000$$
$$Profit = \$100(10) + \$300(6) = \$2,800$$
$$Profit = \$100(5) \ + \$300(7) = \$2,600$$

In this case, therefore, the optimal solution is to audit 35 short forms and one long form per day. This solution makes the most money and meets all the imposed constraints. Clearly, had the figures been changed only slightly, the solutions would have been more difficult to calculate by hand. It is possible, of course, to make other combinations (for example, 20 short forms and only three long forms), but everything below the diagonal line is a suboptimal solution. Hence we concentrate on the point on the diagonal line where profit is maximized.

Clearly, this technique can be of considerable help in planning operations, provided that the necessary data are available and reliable. It hardly makes sense to use a sophisticated algorithm such as this when the measurement does not permit accuracy or reliability of findings. In addition, when the constraints overlap (in the example, they did not), the solutions become increasingly difficult, and the decision maker will likely need a computer program to process the algorithm.

***Heuristic rules.*** Heuristic rules provide guidelines for decisions, but they do not lead to unique choices or solutions (see Boguslaw, 1965:13). Heuristic rules are used more commonly in administrative decision making than are algorithms. There are two general classes of heuristic rules: specified and unspecified. Specified heuristic rules are formal or known to the decision maker. These rules can in turn be incorporated into computer programs, such as the General Problem Solver and Simula (see Newell, 1959). Unspecified heuristic rules govern or direct choice, but the decision maker either has not formalized or cannot formalize the rules involved. In short, the decision maker senses they are there. Examine each of these two classes of heuristic rules more closely.

*Specified heuristic rules.* Development is a rule of thumb in chess in which each player attempts to move his or her pieces to maximize the number of moves available on the next turn (see Boguslaw, 1965: 75). General Problem Solver and a number of other problem-solving computer programs can use the same rule in playing chess that an individual might use. Now consider the role of specified heuristic rules in administrative behavior. Over a generation ago, Fayol (1949) proposed 14 principles of management; among them were the following guidelines: divide work, maintain the unity of command, and maintain the unity of direction. Each of these are specified heuristic rules that Fayol thought administrators would find useful. Each is a rule of thumb that Fayol and the many who followed him consciously used to improve management. Of course, it is also clear that these rules are only guidelines; they do not provide a unique and definite solution to the problem of management. Instead, they are guides to choice that, it is hoped, will result in more effective and efficient pursuit of organizational goals. Not surprising, there are a number of these specified heuristic rules, and they vary from one bureaucratic organization to another (see also Massie, 1965:387-422).

Quite often specified heuristic rules are communicated through the cybernets in an organization. And these heuristic rules might not always be consistent. For example, one's supervisor might suggest that the work pace be hastened, while other workers could suggest that the work pace be maintained or even slackened. A classic example of a conflict in specified heuristic rules is found in law enforcement. A traf-

fic officer is supposed to enforce the law but also keep traffic moving. When congestion builds at a four-way stop, for example, the traffic officer may wave people through the stop signs to get traffic moving, although this is technically a violation of the law requiring motorists to come to a complete stop when the appropriate sign is displayed. Imagine the similar dilemmas faced by supervisors when they are told to keep employees happy but increase production because the plant is behind schedule.

*Unspecified heuristic rules.* This is a more subtle form of decision making. Here there appear to be general rules guiding choice, but the decision maker is not fully conscious of them (see Polanyi, 1967). Winch (1973:52) notes that the test of rule-guided behavior is not whether the individual can formulate a rule, but whether the individual can distinguish a right and wrong way of doing the things he or she does.

Unspecified heuristic rules are part of the image people acquire of their organizations and their roles in those organizations. Although the rules are not formulated, they are enormously important in guiding choices that lead to various forms of activity within the organization. For example, employees might sense how much talking or how much loafing they can do before the supervisor intervenes. Similarly, employees might have some vague idea about the kinds of things the supervisor would like to see during work, even though these cannot be specified clearly.

Suppose you are a patrolman on a major freeway. Although the posted speed limit is 55 miles per hour, the average car appears to be moving closer to 60 miles per hour. You are willing to let this speed continue, but you watch closely for cars that appear to be moving faster than the norm of 60 miles per hour but slow down when they see your patrol car. You have some implicit ideas about how a driver acts or how a car appears relative to other traffic when the driver is moving faster than the traffic flow and attempts to slow down when he or she spots your vehicle. You might not be able to specify all the characteristics, but you are sufficiently sure that you pull onto the freeway, follow the car at a distance, and wait for the driver to speed up beyond the flow of traffic. Analogous situations occur in a personnel office, welfare office, and so forth, when feelings about the personal contact do not match the formal information on the application for a job or service. These "feelings" might be sufficient to trigger further questioning or attempts to verify the information supplied by an applicant.

### Overview

Decision are made by using rules. These rules might be part of an image or they might be communicated through the cybernets in an organization. Taken together, this package of rules helps govern behavior. Some rules provide unique and specific solutions (algorithms), while other rules provide only general guidelines but no unique or specific solution (heuristic rules). In turn these rules might be known formally or they may be unformulated. During normal decision making this package of rules is sufficient to guide choice. But on some infrequent occasions the package of rules itself is transformed radically. When this occurs there also is a transformation in the organizational image and perhaps a change in the operating cybernets in the organization.

### CONCLUSION

Our study of bureaucratic decision making has focused on three basic issues: How are the scope and frequency of choices limited in bureaucratic organization? What are the consequences of the choices available in bureaucratic decision making? When choices exist, how are decisions made? We have seen that the dynamic equilibrium in power channels limits the scope of choice. Leadership expands choice, while managerial maintenance limits choice. The delegation and specialization of authority expand choice, but centralizing power and differentiating the organization help check this expansion of choice. Discretion expands the frequency of choice, but appropriate organizational images help check the exercise of discretion. And questions of value drastically expand the problems of choice in decision making. Further we have found that a wide scope or frequency of choice tends to make bureaucratic activity less regular and more unpredictable, but limiting the scope and frequency of choice tends to foster incremental decisions and thus enhances regularity and predictability.

The process of making decisions occurs at two levels. Sometimes problems arise that virtually require a transformation of the usual "programs" used in making choices. When this occurs, one organizational image replaces another. More frequently decisions do not require a change in image or "program." Rather, rules contained in this image are communicated through cybernets made possible by an organizational image to help guide choice. Algorithmic rules provide unique solutions to a problem of choice, while heuristic rules only provide guidelines for choice. Finally, some of these heuristic rules are specified and known, while others are operative at a less conscious level. Normal bureaucratic decision making is guided by rules. The choices made might not always be predictable, but they seldom are random.

### REFERENCES

Arnold, T. *The symbols of government.* New York: Harcourt Brace Jovanovich, Inc., Harbinger Books, 1962.

Arrow, K. *Social choice and individual values.* New York: John Wiley & Sons, Inc., 1951.

Benn, S. I., and Weinstein, W. L. Being free to act and being a free man. In R. E. Flathman (Ed.), *Concepts in social and political philosophy.* New York: Macmillan, Inc., 1973.

Boguslaw, R. *The new utopians.* Englewood Cliffs, N.J.: Prentice-Hall, Inc., 1965.

Brams, S. J. *Paradoxes in politics.* New York: Free Press, 1976.

Edelman, M. *The symbolic uses of politics.* Urbana, Ill.: University of Illinois Press, 1967.

Fayol, H. *General and industrial management* (C. Stours, trans.). London: Sir Isaac Pitman & Sons Ltd., 1949.

Geertz, C. The impact of the concept of culture on the concept of man. In J. Platt (Ed.), *New views on the nature of man.* Chicago: University of Chicago Press, 1965.

Gerth, H. H., and Mills, C. W. (Eds.). *From Max Weber.* New York: Oxford University Press, Inc., Galaxy Books, 1958.

Goldstein, J. Police discretion not to invoke the criminal process: low visibility decisions in the administration of justice. *Yale Law Journal,* 1959-1960, *69,* 543-594.

Hillier, F. S., and Lieberman, G. J. *Operations research* (2nd ed.). San Francisco: Holden-Day, Inc., 1974.

Kuhn, T. *The structure of political revolutions* (2nd ed.). Chicago: University of Chicago Press, 1970.

Lasswell, H. D. *The decision process: seven categories of functional analysis.* College Park, Md.: University of Maryland Press, 1956.

Lindblom, C. The science of muddling through. *Public Administration Review,* 1959, *19,* 83.

Lindblom, C. *The intelligence of democracy.* New York: Free Press, 1965.

Long, N. Public policy and administration: the goals of rationality and responsibility. *Public Administration Review,* 1954, *14,* 22.

Mannheim, K. *Ideology and Utopia* (L. Wirth and E. Shils, trans.). New York: Harcourt Brace Jovanovich, Inc., Harvest Books, 1936.

Massie, J. Management theory. In J. G. March (Ed.), *Handbook of organizations.* Skokie, Ill.: Rand McNally & Co., 1965.

Mead, G. H. *On social psychology* (A. Strauss, ed.). Chicago: University of Chicago Press, 1964.

Neumann, J. von, and Morgenstern, O. *Theory of games and economic behavior.* Princeton, N.J.: Princeton University Press, 1953.

Newell, A., Shaw, J. C., and Simon, H. A. Elements of a theory of human problem solving. *Psychological Review,* 1958, *65,* 151-166.

Newell, A., Shaw, J. C., and Simon, H. A. Report on a general problem-solving program. Rand paper P-1584. Santa Monica, Calif.: Rand Corp., 1959.

Newell, A., Simon, H. A., and Shaw, J. C. *The process of creative thinking.* Santa Monica, Calif.: Rand Corp., 1959.

Polanyi, M. *The tacit dimension.* New York: Doubleday & Co., Inc., Anchor Books, 1967.

Seitz, S. T. Ideology and public policy (Doctoral dissertation, University of Minnesota, 1972). *Dissertation Abstracts International,* 1973, *33,* 11-A. (University Microfilms No. 73-10696, 6422).

Seitz, S. T. Political ideologies and the essence of politics. In L. E. Shaw (Ed.), *Modern competing ideologies.* Lexington, Mass.: D. C. Heath & Co., 1973.

Simon, H. A. *Administrative behavior* (3rd ed.). New York: Free Press, 1976.

Taylor, D. W. Decision making and problem solving. In J. G. March (Ed.), *Handbook of organizations.* Skokie, Ill.: Rand McNally & Co., 1965.

Tiryakian, E. A model of societal change and its lead indicators. In S. Z. Klausner (Ed.), *The study of total societies.* New York: Doubleday & Co., Inc., Anchor Books, 1967.

Vickers, G. *Value systems and social processes.* Baltimore: Penguin Books Inc., Pelican Books, 1970.

Wald, G. Determinacy, individuality, and the problem of free will. In J. Platt (Ed.), *New views on the nature of man.* Chicago: University of Chicago Press, 1965.

Weaver, W. Recent contributions to the mathematical theory of communication. In C. E. Shannon and W. Weaver, *The mathematical theory of communication.* Urbana, Ill.: University of Illinois Press, 1949.

Winch, P. Nature of meaningful behavior. In R. E. Flathman (Ed.), *Concepts in social and political philosophy.* New York: Macmillan, Inc., 1973.

# PART THREE

# Applications

# CHAPTER 11

# Bureaucracy and democracy

Confusing structure and function, some critics charge that bureaucracy in America is oligarchic and hence undemocratic. Under conditions of routine decision making, bureaucracy's primary function is administrative. Control over bureaucracy is exercised by policy makers through a complex system of checks and balances. Under conditions of critical decisions, however, bureaucracy might assume extraordinary policy-making functions that carry with them a legitimate threat of bureaucratic totalitarianism.

## DILEMMAS OF BUREAUCRACY

Bureaucracy, democracy, and totalitarianism are special forms of social organization that provide procedures for structuring political action. Other forms of social organization, particularly kinship and ecclesiastical authority, fuse substance and procedure when structuring political action. Bureaucracy, democracy, and totalitarianism divorce substance from procedure. During the twentieth century, for example, democratic governments have pursued laissez-faire policies (that government is best which governs least), welfare-state policies, and a variety of socialist policies. Similarly, some totalitarian regimes have pursued the radical reforms of communism, while others have been staunchly conservative. For example, with some changes the bureaucracy in Germany served both a democratic government and the Nazi government of Adolf Hitler (see Renner, 1946; see also von Borch, 1954). All these examples illustrate the extraordinary flexibility of social organizations that divorce procedure from substance.

Bureaucracy is a procedural device for elaborating and administering substantive guidelines for structuring political action through the delegation and specialization of authority. Democracy is a procedural device for establishing substantive guidelines for structuring political action through the free, periodic election of officials, competition for office, regular turnover of officials, and constitutionally limited authority (see Seitz, 1973:11; see also Lipset et al., 1956). Totalitarianism is a procedural device for establishing substantive guidelines for structuring political action through a self-recruiting elite that exercises relatively unlimited authority (see Lippincott, 1965). While bureaucracy elaborates and administers substantive guidelines, democracy and totalitarianism establish these guidelines. In turn democracy differs from totalitarianism in its open rather than closed methods of recruiting officials and in the limits imposed on official authority.

### Bureaucracy and oligarchy

Democratic critics of bureaucracy in America might be divided into two schools of thought. The first, represented by Mills, contends that America does not have a genuine bureaucracy, because its officials cannot weather changes in political administrations and because it is little more than a tool of a power elite (Mills, 1956:236-241). Mills cites several reasons why the civil service reform did not abolish the spoils system in America:

1. Top bureaucratic officials, those more likely involved in critical rather than routine decisions, are appointed by the President and confirmed by the Senate. (For a discussion of critical versus routine decision, see McFarland, 1969:70-92.)
2. The Civil Service Commission can change with changing administrations.
3. Creation of new agencies can bypass competitive recruitment, and abolition of agencies can make civil service tenure meaningless.
4. Jobs can be classified under civil service regulations and easily declassified from those regulations (Mills, 1956:237).

In Chapter 7 we saw two reasons why politicians recruit bureaucrats through a spoils system: there is a need to limit bureaucratic authority to that delegated, and the principal means to do so is to make tenure of office dependent on the wishes of those who delegate authority; and bureaucratic offices are considered the property of those in positions of policy making. Under these conditions, according to Mills, the Civil Service Commission has been unable to recruit superior talent, morally qualified personnel, and intelligent administrators. Lacking the necessary independence, the bureaucracy cannot assemble a group of expert administrators who reach beyond unreflective conformity to make a skilled judgement of policy alternatives (Mills, 1956:241). In short, the bureaucracy has little power in the executive arena where critical decisions are made. At best the bureaucracy is confined to the routine decisions that reflect conformity to the critical decisions made by the power elite (see also Quinney, 1974).

Another school of thought contends that bureaucratic organization centralizes power in the hands of a few, thereby threatening the freedom essential to democracy (see Bendix, 1945:194-209; see also Neumann, 1942; von Mises, 1946). Blau and Meyer (1971:166-167) cite three ways that bureaucracy endangers democracy: (1) the hierarchical organization of bureaucracy creates profound inequalities of power; (2) these organizations discourage the democratic participation necessary for developing civic responsibility; and (3) bureaucratization tends to block the free exchange of opinions and ideas. Finally, Michels argues that bureaucratization threatens democracy because bureaucratic leadership is incompatible with democracy and bureaucratic organizations soon become ends to themselves. According to Michels (1962: 365) bureaucratic organizations soon become oligarchies: totalitarian organizations where an elite group exercises power for private ends.

Clearly, these two schools are not entirely consistent in their critique of bureaucracy. Proponents of the first school see bureaucracy as a tool of a totalitarian elite because it lacks the independence necessary for a genuine bureaucratic system. However, they feel that bureaucracy might be a check on power if bureaucratic decision makers are included in critical decisions. Proponents of the second school see bureaucracy as a totalitarian elite, precisely because it is independent of democratic policy makers. They feel that bureaucracy is a centralized power that participates in critical decisions to the detriment of democracy.

### Bureaucracy and democracy

The story is told of six blind men who, having touched various portions of an elephant, were asked to described an elephant. Needless to say, the six blind men "looked" in different places, found different things, and described the elephant in six different ways. Do we have a similar phenomenon among the democratic critics of bureaucracy? It appears that the first school concentrates attention on the processes that limit the scope and frequency of bureaucratic decision making, while the second school concentrates on the processes enhancing bureaucratic leadership. In Part II we saw both processes, as well as others, at work.

In Part I we saw that social complexity enhances bureaucratic development. Bureaucracy provides the needed flexibility to meet radical social change because it divorces substance from procedure. Bureaucratic organization provides the needed social coordination for exploiting natural resources and increasing material production. Bureaucratic organization helps maintain coordination through such social control devices as the criminal law, the civil law, and containment forces during civil unrest. Bureaucratic organizations, from the nation-state to the multinational corporation, increasingly influence the pattern of international relations.

In Part II we saw that advanced bureaucratic states have multiple bureaucracies. Certain recruitment and personnel policies enhance the power of bureaucratic organizations, exemplified by bureaucratic leadership. Communication is the primary device for shaping and sharing power within a power channel and within an organization. Bureaucratic management is the process of shaping and sharing power in the pursuit of organizational goals. Several processes limit the scope and frequency of bureaucratic decision making, and the normal process of bureaucratic decision making involves the use of decision rules that help make decisions predictable.

From our dicsussion in Parts I and II, we know that neither picture given by the critics of bureaucracy and democracy is entirely adequate. Instead, bureaucratic organizations become "infused with value" and then seek self-preservation and protection of established organizational goals. However, the tendency toward self-preservation and protection of established goals does not

necessarily mean that the bureaucracy is totalitarian. This view overlooks the complex power channels of which bureaucracies are a part and the complexity of cybernets and organizational images that foster the collective intent necessary for the pursuit of organizational goals. Both views generally overlook the creation of new bureaucratic organizations to serve as advocates for emerging social problems.

Ultimately the charges of bureaucratic totalitarianism rest on a confusion of bureaucratic function with bureaucratic structure. It is certainly the case that bureaucracies have relatively closed (non-participatory) recruitment and decision-making procedures. In this respect the structure of bureaucratic organization more closely resembles that of totalitarianism than that of democracy. For Mills and proponents of the first school, a power elite external to bureaucracy determines recruitment. For Blau and Michels, a power elite within bureaucracy determines recruitment. Hence the criticisms appear to concentrate on some similarities of structure between bureaucracy and totalitarianism.

Similarity in structure does not prove similarity in function. Supposedly, bureaucracy fills a policy-administration function, while democracy and totalitarianism fill policy-making functions. However, we have seen instances where this distinction becomes blurred. Under stable conditions, routine decisions are typically incremental because the scope and frequency of choice are limited. Here the separation of policy making and administration is more readily observed. Under conditions of rapid change, critical decisions often find bureaucracies defining problems, elaborating alternatives, and offering judgements about alternatives. Although politicians supposedly make the final decisions, the influence of bureaucracies is enormous. In advanced bureaucratic states the dangers of bureaucratic totalitarianism become most clear when the scope of choices becomes extremely broad.

### Political action and history

We learned in Chapter 2 that political action is people's deliberate efforts to attend to the arrangements of society. People structure political action to secure the needed coordination for exploiting natural resources and expanding material production, secure the needed coordination involved with any distribution of privilege and obligation in society, and help govern the interaction among societies. To achieve these ends people need procedural devices for selecting, elaborating, and administering substantive guidelines. These procedural devices, among them bureaucracy and democracy, require choices. Most of these choices are routine; that is, the scope of choice is small, and the frequency of choice often is high. Some choices are critical; that is, the scope of choice is broad, although the frequency of such choices usually is quite low.

When decisions are routine, each decision is of relatively small consequence. Taken together over time, these decisions add up in a way intended by no one person or group of people. Routine decisions suggest that the normal adjustive mechanisms are at work and the course of history is something like a drift within established boundaries. When decisions are critical, each decision is of enormous consequence for a society. These decisions help establish new boundaries for political action, and they help address conditions of radical social change. Here history is not left to fate. Its contours are the products of key decision making at key moments. The political capitalism of the military-technology complex, for example, suggests that there are some broad choices entrusted to key procedural devices (see Mills, 1956:20-25).

If we grant that America has some semblance of a democracy and hence grant that bureaucracy can coexist with democ-racy, then we might ask two basic questions about our procedural devices for structuring political action in the United States. What are the dynamics among bureaucracies, policy makers, and the public under conditions of routine decision making? What are the dynamics among bureaucracies, policy makers, and the public under conditions of critical decision making?

### ROUTINE DECISIONS

Four interactions in complex power channels are particularly important here: the interactions among bureaucracies and the executive branch of government, those among the bureaucracies and the legislative branch of government, the interactions among bureaucracies and the judiciary, and those among bureaucracies and the public. (A fifth set of interactions in complex power channels—those among bureaucracies—was examined in Chapter 6.) Examining these interactions will help us determine how power is shaped and shared among bureaucracies, policy makers, and the public and how these interactions affect public policy.

### Bureaucracies and the legislature

We tend to think of public bureaucracies as servants of the executive, legislative, and judicial branches of government. In some respects this is true. There are, of course, at least 51 independent agencies, among them the Interstate Commerce Commission (1887), the Federal Trade Commission (1914), the Federal Power Commission (1930), the Federal Communications Commission (1934), the Securities and Exchange Commission (1934), the National Labor Relations Board (1935), and the Civil Aeronautics Board (1938) (see Schwartz and Wade, 1972:26-34). Although these "big seven" do have considerable independent regulatory power, they account for only 0.4% of federal civilian employment and less than 0.01% of all federal expenditures (Gellhorn and Byse, 1974:45). Clearly, a large segment of the public bureaucracy falls under the supposedly direct supervision of policy makers.

**Statute.** One important source of legislative control over administrative agencies is the statute required to activate many agencies, define their fields of activity, and define their organizational goals. In theory, the Congress cannot delegate its legislative power. In practice, however, the courts have interpreted this limitation rather broadly, allowing Congress to transfer power to the executive and administrative components through statute. In general the courts allow this transfer of power because it supposedly does not involve a transfer of law-making authority. The reasoning appears to be that, through statutory transferrals, the Congress has made the laws, but the menial task of attending to particulars is left to subordinates (Gellhorn and Byse, 1974:60).

To be sure, there are limits to the scope of power that may be delegated by statute. Two critical cases decided before the Supreme Court have established some boundaries for statutory delegation. In *Panama Refining Company* v. *Ryan* (1935), Chief Justice Hughes established three criteria for judging the legality of such transfer of power: (1) whether the Congress has declared a policy in the area authority is transferred, (2) whether the Congress has established a standard to guide Presidential action, and (3) whether the Congress has required some reasons from the President before exercising the delegated authority. In *Schechter Poultry Corporation* v. *United States* (1935), Chief Justice Hughes distinguished between the statutes allowing independent agencies to prescribe codes for regulation and the statutes conferring similar power on the President. The statutes allowing independent regulatory agencies to prescribe codes were constitutional because they included procedures for formal complaint, notice and hearing,

fact finding, and judicial review. Without these procedural provisions the statutory delegation of regulatory authority is unconstitutional.

**Appropriations.** Congress has the power of the purse over administrative agencies (see Wildavsky, 1964; see also Fenno, 1966). This power is perhaps the most important control Congress might exercise over the activities of public bureaucracies. Congress might enhance or drastically curtail the activities of various agencies by simply expanding or contracting the available operating budget. Often agencies seek proponents in the House or Senate who will advocate their interests during the budgetary process. And, of course, the agencies might lobby on their own behalf. But congressional displeasure might be reflected in prohibiting the use of funds for certain activities within an agency and prohibiting the use of funds for certain personnel. In 1943, for example, Congress forbade use of appropriations to the Office of Price Administration for paying salaries of people not experienced in business, industry, or commerce but engaged in setting prices (Gellhorn and Byse, 1974:112). This particular prohibition was apparently aimed at professors, lawyers, and economists employed by the Office of Price Administration. Congress wanted the job left to practical businessmen.

Although the power of the purse is the most important control Congress might exercise over administrative agencies, it seldom exercises that control to its limits. The federal budgetary process is extremely complex, does not permit Congressional decision makers either the time or information to review adequately all parts of a proposed budget, and cannot be easily couched in terms of algorithms for optimizing policy decision. In turn the appropriations process is usually incremental, and it can easily be simulated by some simple, crude heuristic rules (see Davis et al., 1966:543). The implication is straightforward: the appropriations process normally involves routine decisions, and its impact on public policy does little more than introduce marginal changes.

**Legislative oversight.** The third interaction among bureaucracies and the legislative branch falls under the rubric of legislative oversight. Congress has a number of standing committees, each with specific tasks and jurisdictions. The oversight function is performed with varying degrees of success, ranging from congressional reliance on agency personnel for information and policy direction to legislative intrusion into agency decision making supposedly free of political influence (see Scher, 1960). Congress also has some watchdog committees specifically established to monitor agency activities in particularly complex areas, such as atomic energy, Through the Atomic Energy Act of 1946, for example, Congress established the Joint Committee on Atomic Energy, a joint committee of the House and Senate charged with monitoring the Atomic Energy Commission. Because these committees are extremely time consuming, Congress has been rather restrained in establishing watchdog committees over particular agencies (see Gellhorn and Byse, 1974:115-116).

With increasing regularity throughout the twentieth century, Congress has exercised legislative oversight through congressional investigations of agencies, their goals, and their pursuit of goals. Huntington (1965:25) points out that each Congress since 1950 onward has conducted more congressional investigations than all the Congresses in the nineteenth century combined. The congressional investigation has become a primary tool of congressional maintenance in the power channels of modern government. Although these investigations drain congressional time and even more time from agency personnel, the simple probability of periodic congressional investigations dramatically circumscribes agency discretion.

**Legislative intercession.** On behalf of constituents, both individuals and organizations, most congressmen will contact agency personnel as an advocate of constituent's interests. The need for such intercession appears to rest on the complex labyrinth of federal agencies, programs, and overlapping jurisdictions, coupled with enormous red tape, delay, and impersonal civil servants who bear no direct responsibility to individual citizens (see Gellhorn and Byse, 1974:119-121). During the past 10 years, for example, federal aid to state and local governments grew to $60 billion annually, a 400% increase over the previous decade. At the same time, these monies are administered through more than 1,000 programs, each added one at a time and each generating its own regulations and bureaucracy (Shafer, 1977:40). Commenting on the resulting administrative monster, Senator Edmund Muskie of Maine noted that the problem arose by responding to social problems on a piecemeal basis (Shafer, 1977:40). Here congressional incrementalism helped create the need for legislative intercession, because that incrementalism created an administrative labyrinth unintended by any one decision made during the past decade.

Of course, there is a second side to legislative intercession. The key issue centers upon the "legitimacy" of congressional requests. Again there is a myriad of ethical shadows. Why should one case be given preferred treatment, while others must await the normal processing time? How often does intercession influence the actual decision making in agencies? Are the statutory, investigative, and appropriations powers levers to gain considerations for particular people, groups, organizations, and local governments? Often intercession is limited to routine inquiries, forwarding information, complaints, and claims to the appropriate agency and monitoring the agency as it attends the matter. But there are times, as the scandals of the 1970s revealed, in which intercession becomes advocacy for an interest, a particular decision, or a special favor. These matters clearly go beyond the formal role of intercession and tax the uniformity, consistency, and fairness of agency decisions (see Gellhorn and Byse, 1974:120-121).

**Appointments.** Most of the administrative positions not subject to civil service examination but available to the President for appointment (about 2,200 jobs in 1977) require the advice and consent of the Senate. Seldom does the Senate reject appointments made by the President. Appointments to regulatory agencies, for example, rarely have been rejected, with the past two rejections occurring in 1950 and 1973 respectively (see Gellhorn and Byse, 1974: 122). This record is particularly interesting, given the independence of regulatory commissions and the rapid turnover of top personnel. Such turnover allows the President to guide the regulatory commissions in a preferred direction within a 2- or 3-year period, under normal conditions.

In 1973 President Nixon attempted to dismantle the Office of Economic Opportunity by appointing an administrator favorable to his plans for an indefinite period as acting director, thereby attempting to circumvent the Senate's constitutional right to confirm appointments. In *William v. Phillips* (1973), the District Court for the District of Columbia ruled the President's attempt unconstitutional, and hence the power of temporary appointment was limited (Gellhorn and Byse, 1974:122). Under extraordinary conditions, therefore, the Senate power of confirmation might be critical to the life or death of an agency, but under normal conditions the power seldom is used.

**Overview.** The Congress has a number of mechanisms to guarantee that administrative agencies carry out the designed legislative intent of law making. By statute the Congress can delegate authority to administer programs, establish regulatory commissions, and delegate considerable discretion to the President, provided that standards or guidelines for policy are delegated and provided that procedural devices for open decision making are established when rule-making authority is delegated. In the same vein, through statutory power the Congress can terminate programs and agencies. During the life of an agency, Congress might exercise the power of the purse, legislative oversight, legislative intercession, and the right to confirm appointments to key positions not covered by civil service. However, under routine decision making, appropriations usually are incremental and the right to deny an appointment is seldom exercised. Most congressional control over the agencies appears to be exercised through legislative oversight, although the full scope of legislative intercession as a means of advocating certain decisions is unknown.

### Bureaucracy and the executive

Apart from the independent regulatory agencies, most public agencies are under the executive branch of government. In fact, the growth of executive power under Franklin Roosevelt was institutionalized through the growing administrative apparatus he created while in office. Neither Roosevelt nor his successors were willing to drastically curtail the scope of administrative agencies inside or outside the executive branch. In 1940, for example, President Roosevelt vetoed the Walter-Logan Bill, which sought to abolish many of the independent regulatory agencies. Earlier, in 1937 President Roosevelt rejected recommendations by the President's Committee on Administrative Management that administrative agencies be abolished and absorbed into the Executive Departments (see Gellhorn and Byse, 1974:13). In 1977 President Carter received Congressional approval to reorganize the federal bureaucracy, but the progress to date has been very slow.

***Appointment and removal.*** The most obvious control exerted by the President over administrative agencies is the authority to appoint and remove key officials from administrative office. Within his first year in office, President Nixon had appointed either Republican majorities or Republican chairmen to all the major regulatory agencies (Lyndon, 1970:36). In most of these cases he had both a Republican majority and a Republican chairman. During planning for his second administration, Nixon asked for the resignation of all Presidential appointees plus the resignation of employees appointed by agency heads (1,400 to 1,800 jobs). He required the resignations to allow him to mold the bureaucracy more in his image because, as he commented to government officials and newsmen, the bureaucracy was insufficiently responsive to his directives during the first administration.

On occasion Congress has sought to restrict the presidential authority of removal, particularly by setting fixed terms of office and then requiring Senate approval before removal if the term has not expired. In *Myers* v. *United States* (1926), the Supreme Court found this restriction unconstitutional. Chief Justice Taft argued that the President had the authority to remove appointees from office to ensure the unitary and uniform execution of law. However, in *Humphrey's Executor* v. *United States* (1935), the Supreme Court noted that a commissioner appointed to the regulatory commissions could be removed only for inefficiency, neglect of duty, or malfeasance in office. While the Myers case involved purely executive officers, the Humphrey case involved appointees to independent regulatory commissions. Two additional cases are particularly relevant. In *Wiener* v. *United States* (1958), the Supreme Court declared President Eisenhower's attempt to remove a Truman appointee to the War Claims Commission unconstitutional. The court declared that the commission had a judicial charge from Congress and hence the President could not intervene by removing a commissioner. On similar grounds the District Court for the District of Columbia declared the firing of Special Watergate Prosecutor Archibald Cox unconstitutional, in *Nader* v. *Bork* (1973)(see Gellhorn and Byse, 1974:128-133).

***Executive direction.*** In the Myers case the Supreme Court justified removal of executive officers on the grounds that the administration of law should be unitary and uniform. That decision follows from a general view that the President is the chief executive officer and therefore is entitled to direct the decisions of subordinates in administrative agencies subject to the executive branch of government. Of course, Congress can and often does attempt to limit the scope of Presidential choice by specifying detailed rules in the statutes that authorize various programs and agencies. Still, the range of possible discretion available to the President is rather enormous.

Here the incredible number of administrative agencies in the federal government helps limit the power of the Presidency in any scheme for overall management. Each of these agencies derives its authority from different statutory delegations. As noted in Chapter 6, the fragmentation of the sources from which bureaucratic organizations derive their authority and legitimacy also tends to fragment bureaucratic organization. In turn the enabling legislation seldom fixes agency relations in a hierarchy of authority, so the likelihood of centralized coordination decreases accordingly. In addition, the complexity of different policy areas, the specialization of authority, and the multitude of cybernets in a complex power channel make effective reorganization virtually impossible without substantial revisions and consolidations in the enabling legislation and without considerable dismantling of existing agencies. The second point—dismantling existing agencies—becomes even more obvious in light of our discussion of organizational images and the tendency for each agency to become "infused with value" and thus an end to itself. Add to all this the limits of information available and the limits on the amount of information that can be processed. When delegated authority is specialized, the demands for elaborating and administering substantive guidelines are both numerous and complex, and the political system deliberately fragments power to prevent abuses, it is virtually impossible for a monistic world of administration to emerge during routine decision making (see Corwin, 1957:98).

**Budgeting.** Perhaps the more obvious point where the President might seek control over the administrative agencies is in the budgeting process. In 1921 the Budgeting and Accounting Act established a Bureau of the Budget. This bureau was quickly transferred from the Treasury Department to the Executive Office of the President. In 1970 the Bureau of the Budget was transformed into the Office of Management and Budget (OMB) (see Gellhorn and Byse, 1974:135). All appropriations requests supposedly are transferred from agencies to OMB, which then forwards a comprehensive budgeting package to Congress.

The Office of Management and Budget exercises considerable control over individual administrative agencies. Requests for funds must be channeled through it. This applies to both the independent agencies and those under the direct supervision of the chief executive. Requests for necessary legislation must be channeled through it. Often the independent agencies do not channel their requests through OMB. In addition, some of the agencies explicitly have been granted the privilege of making requests directly to Congress without clearance of OMB. OMB can detail how funds allocated to an agency are supposed to be spent, subject to any specific restrictions imposed by Congress. OMB can

freeze an agency's funds if it determines that the agency is using appropriations contrary to the intent of OMB directives.

In theory it would appear that the Office of Management and Budget is the President's bureaucracy for controlling other federal bureaucracies, including the independent regulatory commissions. However, actual practice illustrates some major limits on the power of OMB. Most agencies maintain regular contacts with key senators and representatives. Further, inappropriate decisions by OMB often are challenged during the budgetary hearings. The Office of Management and Budget never has discovered or implemented a truly effective budgeting device that allows the type of comprehensive planning and program development necessary for centralized executive direction in government. Of course, there have been several attempts, among them planning, programming, budgeting systems (PPBS), management by objectives (MBO), and zero-based budgeting (ZBB). PPBS was used under the Kennedy and Johnson administrations, MBO under the Nixon administration, and ZBB under the Carter administration. Let us briefly look at each of these management devices.

*Planning, programming, budgeting systems.* In 1961 Carey (1961:175-177) of the Bureau of the Budget noted that the administrative process in the United States does reasonably well in program execution, but it does not do well in anticipating change or in reflecting future needs in present decision making. Preparing for the fiscal 1963 budget, each agency was given planning guide budget figures based on fiscal projections for a 5-year period. In turn agencies were asked to use these planning guides in preparing and submitting budget requests to the Bureau of the Budget. By 1965 the Bureau pushed PPBS, the management system growing out of the attempts in 1961 to combine planning and budgeting. Partly because the new system was pushed too fast and hence generated some major budgeting problems and partly because PPBS was a Democratic idea, the Nixon administration laid PPBS to rest in 1969. (For a discussion of PPBS, see Turnbull, 1976:602-612).

The rudiments of PPBS are as follows. Item budgeting is replaced by programming budgeting. In an item budget, entries are made for various material and personnel costs, but these costs are not related to specific agency activities. In program budgeting, on the other hand, budget costs are assigned to program elements or action packages. Once the program elements are specified, various alternatives for achieving these programs are analyzed and evaluated in terms of costs and benefits over a multi-year period. Similar program elements from various agencies are analyzed together, compared, and when possible consolidated into one common program package. Budgeting requests reflect those alternatives that prove more cost effective and attempt to centralize program activities.

The discovery that budgeting is an important technique for administrative control is not new. The Hoover Commission of 1949 proposed program and performance budgeting. Early proponents of the planning, programming, budgeting system make a distinction between the program budget and a performance budget (see Snyder, 1960:98-99). The program budget is a tool for policy making where policy makers can approve or disapprove various action packages as they are presented in the budget. The performance budget is a managerial tool for policy implementation where supervisors use this budget as a guide to implementation and a means of controlling costs.

There are several reasons why PPBS did not provide the presidency more centralized control over the public bureaucracies in the federal government. First, it is extremely difficult to isolate programs pursued by agencies, particularly if these programs are supposedly defined by the goals they pursue. What the agency actually accomplishes sometimes bears little relation to the statutory goals once defined by Congress. And more often the multiple goals of most agencies cannot be divided into neat packages.

Second, the demand for information and the facilities needed to use that information —both mechanical and human—are so enormous that adequate assessment of costs and benefits are virtually impossible. The problem becomes particularly critical when the actual performance of any one program or set of programs is contingent on the activities and programs of another, unrelated agency. Under the myriad programs currently operating at the federal level alone, the impact of any one program often is dependent on the existence of other, sometimes unknown, programs administered by other agencies.

Third, the fragmentation of statutory authority and the fragmentation of bureaucratic organizations make it extremely difficult for a comprehensive management system to plan programs and adapt a budget in a highly pluralistic environment without massive and radical statutory reform and radical reorganization, including termination of agencies. In turn, of course, this type of threat simply exaggerates the trend of established agencies to secure self-preservation.

Fourth, it is incredibly difficult to translate planning and programming into actual budgetary decisions. This gap between the comprehensive and abstract on the one hand and the narrow and concrete on the other tends to generate tension and huge communication gaps. Couple this with the time pressure that most budget officials face, and there is a serious problem in simply integrating budgeting and planning.

*Management by objectives.* Like PPBS, management by objectives (MBO) is a comprehensive budgeting-planning system, in use in the private sector since Drucker made it popular in 1954 (see Billings, 1976:71-92; Drucker, 1954). Like PPBS, MBO attempts to remedy the problem of planning for the future that the present administrative agencies generally avoid in favor of incremental decisions. MBO was not actually implemented in the federal government until early 1973. Although President Ford continued MBO after the Nixon resignation, it was terminated under the Carter administration.

The rudiments of MBO are as follows. Supervisors are encouraged to consider overall organizational objectives, enforced by contracts with higher supervisors that specify goal and performance measures and encouraging commitment to overall goals through supervisory participation. Supposedly, MBO can build responsibility and performance among supervisors through the motivation of contracts, knowing what to do and how to do it, seeing how one's actions contribute to the overall goals, getting feedback necessary to correct one's actions, and integrating personal goals with organizational goals through participation. Goals and objectives are specified at all levels of the hierarchy. In turn these goals and objectives are supposed to be integrated at each level in the hierarchy so that the overall performance contributes to the objectives of the agency as a whole. When goals and objectives have been specified, action plans are devised and implemented to achieve these goals and objectives. At each stage of action the individual receives feedback regarding performance as measured against an agreed standard, and each individual is given the opportunity to correct action plans that do not achieve the agreed standards or that do not contribute to the established goals and objectives at that level in the bureaucratic hierarchy.

Under MBO, the Office of Management and Budget could affect agency activity in one of two basic ways. The OMB could establish goals for each agency, reject other goals purportedly pursued by an agency, and make budgetary decisions in accord with the goals OMB wished each agency to pursue. And the process of management by objectives could encourage more effective and more efficient implementation of budget and policy decisions by measuring performance against stated objectives and through periodic review of an agency's progress. Although many agencies feared that OMB would attempt to dictate agency goals, this strategy was not followed before Nixon resigned. By and large, agency budgets did not change under MBO. Some agencies had a particularly difficult time using the philosophy of MBO to motivate workers. Its success appears restricted to higher level supervisors, with little impact on motivating effectiveness or efficiency at the lower levels of the bureaucratic hierarchy (see Billings, 1976:78-85).

Again there are several reasons why MBO did not provide the centralized control promised by this comprehensive system of management. Had the Office of Management and Budget attempted to establish goals for each agency or reject existing goals, it is likely that the matter would have ended before the Supreme Court on grounds that the Office of Management and Budget had deliberately thwarted the legislative intent underlying the affected programs. Although court battles were hardly unusual during the Nixon administration, this type of OMB dictatorship would almost certainly paralyze the administrative agencies and mobilize Congress against both OMB and the President. In short, the Office of Management and Budget did not have the legal or pragmatic power to centralize administration through establishing or rejecting agency goals.

Some objectives cannot be stated in measurable form. What is, for example, the quantitative measure of justice? In a similar vein, progress cannot always be measured. For example, HEW seeks a cure for cancer, but what is the measure of progress in cancer research? (see Billings, 1976:79). By the same token, if objectives are not quantified and progress not readily measured, how can management by objectives improve the performance and efficiency through a contract between supervisory levels?

Agency officials were asked to translate their own goals and objectives into statements consistent with the President's general outlook on policy. This becomes increasingly difficult as the program or activity becomes more specialized. We have already noted the problems that arise when officials attempt to move from general policy to specific decisions. In addition, it is not clear that all agency goals were, in fact, consistent with the President's direction. This is one reason why the President attempted to dismantle the Office of Economic Opportunity by appointing an acting head for an indefinite period of time.

*Zero-base budgeting.* Zero-base budgeting really is an outgrowth of PPBS. Both are comprehensive planning devices, and both emphasize budgeting by program (see, for example, Pyhrr, 1973; Turnbull, 1976:609-610; Anthony, 1977:22). As a special form of PPBS, zero-base budgeting was implemented by the governor of Georgia in 1971 (now President Jimmy Carter). In the private sector ZBB currently is used by more than 50 companies on *Fortune's* list of 1,000 companies. In the public sector the budgeting system has been used for 3 years in New Jersey and also is being used in Texas and parts of Illinois and by the Environmental Protection Agency (see Stonich, 1977:19).

The rudiments of zero-base budgeting roughly parallel those of PPBS. Item budgeting is replaced by program budgeting. Each program pursued by an agency is presented as a "decision package," which allows policy makers to choose among decision packages if a budget cut is necessary or justified by the merit found wanting in a particular decision package. Agency officials are supposed to rank the decision packages pursued by their agency. Depending on budget expansion or contraction, low-ranked decision packages can be dropped or funded for that year. Each decision package should contain a projection of benefits of costs associated with that package. The system can be added to a PPBS system, allowing consolidation of programs across agencies and a cost-effective comparison of existing programs.

In theory zero-base budgeting requires each agency to justify anew each year the decision packages comprising its activities. And in theory ZBB supposedly gives policy makers a broader set of alternatives and better control when reducing expenditures or eliminating program duplication. In practice, however, ZBB is enormously incremental, with each agency in Georgia automatically receiving 80%, not 0%, of its budget from the previous year (see Anthony, 1977: 22; Turnbull, 1976:610). In turn decision making centers on increments above 80% of the existing agency budget, based on comparisons and rankings of decision packages.

Zero-base budgeting does not centralize power in the executive or move far beyond incremental budgeting, for several reasons. Central decision-makers simply cannot review or rank the large number of decision packages generated by a complex bureaucracy. In Georgia 11,000 decision packages were generated. Anthony (1977:22) estimates that it would have taken the governor 4 hours a day for 2 months to devote 1 minute to each of these 11,000 decision packages. And 1 minute per package is hardly sufficient for a comprehensive evaluation of projected costs and benefits. The time demands alone force the true base for budgeting upward, closer to 70% or 80% for large organizations. In a set of bureaucracies as complex as the federal government the base may reach even higher. But the further away this base gets from zero, the more incremental decisions become and the less powerful this technique becomes as a means for reducing program duplication, increasing efficiency, or reducing a budget.

Where it has been tried, few existing programs have been rejected out-of-hand (see Turnbull, 1976:610). Under an expanding budget it is somewhat easier to get funding for a new program than under MBO, but it is still difficult to take money from one program to implement another. As we have seen, most agencies, once established, look after their own interests, and they will lobby in Congress if necessary to protect current operations. As the true base is pushed down toward zero, ZBB creates a curious form of panic and hysteria among organizations. The constant anxiety impairs the process of image building and thereby impairs management, the pursuit of organizational goals, effectiveness, and efficiency. In short, when it does work it generates some strongly negative unintended consequences. Like the more successful versions of PPBS and MBO, if ZBB actually were successful it is likely that the budgeting system would interfere with the legislative intent underlying the statutory authority establishing programs and agencies. In short, incrementalism may help ZBB avoid some serious constitutional questions about the relative power of Congress and the presidency over the administrative agencies.

In summary, each of the three budgeting systems used in the Bureau of the Budget or the Office of Management and Budget attempts to create greater flexibility in planning through budgeting, inject greater rationality into the budgeting process, and give policy makers greater control over administrative agencies. In practice, each of these devices is a set of specified heuristic rules—guidelines for action that do not provide one unique solution to the problem of planning, rationality, or control. Curiously, however, proponents of each system tend to believe that these devices are more like algorithms than heuristic rules and hence believe that the devices can lead to optimal solutions to social problems through the budgetary process. It is further interesting to note that none of these devices has altered the crude heuristic rules governing the actual budgetary process. These rules are stochastic, meaning that the single best predictor of next year's appropriations is a simple weighting of this year's appropriations. Stated differently, budgets reflect past probabilities for funding. This can only occur if the complex network of policy makers and bureaucracies stand in some form of equilibrium with one another, where most decisions are routine and where the shaping and sharing of power in complex power channels tends to limit the scope of choices to those with marginal impact on the overall course of public policy. There are, of course, exceptions, as we shall note later in this chapter. Under normal conditions the push and pull of forces in the power channel tend to minimize the impact of appropriations as a control device by the chief executive.

***Executive decisions.*** The final form of interaction between the President and the public bureaucracies is the presidential authority, in certain instances, to make the final decision for an administrative agency. For example, the President generally has final say over tariff regulations proposed by the Tariff Commission established by the Tariff Act of 1930. Similarly, the President has final say when a foreign air carrier seeks an operating permit in the United States and when a domestic carrier seeks to engage in overseas air transport (Gellhorn and Byse, 1974:137, 138). These circumstances are relatively few in number; for the most part, administrative agencies have final say over most regulatory decisions, subject to judicial review.

***Overview.*** We have identified several

forms of interaction between the chief executive and administrative agencies at the federal level. The President has the authority over appointment and some authority over removal of administrative officers. The President might seek to impose executive direction over administrative agencies through removal, appointments, reorganization, and budgeting. Further, in some limited instances the President has final say over administrative decisions. For the most part, the President does exert enormous influence over both Congress and the administrative agencies but is hardly in a position to impose autocratic direction, given the fragmentation of power and the plurality of actors at the federal level. The same pattern, although to varying degrees, can also be found at the state and local level across the 50 states. As Eisenhower discovered, the federal bureaucracies are not like the military bureaucracy from which he came. An order in the military usually will produce the expected results; in the Presidency, given the pluralism of the federal bureaucracy, an order may have no real consequences whatsoever.

### Bureaucracy and the judiciary

The interactions among the bureaucracies and courts are not as visible as those among bureaucracies and either the legislative or executive branches. However, the courts exercise enormous control over administrative activity. Through decades of case law the courts have come to occupy a central role in monitoring administrative decisions and making sure that administrative decisions properly follow from the enabling legislation of the Congress. Some of the more important interactions include judicial review, control over administrative rule making, control over the application and elaboration of administrative rules, control over administrative adjudications, and checks on administrative biases. In addition, the administrative agencies may turn to the courts for access to information and sometimes protection against interference from other government officials. Let us examine each of these matters more closely.

*Judicial review.* Although there are instances where a reviewing court might reverse the decisions of an administrative agency, the primary role of judicial review is to determine whether the agency has acted within the scope of authority delegated to it by the legislature. Legal scholars tend to agree that the primary value of judicial review is its deterrent effect on overzealous administrative officials. Very often judicial review is too costly, too slow, or too late to really remedy a problem arising from administrative activity. However, the threat of judicial review is a constraint that likely reduces the need for such review (Gellhorn and Byse, 1974:143, 144). Historically the courts have claimed jurisdiction for judicial review from the statutes creating the agency or from common law or constitutional law that has been extended to cover administrative activities. In the first case judicial review follows the express intent of the legislature. In the second case judicial intervention must be justified on other grounds, among them that administrative action somehow infringes on the constitutional or common-law rights of an individual.

*Who can seek judicial review?* In the Administrative Procedure Act of 1946 (approved June 1946, amended June 1967), Congress specifically authorized that any person suffering legal wrong because of an agency action or any person adversely affected or aggrieved by agency action within the meaning of a relevant statute is entitled to judicial review. Although this act appears to extend the right to seek judicial review to a large number of people, regardless of specific statutory provisions permitting judicial review for particular programs, the Supreme Court has been somewhat modest in extending the right to seek judicial review of agency actions.

When statutes explicitly grant judicial review to aggrieved parties, the courts use a less rigorous standard in determining the right to seek judicial review than those required in injunction suits or suits for declaratory judgments (see Gellhorn and Byse, 1974:170). In *Federal Communications Commission* v. *Sanders Radio Station* (1940) and *Scripps-Howard Radio, Inc.,* v. *Federal Communications Commission* (1942), the Supreme Court laid the foundations for private litigants acting in the public interest and threatened financial loss as a measure of a person aggrieved. In turn these two principles allow suits by consumers against administrative actions. In the *Joint Anti-Fascist Refugee Committee* v. *McGrath* (1951), the Court clearly established the right to judicial review when administrative action violates a legally protected right. In *Association of Data Processing Service Organizations* v. *Camp* (1970) and *Barlow* v. *Collins* (1970), the Supreme Court noted the trend toward enlarging the class of people who might protest administrative action. Citing the Administrative Procedure Act, Justice Douglas delivered the Court opinion that the Administrative Procedure Act grants the standing to sue, even though the specific statute governing an agency or program does not. Here aggrieved persons were held to include not merely economic harm but also aesthetic and environmental well-being. And in *Sierra Club* v. *Morton* (1972), the Court required that a petitioner establish himself or herself among the injured affected by an agency action (see Gellhorn and Byse, 1974:167-217).

*Uses of judicial review.* Judicial review may be sought by eligible parties, providing the relevant statute does not preclude judicial review and the agency action is by law delegated to agency discretion. In *Abbott Laboratories* v. *Gardner* (1967), the Supreme Court decided that it would admit a presumption of judicial review unless there was clear and convincing evidence that Congress wanted the courts to restrict access to review (see Gellhorn and Byse, 1974:217). However, as the Court illustrated in *Myers* v. *Bethlehem Shipbuilding Corporation* (1938), plaintiffs are expected to exhaust all administrative remedies before seeking judicial review. There are some circumstances, particularly when an agency clearly acts beyond its authority, when the courts will grant review before administrative remedies are exhausted. In addition the courts generally attempt to reserve judicial review until agency actions are final, thereby avoiding judicial entanglement in administrative matters during the normal process of administrative decision making. Finally, the courts often choose to stand aside when the primary jurisdiction of another body will enhance the uniformity of decisions or help make use of relevant expertise (see Gellhorn and Byse, 1974:217-310).

Historically there has been a major impediment to judicial review as a device for judicial control over the bureaucracy. Although the guideline is unwritten, the courts generally have recognized a rule that forbids a suit against the sovereign unless the sovereign waves rights to this immunity. The courts attempted to circumvent this rule by arguing that an agent of the sovereign who steps outside legal bounds is thereby stripped of official position and might therefore be sued as a private individual (see Gellhorn and Byse, 1974:311). In *Larson* v. *Domestic and Foreign Commerce Corporation* (1949), the Court cited two types of cases where a suit against agency personnel might be permitted: when an official acts beyond his statutory authority, and when the statute on which an official takes action is itself declared unconstitutional.

*Scope of judicial review.* The Administrative Procedure Act generally establishes the scope of judicial review of agency actions. In particular the courts are supposed to compel agency action unlawfully withheld or unreasonably delayed and hold unlawful and set aside those actions that are arbitrary, capricious, abuse discretion, or are not in accordance with the relevant statute; are contrary to constitutional rights, power, privileges, or immunity; are in excess of statutory jurisdiction, authority, or limitations, or short of statutory right; are without observance of the procedures required by law; are unsupported by substantial evidence; and are unwarranted by the facts to the extent that the facts are subject to trial de novo by the reviewing court.

In *Universal Camera Corporation* v. *National Labor Relations Board* (1951), the Supreme Court concluded that the Administrative Procedure Act required the courts to assume more responsibility for the reasonableness and fairness of agency decisions than had been characteristic of earlier court decisions. For the most part, however, the courts recognize a general restriction on a complete, new review of facts once an agency has made a ruling. In the same case, the Court accepted an agency's interpretation and application of a statute. Earlier, in *Gray* v. *Powell* (1941), the Court concluded that an agency's application of a statutory term to unquestioned facts is acceptable so long as it has a rational basis. When administrators make determinations of law that exceed the boundaries established by the appropriate congressional statutes, the courts will, as in *Addison* v. *Holly Hill Fruit Products, Inc.*, (1944), hold invalid an administrative decision. In that case Justice Frankfurter pointedly observed that the agent to whom authority is delegated cannot determine the scope of authority delegated. Congress must make that determination (see Gellhorn and Byse, 1974:378-485).

**Rule making.** Within the confines of policies established by legislative statute, some administrative agencies have the authority to make rules that can deprive people of liberty or property. Constitutionally these deprivations require due process of law. When administrative agencies engage in these activities, the courts generally have required that they too extend due process to those affected by their actions. In *Londoner* v. *Denver* (1908), the Supreme Court held that subordinate bodies of a legislature entitled to fix a tax must first extend due process of law to those affected by the tax. In particular the Court required a hearing before the tax could be permanently fixed. When hearings are required, the Court also requires that they be fair and impartial. These principles were further extended in *Goldberg* v. *Kelly* (1970). Here the Supreme Court required evidentiary hearings before welfare benefits might be terminated.

Consistent with this emphasis on due process, the Administrative Procedure Act requires specific procedures when an agency formulates, amends, or appeals a rule. In particular the agency must state the time, place, and nature of rule-making proceedings; cite the legal authority under which the rule is proposed; and state the terms or substance of the proposed rule or a description of the subjects and issues involved. In *United States* v. *Florida East Coast Railway Company* (1973), the Supreme Court made an explicit distinction between administrative hearings for promulgating policy-type rules and administrative hearings to adjudicate disputed facts in particular cases. In the first instance the administrative agency hearing should parallel the type of hearings common to legislative bodies when substantive guidelines are being debated or discussed. In the second instance, when the administrative agency serves a judicial rather than a legislative function, the hearing should more closely approximate those used in courts (see Gellhorn and Byse, 1974:575-752).

**Application and elaboration of rules.** To a great extent, administrative agencies devote their attention to the application and elaboration of rules derived from policies specified in statutes. Of course, there is room for considerable scope and frequency of choice here, because general guidelines often permit a variety of translations into concrete programs and decisions. Although granting considerable discretion to administrative agencies in both questions of fact and questions of law, the courts do require that (1) an agency's judgment or rule conform to the grounds offered in its defense or explanation and (2) these grounds must be clear and understandable. So long as an agency meets these two criteria, as demonstrated in *Securities and Exchange Commission* v. *Chenery Corporation* (1947), the Supreme Court generally is willing to uphold the determination of an agency, provided that action is within the scope of delegated authority.

The Supreme Court also encourages administrative agencies to develop either rules or adjudicative precedents that allow clients to predict the forthcoming decisions. In general the courts tend to frown on a malaise of administrative procedures where agencies do not narrow, clarify, and explain their statutory directives so that decisions might be intelligible and predictable. When failures do occur, the case might be brought to court for adjudication. Hence, in addition to offering grounds for a decision that are clear and understandable and related to the decision, the courts generally expect some consistency in the application of rules or the adjudication of disputes (see Gellhorn and Byse, 1974: 753-859).

**Administrative adjudication.** Both the Administrative Procedure Act and the courts distinguish between the quasi-legislative activities of administrative agencies and their quasi-judicial activities. In turn the courts hold different requirements for agency action, depending on which function is more prominent in any given decision. Adjudication requires a search for relevant facts. In the American system of justice an adversary process is used, where witnesses confront one another and cross-examination procedures attempt to establish the "truth." In many European courts, on the other hand, the process of fact finding is more investigatory than adversarial. Although administrative agencies in the United States might use both techniques, the courts impost strict limitations on investigation divorced from cross-examination.

Generally speaking, the courts tend to use the following rules when judging the adjudicative behavior of administrative agencies.

1. Evidence from investigations can be used in adjudication, but it must be supplemented whenever possible by testimony under cross-examination.

2. Although the requirements of evidence might be less rigorous than those expected in a court, the use of hearsay evidence must be consistent with other evidence presented during the hearing. If it is not, the contradictory information should outweigh hearsay evidence.

3. In *Ohio Bell* v. *Public Utilities Commission of Ohio* (1937), the Supreme Court held that evidence used in making adjudications must be made known to affected clients and those clients must be given a chance to refute that information (see Gellhorn and Byse, 1974:860-944).

**Administrative biases.** As in other arenas of decision making, biases might undermine the due process guaranteed to the clients of administrative agencies. We can distinguish two general types of biases: the decision maker has some preconceived notions about rules and their applications, and the decision maker has some personal interest that interferes with his or her judgment of a particular case. Although the courts generally will not disqualify an administrator for demonstrated biases of the second form, in *Tumey* v. *Ohio* (1927), the Supreme Court held that a trial judge with a personal monetary interest in the outcome of a case legally was disqualified from hearing that case because he could not guarantee the fair trial demanded through the due-process clause in the Constitution. The same type of principle has been applied to administrative decision makers (see Gellhorn and Byse, 1974:945-1035).

***Overview.*** The courts exercise control over the administrative agencies in a number of ways. These include judicial review; guarantees of due process during rule making, rule elaboration, and application; adjudication; and protections against administrative bias. The various cases and principles outlined here comprise a set of specified heuristic rules that guide judicial decision making and guide administrative behavior in light of the restraints imposed by the courts. Although the rules are not always consistent, they provide a basis on which agencies can predict court reactions and thus confine their activities within these expected guidelines. Under conditions of routine decision making, such rules provide added stability to the power channels and help limit the scope and frequency of choices available to administrative agencies.

### Bureaucracy and the public

In chapter 6 we noted some strong trends toward fragmenting power in the United States. Relative to routine decisions, our discussion thus far has amply illustrated the extent to which power is fragmented in fact. Since the first administration of Franklin Roosevelt the administrative agencies of the federal government have expanded enormously. However, those agencies soon assumed a circumscribed place in a complex power channel in which the executive, the legislative, and the judiciary branches all help control the activities of administrative agencies. Coupled with the tendency for established organizations to foster "organizational images" and thus self-preservation, the fragmentation of policy-making authority has

helped fragment bureaucracies as well. During the past two generations the national government has grown increasingly. But a strong national government does not in itself mean that power also is centralized in the hands of a few.

The fragmentation of power has three obvious consequences for the public. First, fragmented power helps check the abuses of power. Admitting that power sometimes is necessary does not mean that it will not be misused. The Supreme Court serves as a guardian of a Constitution that sharply restricts the uses of power by granting to ordinary citizens a number of substantive and procedural rights. Through case law the courts have extended many of these rights against the actions of administrative agencies. Second, fragmented power implies inefficiency. The administrative malaise, the extensive red tape, and the profusion of agencies attest to this inefficiency. Liberal governments, Lowi tells us, cannot plan; and a government like that in America is most efficient when it attempts to preserve something, least efficient when it looks to the future (Lowi, 1969:61). Third, fragmented power implies incrementalism (see Lindblom, 1965). Fragmented power increases the number of political actors, increases the number of pressures maintaining a given state of affairs, increases the complexity of nonincremental change, and makes the probability of nonincremental change rather small by reducing the scope and frequency of choice available to any actor in the political arena. Administrative actions are no exception to this trend. Agencies typically receive incremental budgets, they are encouraged to develop standards that make their actions predictable, the scope and frequency of choice is limited by executive, legislative and judicial action, to say nothing of the activities of other administrative agencies and their clients normally have recourse to the courts if an action appears to lead beyond delegated authority.

***Target clientele.*** In Chapter 6 target clientele were identified as (1) a collection of individuals commonly affected by a social problem arising from the actions of others and as (2) a collection of individuals organized by policy makers and policy administrators in the process of attending existing social problems. Social problems seldom affect all members of a society. In fact, as we observed in Chapter 6, social problems help fragment the public because some of those affected by one problem also might be affected by another, thereby creating a set of overlapping publics, and the compound effects of overlapping publics create unusual problems for policy makers and administrators. In this context the duplication of programs, the proliferation of agencies, and the variety of public programs all make some sense, because there is no *one* public for which there is *one* appropriate program. Consequently, multiple bureaucracies help match the pluralism of power with the pluralism of society.

***Participation.*** Critics of pluralism long have noted that publics can exist without the appropriate attention from policy makers or policy administrators. Only those publics with sufficient resources to organize themselves readily gain access to decision makers. The critics conclude, therefore, that more widespread participation is necessary to bring unorganized publics into the legislative, administrative, and judicial processes of government (see, for example, Green and Levinson, 1970; Cook and Morgan, 1971). We might separate the issue of participation into two distinct problems: participation as a mechanism for getting policy makers and policy administrators to organize a target clientele, and participation as a mechanism through which an organized target clientele can influence the decision of policy makers and policy administrators.

*Organizing target clientele.* Ever since Marx, scholars have noted an important distinction between manifest and latent interests in society. Manifest interests, Dahrendorf (1959:178) suggests, are those represented in the programs of organized groups. Latent interests are no less real, but they have not entered awareness in a way that allows those affected to note their similarity of condition and devise programs accordingly. Hence latent interests are without programs. The distinction between latent and manifest interests brings to the fore a critical question regarding participation as a mechanism for getting policy makers and policy administrators to organize a target clientele: Does participation translate latent interests into manifest interests?

If policy makers and policy administrators translate latent interests into manifest interests, then the role of participation centers on ensuring that policy makers and administrators act on the programs they have defined. In this respect numbers might well be critical in a democratic calculus of power. But the claims for participation go beyond this. Participation mobilizes the politically silent, allowing them to translate latent interests into manifest interests. What do the advocates of participation have in mind here?

There is no magical way in which participation can translate latent interest into manifest interest by itself. Part of the confusion here appears to rest on an analogy drawn between a political arena and the marketplace (see Hirschman, 1970; Mill, 1947). In the marketplace the consumer can express discontent with a product or service by refusing to buy that product or by switching to another. In the political arena a slightly different mechanism is at work. When a citizen does not like the course of policy or a particular program, the individual can voice his or her discontent through voting, hearings, and so on. In both the marketplace and the political arena these mechanisms can inject recuperative pressures on organizations or governments that appear to go astray.

However, the opportunities to exit from the marketplace or have a voice in the political arena are meaningful only to the extent that alternatives are available. Neither mechanism determines, in itself, the alternatives that might be made available by competing firms or competing political elites.

In a similar fashion, participation cannot break political silence unless several conditions are met:

1. Participation must serve as a vehicle for making people aware of latent interests.
2. Participation must serve as a vehicle for elaborating definitions of the problem and alternative solutions to the problem.
3. Participation should be a vehicle for choosing among alternative solutions.

Although the third condition can be resolved through participation, it is not entirely clear that participation creates the necessary marketplace of ideas where people might become aware of latent interests and define alternative strategies for resolving the problem. In fact, the Founding Fathers were convinced that such forums would disintegrate into factions motivated by passions of the moment and given to tyranny.

*Influencing decisions.* We can divide this stage of participation in two basic ways: participation in the actual decision process or participation to limit the scope or frequency of choices exercised. The classic example of the first form of participation in administrative decision processes occurred during the Johnson Administration. The Community Action Program of the Office of Economic Opportunity sought to maximize citizen participation in community programs sponsored by the federal government. Although the conclusions drawn from this experiment vary considerably, most scholars agree that participation in the decision process did have con-

siderable impact on these programs (see, for example, Greenstone and Peterson, 1973; Krause, 1971:420-421; Moynihan, 1969). In particular, as participation became more extensive, the participants began questioning even routine decisions, so that conflicts and misunderstandings escalated and program delays and costs became excessive. In short, things got pretty complicated.

Although less visible, the second form of participation might be a more meaningful way to influence the decisions of administrative personnel. In his discussion of police administration, for example, James Q. Wilson (1972:286-287) distinguishes between an institutional model and a communal model. The institutional model concentrates on the uniform application of laws and sanctions, reflected in strict adherence to the specified heuristic rules established by key police administrators and other agents of criminal justice. The communal model concentrates on understanding communal norms, even though these be unspecified heuristic rules, to adapt law enforcement to the notions of substantive justice held by the citizenry.

Under the institutional model, participation by the community does little to limit the scope or frequency of choice exercised by patrolmen. This function is left to supervisors and key decision makers in the criminal justice system. Under the communal model, however, participation by the community is the primary mechanism for limiting the scope and frequency of choice exercised by patrolmen. Participation in this sense does not mean formal voting or formal hearings. Nor does it mean community control programs like those advocated by the Black Panthers. Rather, here participation means that the heuristic rules defining justice for the community are made part of a patrolman's thinking through a process of socialization with the neighborhood and given considerable weight in law enforcement decisions. This approach to law enforcement is quite common in England, and it has been used in a number of older cities in the United States. In general, the device is quite successful in incorporating the community in routing law-enforcement decisions.

### Overview

Routine decisions by administrative agencies are controlled in a number of ways. The legislature, executive, judiciary, and community help limit the scope and frequency of choices available to administrative decision makers. In addition, the fragmentation of power severely limits the power exercised by administrative agencies, but it also contributes toward administrative inefficiency and incremental or marginal decision making. Clearly, the peculiar fragmentation of power and bureaucratic organization in America helps maintain stability, protect individual rights, and guard against the disruptive influences of concentrated power. But what happens when social conditions require radical change?

### CRITICAL DECISIONS

In the life of any society there are times, normally few in number, when critical decisions must be made. Critical decisions imply that the scope of choices is considerably broader than usual, that history no longer is left to drift, and that the normal boundaries for decisions simply are inadequate for providing solutions to impending problems. In Part I we identified a number of these radical problems, including revolutions in the means of production; serious changes in the way a society views the legitimate distribution of rights, privileges, and rewards; and the threat of war. During the twentieth century, America has faced a number of such crises. In Chapter 5, for example, we examined the Cold War crisis and the emergence within one generation of a military-technology complex that has moved the United States into a game of credibility chess with other superpowers around the globe.

### Political vision

What conditions lead people to expand the scope of choices available to policy makers? Historically, two have been very important: the pursuit of a vision and the response to crisis. All societies have ideals. When the gap between these ideals and existing conditions is extremely large, strong social pressures motivate policy makers to broaden the scope of choices and hence move a society from its current state of affairs into a condition more congruent with these ideals. This pressure to change what is into what ought to be is both visionary and dynamic (see Lindsay, 1962; Bell, 1962; Seitz, 1973:1-15). It can create violent dissatisfaction with existing conditions. During the twentieth century we have seen a number of states expand the scope of choice in the pursuit of a vision, among them the communist countries, Nazi Germany, Fascist Italy, and some developing countries of the Third World.

In the nineteenth century the role of vision in politics was demonstrated by a trend toward greater democratization. By contrast, in the twentieth century that role is amply demonstrated by the trend toward dictatorships (see Cobban, 1939; Lippincott, 1965:10). In several countries, including Germany and Italy, free democratic elections have served as vehicles for victory by totalitarian parties. In most of these cases, existing social conditions had fallen far short of social ideals, and a totalitarian party promised radical programs to transform existing conditions.

Consider the case of France. At the time of this writing, the Socialists and Communists have a fair chance of winning the March 1978 elections. (For some time, many French labor unions have been dominated by communists.) The Communist Party promises nonrepressive and nonbureaucratic politics if it wins the elections (see Laqueur, 1977:12). Of late, however, radical-left French intellectuals have begun juxtaposing the promise of Communism with its performance. In particular they note that the totalitarian party and the extensive state apparatus needed to nationalize French industry do not square with nonbureaucratic politics and that communist parties, once in power, have not made concessions to democratic ideals. (For a classic discussion of the totalitarian party, see Lippincott, 1965).

Suppose we look more closely at the discrepancy now being debated by radical-left French intellectuals (see also Garaudy, 1970). The theory of communism translates latent social interests such as the inequitable distribution of resources in society and the concentration of capital in the hands of a few into manifest interests. Further, it defines programs that mobilize the politically silent by offering them a meaningful alternative to existing programs (see Bell, 1962:400-401). In short, the theory of communism expands the scope of political choice, making political participation in elections meaningful and social mobilization (changes in the aspirations of individuals, groups, and organizations) possible (see Huntington, 1968: 34).

However, the practice of communism must limit the scope of choice. Once the electorate has given approval for radical program revisions and the required critical decisions have been made, the regime must consolidate its own power position and regularize the administration of its programs. To do so, the bureaucracy becomes a tool of the party elite, used to implement and then sustain critical decisions. Equally important, the new power elite typically uses the bureaucracy to maintain its consolidated power and newly acquired position of authority.

During the transition to communist programs, the party elite attempts to control the scope of choices available to both the citizenry and to bureaucratic decision makers. Once planning and coordination become regularized and hence decisions become routine, there is a tendency for the bureaucracy to gain some independence from the party elite. Under Breshnev in the Soviet Union, for example, the bureaucracy appears to be more independent of the party elite than at any time since the Communist takeover in 1917. As we noted in Chapter 10, no society can tolerate lengthy periods where both the scope and frequency of choices are high. Although the politics of vision expand social choices, the bureaucracy helps narrow the scope of choices over time. Does the same phenomenon occur when crises force decision makers to expand the scope of choices?

### Response to crisis

The second condition expanding the scope of choice is crisis. A crisis is an unusual, unstable moment when crucial decisions are required. These moments are unstable and unusual precisely because politics as usual cannot provide the necessary solutions and, without radical action, more severe and drastic consequences might follow. Historically crises tend to occur simultaneously with social mobilizations for radical social change. However, some countries, particularly the United States, have been more pragmatic and less visionary in responding to crises than have other countries, particularly when compared with those in Europe. That pragmatism has led Americans to favor problem-solving politics rather than bitter ideological debates.

Like the politics of vision, solutions to crises require expanding the scope of choices. Although political mechanisms in the United States operate to maintain routine decisions and hence drastically limit the scope of available choices, crises have triggered periodic outbursts of critical decisions that have altered the norm state around which adjustive mechanisms operate when the balance of power is restored to complex power channels. Burnham (1970), among others, describes periodic critical elections in the United States, in which the groups supporting political parties shift, as do the party platforms and resulting administrative programs. These critical election periods are relatively short, and then the electoral process quickly resumes a new but stable politics-as-usual status.

One serious crisis was the Great Depression of the 1930s. The American response to that crisis, although pragmatic in its orientation, has had a profound impact on American politics. The enormous proliferation of administrative agencies began in earnest under the New Deal of Franklin Roosevelt. Roosevelt and his advisors identified pressing social problems in several areas of life and established administrative agencies to address each problem. To do so, Roosevelt required unusual cooperation from the Congress. In normal times the Congress serves to check the power of the President. But during this crisis Roosevelt exacted enormous concessions from Congress to quickly implement social reforms. Roosevelt also required enormous concessions from the Supreme Court. These concessions were slow in coming, and Roosevelt threatened to change the size of the Court before decisions favorable to his programs began to emerge. Further, in response to the growing number of administrative agencies, the courts rapidly developed case laws governing agency activities. Because the social problems were national in scope, Roosevelt's programs shifted the focus of political action from the states to the federal government. After Roosevelt the federal system of government never would be the same. Still, America quickly returned to a new state of routine decision making, fostered by the stabilizing influence of bureaucratic organizations in a pluralist power channel.

Politics as usual in the United States is deliberately conservative. It fosters routine decisions and avoids critical decisions whenever possible. The power of government at all levels is extraordinarily fragmented, and the resulting decisions usually are marginal or incremental. The normal balance of power does not admit visionary demands, nor does it permit radical reform. Long-range planning is virtually impossible because the balance of power does not permit comprehensive uses of power. To trigger critical decision making, a crisis first must disrupt the normal balance of power. Only when this occurs can we see the enormous flexibility of democracy and bureaucracy as procedural devices capable of responding to radical social problems. It is important to note that the balance of power resulting from the fragmentation of authority in America is the key to conservative politics, not the existence of bureaucracy or democracy. It is precisely during times of crisis, however, that government in America most approximates an oligarchy. The need to centralize power and make consistent, effective responses to radical problems tends to decrease the utility of majority participation in implementing critical decisions, while it tends to increase the importance of bureaucratic expertise for defining problems and elaborating alternatives. Here Blau's and Michels' critiques of bureaucracy are most relevant.

## CONCLUSION

Is bureaucracy the tool of an oligarchy in America? Is bureaucracy the source of oligarchy in America? Under routine decisions bureaucracy is part of a complex power channel in which power is fragmented and most decisions are marginal or incremental. Here bureaucracy is neither the tool of an oligarchy nor the source of oligarchy. The complex checks and balances of power within the power channel tend to balance policy makers, policy administrators, and the public. In turn, politics as usual generally is more conservative than that observed in many other nation-states of the twentieth century. But there are times when this balance of power disintegrates because crisis and the threat of severe consequences demand a form of decision making that virtually is impossible so long as the prevailing balance of power remains intact. These moments of disequilibrium in the power channel are usually brief, and there is a strong pressure toward a new equilibrium. However, during moments when critical decisions are required, it is possible that bureaucracy might become a tool of an oligarchy (some semblance of this did occur during the Roosevelt Administration), and it is possible that one of the bureaucracies might become an oligarchy in its own right (the military-technology complex is one prime candidate). It is this volatile nature of American politics under conditions requiring critical decisions that makes the future of American politics uncertain and raises the legitimate spectre of bureaucratic totalitarianism.

## REFERENCES

Anthony, R. Zero-base budgeting is a fraud. *The Wall Street Journal,* April 27, 1977, p. 22.

Bell, D. *The end of ideology.* New York: Free Press, 1962.

Bendix, R. Bureaucracy and the problem of power. *Public Administration Review,* 1945, 5, 194-209.

Billings, C. D. MBO in the federal government. In R. T. Golembiewski, F. Gibson, and G. Y. Cornog (Eds.), *Public Administration* (3rd ed.). Skokie, Ill.: Rand McNally & Co., 1976.

Blau, P., and Meyer, M. *Bureaucracy in modern society* (2nd ed.). New York: Random House, Inc., 1971.

Borch, H. von. *Obrigkeit und Widerstand.* Tubingen: J. C. B. Mohr (Paul Siebeck), 1954.

Burnham, W. D. *Critical elections and the mainsprings of American politics.* New York: W. W. Norton & Co., Inc., 1970.

Carey, W. D. Long-range budgeting and planning in the federal government. *Public Administration Review,* 1961, 21, 175-177.

Cobban, A. *Dictatorship: its history and theory.* London: Cape Publishers, 1939.

Cook, T. E., and Morgan, P. M. (Eds.). *Participatory democracy.* New York: Harper & Row, Publishers, Canfield Press, 1971.

Corwin, E. S. *The President: office and power* (4th ed.). New York: New York University Press, 1957.

Dahrendorf, R. *Class and class conflict in industrial society.* Stanford, Calif.: Stanford University Press, 1959.

Davis, O., Dempster, M. A. H., and Wildavsky, A. A theory of the budgetary process. *American Political Science Review,* 1966, 60, 543.

Drucker, P. *The practice of management.* New York: Harper & Row, Publishers, 1954.

Fenno, R. *The power of the purse.* Boston: Little, Brown and Co., 1966.

Garaudy, R. *The crisis in Communism.* New York: Grove Press, Inc., 1970.

Gellhorn, W., and Byse, C. *Administrative law.* Mineola, N. Y.: Foundation Press, Inc., 1974.

Green, P., and Levinson, S. (Eds.). *Power and community.* New York: Random House, Inc., Vintage Books, 1970.

Greenstone, J. D., and Peterson, P. *Race and authority in urban politics.* New York: Russel Sage Foundation, 1973.

Hirschman, A. O. *Exit, voice, and loyalty.* Cambridge, Mass.: Harvard University Press, 1970.

Huntington, S. P. Congressional responses to the twentieth century. In D. B. Truman (Ed.), *Congress and America's future.* Englewood Cliffs, N.J.: Prentice-Hall, Inc., 1965.

Huntington, S. P. *Political order in changing societies.* New Haven, Conn.: Yale University Press, 1968.

Krause, E. Functions of a bureaucratic ideology. In T. E. Cook and P. M. Morgan (Eds.), *Participatory democracy.* New York: Harper & Row, Publishers, Canfield Press, 1971.

Laqueur, W. French Left discovers "Gulag." *The Wall Street Journal,* July 19, 1977, p. 12.

Lindblom, C. *The intelligence of democracy.* New York: Free Press, 1965.

Lindsay, A. D. *The modern democratic state.* New York: Oxford University Press, Inc., 1962.

Lippincott, B. E. *Democracy's dilemma.* New York: Ronald Press Co., 1965.

Lipset, S. M., Trow, M., and Coleman, J. *Union democracy.* New York: Doubleday & Co., Inc., Anchor Books, 1956.

Lowi, T. *The end of liberalism.* New York: W. W. Norton & Co., Inc., 1969.

Lyndon, C. Nixon's influence already apparent in the government's independent regulatory agencies. *The New York Times,* January 14, 1970, p. 36.

McFarland, A. *Power and leadership in pluralist systems.* Stanford, Calif.: Stanford University Press, 1969.

Michels, R. *Political parties.* New York: Macmillan, Inc., Collier Books, 1962.

Mill, J. S. *On liberty.* New York: Appleton-Century-Crofts, 1947.

Mills, C. W. *The power elite.* New York: Oxford University Press, Inc., 1956.

Mises, L. von. *Bureaucracy.* New Haven, Conn.: Yale University Press, 1946.

Moynihan, D. P. *Maximum feasible misunderstanding*. New York: Free Press, 1969.

Neumann, F. *Behemoth*. New York: Oxford University Press, Inc., 1942.

Pyhrr, P. A. *Zero-base budgeting*. New York: John Wiley & Sons, Inc., 1973.

Quinney, R. *Critique of legal order*. Boston: Little, Brown and Co., 1974.

Renner, K. *Demokratie und Bureaukratie*. Vienna: Universum, 1946.

Scher, S. Congressional committee members as independent agency overseers. *American Political Science Review*, 1960, *54*, 911-920.

Schwartz, B., and Wade, H. W. R. *Legal control of government*. New York: Oxford University Press, Inc., 1972.

Seitz, S. T. Political ideologies and the essence of politics. In L. E. Shaw (Ed.), *Modern competing ideologies*. Lexington, Mass.: D. C. Heath & Co., 1973.

Shafer, R. G. Red tape is hobbling federal benefit programs and raising costs, state and local officials say. *The Wall Street Journal*, May 4, 1977, p. 40.

Snyder, R. Reappraising program budgeting. *Public Management*, 1960, *42*, 98-99.

Stonich, P. Zero-base budgeting. Letter to the editors. *The Wall Street Journal*, May 16, 1977, p. 19.

Turnbull, A. III. Rationality and budgeting: is coexistence possible? In R. T. Golembiewski, F. Gibson, and G. Y. Cornog (Eds.), *Public Administration* (3rd ed.). Skokie, Ill.: Rand McNally & Co., 1976.

Wildavsky, A. *The politics of the budgetary process*. Boston: Little, Brown and Co., 1964.

Wilson, J. Q. *Varieties of police behavior*. New York: Atheneum Publishers, 1972.

# Glossary

**adjustive mechanisms** Institutions for maintaining social coordination or functional integration as the intrinsic and extrinsic conditions of a society vary.

**administrative biases** Either preconceived notions held by decision makers about agency rules and their applications or the existence of some personal interest that interferes with judgment.

**administrative adjudication** Quasi-judicial function of administrative agencies through which agencies settle claims and disputes brought before them.

**administrative rule application** Administrative function of agencies through which agencies match rules with cases or problems.

**administrative rule making** Quasi-legislative function of administrative agencies through which agencies translate general policy guidelines into concrete policies.

**advanced bureaucratic state** Society in which authority is delegated and specialized, positive sanctions are used, and in which neither kinship nor religion provide substantive guidelines for political action. Here the substantive guidelines derive from procedures for policy making that are perceived legitimate apart from their substantive guidelines.

**algorithmic rules** Guidelines for choice that provide definite or unique solutions to a problem.

**authority** Legitimate power.

**beginning bureaucratic state** Society in which authority is delegated and specialized, positive sanctions are used, and in which religion and kinship still provide guidelines for structuring political action.

**broken-channel model** Organization set where power relations do not directly link all agencies to one another.

**bureaucracy** Special form of social organization that provides procedures to elaborate and administer substantive guidelines for structuring political action through the delegation and specialization of authority.

**bureaucratic process** Set of ongoing operations within a bureaucratic organization and a power channel that lead to goal achievement.

**centralized decision making** Prerogative to make decisions can be rank ordered such that decisions made at one level might be reviewed and modified by decision makers at a higher rank.

**civil law** Commercial, constitutional, procedural, and administrative rules aimed at maintaining some level of coordination or functional integration in society.

**coalition model** Organization set where agencies have power relations among one another but they cannot be ranked in terms of power vis-a-vis other agencies.

**command cybernet** Special communication network where one actor alters the action probabilities of another through orders accepted as legitimate.

**communication** Interchange of information and meaning between a sender and a receiver through a common set of symbols.

**communication system** Stable and regular process for exchange of information and meaning between a bureaucracy and its environment and among the members of a bureaucratic organization.

**complex judiciary** Advanced form of bureaucratic organization that applies stated rules to legally relevant facts. Authority mainly derives from rational-legal grounds.

**complex society** Cultural group characterized by a large population, considerable social diversity, extensive division of labor, a sophisticated economy, and anonymous relations among most people.

**criminal law** Rules and statutes that define forbidden activities and specify sanctions when these rules and statutes are violated. Unlike civil law, criminal law usually has a moral component, and its violation is considered an act against society.

**cybernetics** Study of control through communication. More specifically, it is the study of communication as a means for shaping and sharing power.

**cybernet** Communication network, identified by the type of message carried, through which one actor alters the action probabilities of another.

**decentralized decision making** Prerogative to make decisions is not ranked, and decisions of one actor are not regularly reviewed or modified by higher authorities.

**decision making** Process of choice leading to action achieved through defining a problem, establishing alternatives, choosing among alternatives, implementing alternatives, and evaluating the resulting action.

**delegation of authority** Condition where the legitimate power to make decisions has been passed from one actor to another.

**democracy** Special form of social organization, which provides procedures for establishing substantive guidelines to structure political action through the free, periodic election of officials; competition for office; regular turnover of officials; and constitutionally limited authority.

**differentiation** Process through which work tasks are simplified (that is, involve fewer operations), but administration becomes more complex in order to synthesize the product of work tasks.

**discretion** State of decision making in which the individual has broad scope of available choices, high frequency of choice, and few rules guiding choice.

**dynamic equilibrium** Range of possible states that a society might experience without requiring definition of a new norm state.

**ecclesiastical authority** Legitimate exercise of power derives from beliefs that the gods make law, authorities are representatives of supernatural powers, and failure to observe laws invites both human and divine sanction.

**economic capitalism** Condition in which business enterprises encourage radical innovations or revolutionary changes in the techniques of production to increase their competitive edge.

**ecosystem** Complex web of physical, chemical, and biological processes that sustain life and create the foundations for evolutionary development.

**egalitarianism** Doctrine or belief that all people have the same inherent worth and dignity.

**entropy** Tendency toward disorder or randomness.

**expertise cybernet** Special communication network where one actor alters the action probabilities of another through specialized knowledge accepted as legitimate.

**extraordinary leadership** Unusual power that helps expand the scope of available choices.

**extrinsic conditions** Social problems arising among societies that require political action.

**feedback** Process for verifying that the receiver has received and understands the meaning and information intended by a sender.

**fragmented policy making** Legislative function is divided among a number of authorities.

**frequency of choice** Number of times decisions might be made.

**functional integration** Coordination of the different tasks performed by members of a society.

**gossip cybernet** Special communication network where one actor alters the action probabilities of another through the informal exchange of meaning and information in forms such as rumor and opinion.

**hereditary privilege** System of bureaucratic recruitment in which claims to office derive from class or social origins.

**heuristic rules** Guidelines for choice that do not provide definite solutions to a given problem.

**hierarchy model** Organization set in which all agencies can be ranked in terms of power vis-a-vis other agencies.

**image building** Process of accumulating information and meaning that create mental pictures of organizations, power channels, and people.

**incrementalism** Bureaucratic action where the scope and frequency of choices are limited and hence the range of behaviors are also limited.

**infused with value** Process through which an organizational image is built and people acquire a mental image of that organization.

**innovative model** Personnel system characterized by emphasis on the individual's job performance, not the position occupied. In addition, advancement and retention are determined by relative job performance.

**intermediate bureaucratic state** Society in which authority is delegated and specialized, positive sanctions are used, and in which religion (but not kinship) still provides guidelines for structuring political action.

**interpersonal communication** Medium for transmitting information and meaning, including conversation, lectures, meetings, and telephone conversations.

**intrinsic conditions** Social problems arising within a society that require political action.

**judicial review** Control over bureaucratic organizations by determining whether the agency has acted within the scope of authority delegated and acted according to due process of law.

**kinship** Form of social organization that defines status relations among people, including prohibitions on marriage and prescriptions for the distribution of economic duties and privileges.

**leadership** Unusual power; power above and beyond that inherent in the actor's position or office.

**legislative intercession** Interaction through which legislators intervene in bureaucratic decision making on behalf of someone or something.

**legislative oversight** Legislative function through which the actions of an agency are regularly reviewed.

**lethargy model** Personnel system characterized by emphasis on job classification rather than the individual holding that position. In addition, advancement is not systematically encouraged, and minimal job performance is sufficient to guarantee tenure.

**management** Process of shaping and sharing power so an organization can pursue its goals.

**management by objectives (MBO)** Managerial device for increasing motivation by measuring performance against stated goals.

**managerial leadership** Process whereby bureaucracies

attempt to adjust to radical disturbances during the pursuit of organizational goals and to alter the collective intent among members of the bureaucracy when changes in goals or unusual adjustments require.

**managerial maintenance** Process whereby bureaucracies attempt to minimize disturbances during the pursuit of organizational goals and to maximize motivation among members of the organization.

**mechanical message** Medium of communication between person and machine, especially computerized information and data processing systems.

**merit system** System of bureaucratic recruitment in which placement and promotion are determined primarily by the skills and talents of the individual applicants.

**military-industrial complex** Condition where the captains of industry work closely with military leaders to enhance military power and business profit.

**military-technology complex** Condition in which military spending spurs advances in applied sciences and advances in applied science enhance military power.

**multinational organization** Bureaucratic organization legally incorporated in several nation-states.

**noise** Memory decay, omission, distortion, information overload, and other factors that impair the communication of information and meaning.

**norm-state** Hypothetical condition where all adjustive mechanisms in a society are at rest and coordination is perfect.

**ordinary leadership** Unusual power that helps expand the frequency of available choices.

**organization sets** Status relations among a set of organizations that result from the systematic exercise of power. These are the products of power channels among multiple bureaucracies.

**paradox of management** Bureaucracies simultaneously need procedures to adapt to radical changes and to maintain some stability.

**personnel system** Process whereby a bureaucratic organization motivates, advances, and retains its employees.

**Peter Principle** Tendency to advance people to a position for which they are minimally competent and above which they are incompetent to rise.

**planning, programming, budgeting systems (PPBS)** Managerial device for comprehensive decision making by synthesizing planning and programs through budgetary controls.

**plebiscite** Governmental procedure where all enfranchised citizens vote on a proposal and choice of ruler.

**policy administration** Deliberative decision process in which substantive guidelines for structuring political action are elaborated into concrete programs and applied to specific cases.

**policy making** Deliberative decision process in which substantive guidelines for structuring political action are established.

**political action** Deliberative efforts to attend to the arrangements of society, enabling people to consciously maintain or to change existing social arrangements.

**political capitalism** Condition in which the modern nation-state encourages radical innovations or revolutionary changes in the techniques used to increase power over other nation-states.

**power** Relation between two or more actors in which X intervenes in the behavior of Y and actor X alters the probability that Y will perform or refrain from performing a particular action without the intervention of X.

**power channels** Systematic power relations among a set of actors.

**queuing** Ordering of communication flows to prevent overload and other factors contributing to noise.

**radical social change** Condition that makes it impossible for a society's normal adjustive mechanisms to maintain a minimal level of coordination or functional integration and hence requires definition of a new norm-state and the institutionalization of new adjustive mechanisms.

**rational behavior** Bureaucratic action that seeks an optimal choice and best behavior for solving a given problem.

**rational-legal authority** Exercise of legitimate power derives from the application of laws and statutes that have in turn derived from a procedural device for making laws and statutes to which a substantial portion of the citizenry grants legitimacy.

**redundancy** Repetition of information and meaning in similar forms or in alternative forms to control noise.

**satisficing behavior** Bureaucratic action that accepts certain choices and the resulting behaviors as good enough.

**scope of choice** Number of options available to decision makers.

**secularization of authority** Claims to the legitimate exercise of power are based on civil rules, constitutions, and other manmade conventions rather than on appeals to divine sanction or God-given privileges.

**simple judiciary** Beginning form of bureaucratic organization designed to supplement traditional mechanisms of social control and conflict resolution. Authority derives from both traditional and rational-legal grounds.

**simple society** Cultural group characterized by a small population, little social diversity, little division of labor, a subsistence economy, and personal contacts among most of the people.

**social arrangements** Patterns of human coordination.

**social organization** Process for systematically coordinating human activities.

**specialization of authority** Condition where the legitimate power to make decisions derives from expert knowledge.

**specialized language** Technical jargon with special meaning to control noise and reduce the volume of communication.

**spoils system** System of bureaucratic recruitment in which tenure of office is dependent on the wishes of policy makers. Typically, bureaucratic offices are the "property" of policy makers.

**target clientele** Either a collection of individuals commonly affected by a social problem arising from the actions of others, or a collection of individuals organized by policy makers and administrators in the process of attending to existing social problems.

**totalitarianism** Special form of social organization that provides procedures for establishing substantive guidelines to structure political action through a self-recruiting elite that exercises relatively unlimited authority.

**transnational organizations** Special form of social organization that might perform a legislative, judicial, or administrative function but whose jurisdiction includes several nation-states or parts thereof.

**written message** Medium of communication, such as letters, records, reports, annuals, and other printed forms.

**zero-base budgeting (ZBB)** Managerial device for comprehensive decision making by requiring agencies to rank action packages and justify funding for each package.

# Author index

# Subject index

## A

Achievement motive, 144
Adjustive mechanisms, 58, 159, 160, 161, 202
Administrative adjudication, 194, 197, 202
Administrative agencies, 54, 55
  facilitative, 100, 101
  nonfacilitative, 100, 101
Administrative biases, 194, 197, 198
Administrative Procedure Act, 195, 196, 197
Administrative rule application, 194
Administrative rule making, 194, 196
Advanced bureaucratic state; *see* Bureaucratic states
Affinal kinship; *see* Kinship
Agricultural revolution, 34
Algorithms, 172, 173, 175, 177, 193
*Association of Data Processing Service Organ v. Camp,* 195
Authority, 181
  charisma, 25
  delegation of, 163, 164, 167
  ecclesiastical, 5-13, 19-26, 29, 30, 37-46, 161, 181
  kinship, 5-13, 19-26, 30, 55, 161, 181
  rationalization of, 8
  secularization of, 20-26, 29-30
  specialization of, 163, 164, 177
  tradition, 5-13, 19-26, 29, 30, 37-46, 161, 181

## B

*Barlow v. Collins,* 195
Barter, 66
Beginning bureaucratic state; *see* Bureaucratic states
Big-push theory, 14
Bolshevik party, 107
Bourgeois social organization, 107
Breach of rules, 45, 46, 47
Broken channel model; *see* Organization sets
Bureaucratic organizations, 23, 26, 90, 159, 165, 182, 183
Bureaucratic states, 5-11, 21
  advanced, 8, 9, 17, 22
  beginning, 6, 9, 17, 22
  intermediate, 7-9, 17, 22
Bureaucratization, 68
Burke, Edmond, 106

## C

Capitalism, 74-76
  economic, 74, 81
  political, 74, 81
Carter, James, 111

Centralization; *see* Ecological process
Civil law, 48, 54
Civil Service Commission, United States, 111, 181
Civil Service reform, 111
Clausewitz, C., 79, 80
Coalition model; *see* Organization sets
Collective images, 139
Collective violence; *see* Violence
Command cybernet; *see* Cybernet
Communal model; *see* Decision making
Communication, 94, 95, 121, 122, 132, 135, 139, 183
  formal system, 123
  informal system, 123
  media of, 129, 135
    interpersonal, 130-133
    mechanical, 130
    written, 130, 134
Communication systems, 122, 123
Complex channel systems; *see* Power channels
Concentration; *see* Ecological process
Conquest; *see* Extrinsic conditions
Coordination, 98-100, 188
Corporatism, 87, 88
  Catholic regime, 87
  Fascist regime, 87
  Salazar regime, 87
  Vichy regime, 87
Countervailing-power theory, 14
Credibility chess; *see* Military strategy
Crime, ecology of, 51
Criminal justice administration, 49
Criminal law, 48
Crisis, 201, 202
Cybernet, 123, 136, 139, 156, 168, 176, 183, 188
  command, 123-129, 132-135, 142, 144-146
  expertise, 123-129, 132-135, 142, 144, 146
  gossip, 123, 124, 128, 131, 133-135, 144
Cybernetic system, 121, 123, 131, 132, 135, 160, 161

## D

Decentralization; *see* Management
Decision making, 159-178
  communal model, 200
  incremental, 201
  institutional model, 200
  stages of, 159-166
    choosing alternatives, 162-164
    defining problem, 159-161
    evaluation, 166
    implementation, 164-166

DATE DUE